PENGUIN REFERENCE BOOK

The Penguin
SHAKESPEARE
DICTIONARY

Sandra Clark is Reader in Renaissance Literature at Birkbeck College, University of London, where she specializes in Shakespeare and the literature of his time. Amongst other works, she is the author of *The Elizabethan Pamphleteers: Popular Moralistic Pamphlets 1580–1640* (Athlone Press, 1983), *The Plays of Beaumont and Fletcher: Sexual Themes and Dramatic Representation* (Harvester-Wheatsheaf, 1994), articles on Elizabethan literature, and two Penguin Masterstudies, *The Tempest* (1986) and *The White Devil and the Duchess of Malfi* (1987). She is currently writing a book on representations of women and crime in the street literature of early modern England.

The Penguin

SHAKESPEARE
DICTIONARY

Edited by Dr Sandra Clark

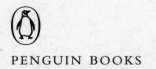

PENGUIN BOOKS

PENGUIN BOOKS

Published by the Penguin Group
Penguin Books Ltd, 27 Wrights Lane, London W8 5TZ, England
Penguin Putnam Inc., 375 Hudson Street, New York, New York 10014, USA
Penguin Books Australia Ltd, Ringwood, Victoria, Australia
Penguin Books Canada Ltd, 10 Alcorn Avenue, Toronto, Ontario, Canada M4V 3B2
Penguin Books (NZ) Ltd, Private Bag 102902, NSMC, Auckland, New Zealand

Penguin Books Ltd, Registered Offices: Harmondsworth, Middlesex, England

First published as the *Hutchinson Shakespeare Dictionary* 1986
This completely revised and updated edition published as
The Penguin Shakespeare Dictionary 1999
1 3 5 7 9 10 8 6 4 2

Typeset in 9/10.5 pt Monotype Bembo
Typeset by Market House Books Ltd, Aylesbury, Bucks
Printed in England by Clays Ltd, St Ives plc

CONTENTS

PREFACE

No writer has at any time been the subject of so much interpretation as Shakespeare. His plays are known the world over and have been translated and adapted into the languages of many countries and cultures. At the end of the twentieth century, they remain vitally alive in the theatre, on the printed page, and, increasingly, in electronic media. His words and phrases have permeated the English language and, though we may not always know it, are constantly on our lips. Critics and scholars, especially in our own century but also since the end of Shakespeare's own, have debated and discussed his style, his language, his characters, his sources; they have argued about his skill in plot construction and his lack of it, his enduring moral values and his religious relativism, his sympathy for women and his misogyny, his reliance on dramatic stereotypes and conventions, and his understanding of human nature. In the midst of such richness and diversity, this book is designed to serve a specific purpose: to make available to the student and to the general reader the basic information, as derived from the most up-to-date scholarship, necessary to a better understanding and enjoyment of Shakespeare's works.

In order to make this information easily accessible, the major part of the book consists of an alphabetical listing with entries on all of Shakespeare's plays and poems (including co-written and apocryphal works), and all of the characters in those plays and poems; the performers, directors, acting companies, and theatres associated with Shakespeare's work, both in his own time and for the centuries to follow; other playwrights, poets, and figures of literary and historical importance in his own period that are relevant of an understanding of his work; and much more. Each play entry contains an account of possible sources for the play and the ways in which Shakespeare deployed them, a brief stage history, a list of characters, and a plot summary. Each of the characters in the plays is given a separate entry. Shakespeare scholarship has undergone changes of many kinds in recent years, and in the provision of information for this dictionary, full use has been made of the most up-to-date research.

The alphabetical listing is preceded by two essays, one on the life of Shakespeare, the other on theatre and play production in Shakespeare's time. There is also an annotated bibliography in seven sections, the entries for which have been specially selected with the needs of students in mind.

The essays are largely the work of Dr David Atkinson, who has also provided invaluable assistance in many other areas.

A SHORT BIOGRAPHY OF SHAKESPEARE

The Early Years, 1564–c. 1587

The exact date of Shakespeare's birth is not known; tradition has it that it took place on St George's day, 23 April 1564, and it is unlikely that he was born more than a few days before April 26, when his baptism was recorded in the parish register of Stratford-upon-Avon. He was the eldest son of John Shakespeare, then a prosperous Stratford businessman, and Mary Arden, his wife. John Shakespeare, the son of a farmer, had left the land in about 1550 and had come to live in Stratford, at that time a town of some 2,000 inhabitants. In some documents he is called a yeoman (a freeholder of land to the annual value of fifty shillings), but at different times he was also a glover and a leather-worker, a seller of barley and timber, and a wool-dealer. After moving to Stratford, he had amassed considerable wealth, and became a man of importance in the community and held numerous civic offices, including those of constable, chamberlain, and alderman. When Shakespeare was four his father was bailiff of Stratford and as such was empowered to grant licences to companies of travelling players. He owned houses in Stratford and elsewhere. The house now designated as Shakespeare's birthplace was not purchased until 1575, and it is possible that Shakespeare was actually born in the adjoining house, to which John Shakespeare had held title since 1556.

The family's fortunes suffered some decline from 1577 onwards, and in 1578 John Shakespeare mortgaged and sold some property that his wife had inherited, although he still possessed substantial properties in Stratford. He was also prosecuted for usury and illegal wool-dealing during the 1570s, and in 1586 he was deposed from his office as alderman because of failure to attend council meetings regularly. The reason for these difficulties remains obscure. It is possible that they arose from John Shakespeare's adherence to the Catholic faith, since by 1577 government hostility to Catholics was increasing. His withdrawal from public life may therefore have been the result of a reluctance to be involved in the corporation's prosecution of Catholics for such offences as non-attendance at church, rather than the consequence of financial difficulties. In 1757 the so-called 'Spiritual Testament' of John Shakespeare is said to have been discovered in the rafters of his house in Henley Street. This was a document of a standard kind, signed by Catholics as a profession of their faith. However, the document has since disappeared, and other Catholics seem to have prospered in Stratford in the 1570s, so that it is not possible to be definite about the faith into which the playwright was born.

Shakespeare's mother, Mary, was a gentlewoman and the youngest daughter of Robert Arden, who had leased the land that John Shakespeare's father farmed. The Ardens were one of the oldest families in Warwickshire, and Robert Arden was sufficiently wealthy at the time of his death in 1556 to make provision for his eight daughters as well as for his second wife. Mary's inheritance included a valuable piece of land at Wilmcote, outside Stratford, called Asbyes, which she brought with her to her marriage. Altogether they had eight children: Joan and Margaret, who died in infancy before William was born, William himself, Gilbert (b. 1566), Joan (b. 1569), Anne (b. 1571), Richard (b. 1574), and Edmund (b. 1580), the youngest; Joan, who died in 1646, was the only one of the eight to outlive William.

The details of William Shakespeare's early life are still a matter of conjecture, since the only documentary evidence from this time consists of the records of his baptism and his marriage. Although Shakespeare became a famous man in his own day, no biography of him was written until Nicholas Rowe's account in 1709. Rowe's work does not pretend to be scholarly and it is not always accurate; he was a playwright, not an historian. As Shakespeare gained recognition as a playwright, his public life became increasingly well documented in terms of published work, court appearances of his dramatic company, legal cases, and property dealings, but there is no fully reliable account of his personal affairs. Some of his contemporaries did record their reactions to him as a man, including Ben Jonson, who said he was "honest, and of an open, and free nature." John Aubrey, the antiquarian, who was not born until after Shakespeare's death but was well acquainted with the Shakespeare mythos, in his *Brief Lives* provides details that may have some historical basis: "He was a handsome well shap't man: very good company, and of a very ready and pleasant smooth Witt." It is from such incidental remarks and what can be inferred from his public life that the outline of Shakespeare's character has to be pieced together.

There are no factual records of Shakespeare's childhood, but Rowe says that he went to a free school, that is, a local grammar school with little or no tuition charges, where the children were instructed in Latin, rhetoric, religion, and possibly some Greek. According to Rowe, Shakespeare left before his education was completed because of straitened family circumstances and "the want of his assistance at Home." Aubrey recounts that "his father was a Butcher, & . . . when he was a boy he exercised his father's Trade, but when he kill'd a Calfe, he would doe it in a *high style*, & make a Speech" (*WS*, ii, 252–53).

The only other pieces of documentary evidence of Shakespeare's life during this period are the marriage licence and bond he obtained in November 1582 to marry Anne Hathaway. Even these documents are not without their mysterious side. The register of licences gives the bride's name as Anne Whateley of Temple Grafton, whereas in the marriage bond she is named as Anne Hathaway of Stratford. The discrepancy is generally laid to the confusion of the clerk who made out the licences, since Rowe and others who knew nothing of the bond recorded Anne's name as Hathaway. The identity of her family is not certain, but she was most probably the daughter of Richard Hathaway of Shottery, who in 1581 left a bequest to his daughter Agnes (which name was then regarded as a form of Anne). The church where the ceremony took place has never been identified, but it was not, as might have been expected, the parish church of Stratford. The marriage seems to have been performed somewhat hastily, for a bond was filed on 28 November 1582, with the Bishop of Worcester, in whose diocese the town of Stratford lay, freeing him from liability since the marriage was to be solemnized without the usual threefold asking of the banns in church. Had Shakespeare and Anne been obliged to undergo this formality they could not have married before mid-January, since by church law the marriage ceremony could not be performed during Advent. At the time of the ceremony Anne was about three months pregnant, and the young Shakespeare's first child, Susanna, was baptized in the parish church on 26 May 1583. William was then nineteen, Anne eight years his senior. Nearly two years later Anne gave birth again, to the twins Judith and Hamnet, who were baptized on 2 February 1585. The unusual names suggest that they may have been christened after Shakespeare's neighbour Hamnet (or Hamlet) Sadler, a Stratford baker, and his wife Judith. Hamnet Shakespeare died when he was eleven, but Judith outlived her own children to die at the age of seventy-seven.

Sometime after mid-1584, Shakespeare left Stratford and eventually made his way to London. The absence of any documentary evidence of his life between the baptism of his younger children in 1585 and the first record of him as an actor and dramatist in London in 1592 has led to this period of his life being dubbed "the lost years". Aubrey thought he came to London in 1584, and perhaps he was already there by the time the twins were baptized; however, there is nothing to indicate even the year-date of his departure, so he may have remained in Stratford for several years after their birth. There has been much speculation as to his reasons for leaving Stratford. Some writers have postulated domestic difficulties, but there is no evidence of this and, since there seems to have been a general economic decline in Stratford about this time, it may have been the necessity to support his family that brought him to London. Rowe connects Shakespeare's departure from home, in a story that is attested to by other sources, with his poaching of deer in the park at Charlecote, which belonged to Sir Thomas Lucy, a local landowner of some importance. So great was Sir Thomas's anger, says Rowe, especially since Shakespeare saw fit to add insult to injury by lampooning the knight in a ballad, "probably the first Essay of his Poetry" (*WS*, ii, 265), that the young man had to flee to London for safety. Inevitably, doubt has been cast upon this account, especially since it was later discovered that Sir Thomas had no park at Charlecote at that time, only a free-warren.

Another account, from William Beeston, whose father Christopher was an actor and member of Shakespeare's company, has it that Shakespeare was for a time a country schoolmaster. This hint has led to the proposition that around 1580–81 the young Shakespeare could have been an assistant teacher in the Catholic household of the Hoghton family in Lancashire. The will of Alexander Hoghton of Lea, dated

3 August 1581, bequeathed his stock of play clothes and musical instruments to his brother Thomas or, if he did not choose to keep players in his service, to Sir Thomas Hesketh, and it went on: "And I most heartily require the said Sir Thomas to be friendly unto Fulk Gyllome and William Shakeshafte now dwelling with me and either to take them unto his service or else to help them to some good master". The name Shakeshafte, it is suggested, could represent an alternative form of Shakespeare, and there is a Stratford connection with Lancashire in John Cottom, the master of Stratford's grammar school who was a native of the county.

On this hypothesis, Shakespeare could have acquired experience as a player as well as a schoolmaster in the Hoghton household, and subsequently in that of another Lancashire Catholic, Sir Thomas Hesketh. The Hesketh family was in turn intimate with that of Lord Strange, Earl of Derby, a known patron of professional players, and Shakespeare could have been recommended to Lord Strange in 1582, or later in 1585 or 1586. The title-page of *Titus Andronicus* connects the play with the Earl of Derby's Men, possibly as early as 1586. The evidence remains highly circumstantial, but if the Lancashire connection were indeed correct, it would mean that Shakespeare was gaining experience as both actor and playwright during the lost years. It would also tend to confirm that the young Shakespeare was a Catholic. However, many English Catholics converted to Protestantism during the 1580s, especially in response to the threat of the Spanish Armada, and it is probable that Shakespeare did the same, since his will is couched in Protestant phrasing, and anti-Catholic sentiments can be traced in his works. Later, in 1606, Shakespeare's elder daughter Susanna was accused and subsequently acquitted of recusancy. At least one report, which originated with an Anglican clergyman who lived in the region of Stratford, has it that Shakespeare reverted to Catholicism on his death-bed.

In fact, though, we know nothing definite about Shakespeare until 1592, when he had already become known as an actor and playwright in London. Some have thought that during the lost years Shakespeare visited Italy, but there is no evidence, not even hearsay, to support the idea. More likely, once he reached London, he earned his living doing theatrical hackwork, revising the plays of others, adding speeches, reworking old material, collaborating—in general, learning the techniques of his trade. Aubrey says that he "was an Actor at one of the Play-houses and did act exceedingly well" (*WS*, ii, 253). This too is plausible. It is essential to presuppose some groundwork laid for Shakespeare's very rapid rise to fame and success after 1592, and not very surprising to find no record of it.

Life in London to 1595

London in the 1590s was a vast, magnificent city by the standards of the rest of England at that time. About a quarter of a million people lived there, mostly in the area known now as the City of London, bounded by Finsbury Fields to the north, the Inns of Court to the west, Aldgate to the east, and the river Thames to the south.

Literary men tended to know each other and maintain close friendships and well-defined enmities. The first printed reference to Shakespeare comes in a pamphlet by Robert Greene, one of the most notorious members of London's literary coterie. Greene—poet, playwright, and pamphleteer—an exceptionally prolific writer, testified in one of his last pamphlets to the fact that Shakespeare had already begun to make his name in the literary world of London. At that time Greene, only a few years older than Shakespeare, was dying in poverty; in *Greene's Groatsworth of Witte* (1592) he recalled his own life and described, not without a slight revelling in the melodrama, the circumstances of his miserable end, warning his friends Marlowe, Peele, and Nashe to avoid the vices of the world and in particular to distrust actors, for they were treacherous fellows who would desert a playwright, however well he had provided them with parts, as soon as they saw a newer one:

> there is an vpstart Crow, beautified with our feathers, that with
> his *Tygers hart wrapt in a Players hyde*, supposes he is as well able to
> bombast out a blanke verse as the best of you: and beeing an absolute
> *Iohannes factotum*, is in his owne conceit the onely Shake-scene in a
> countrey.
>
> (*WS*, ii, 188)

The reference to Shakespeare was unmistakable and unflattering, and in particular alludes to him as something of a theatrical Jack-of-all-trades. He seems to have taken offence at the pamphlet, as did Marlowe, whom Greene had openly accused of atheism. Greene died before the pamphlet was published, but Henry Chettle, who saw it into print and has been suspected of being its true author, made an apology to Shakespeare in the preface to his pamphlet, *Kinde-Harts Dreame*, which came out at the end of the same year:

> my selfe haue seene his demeanor no lesse ciuill than he exelent in
> the qualitie he professes: Besides, diuers of worship haue reported his
> uprightnes of dealing, which argues his honesty, and his facetious grace
> in writting, that aprooues his Art.
>
> (*WS*, ii, 188)

By 1592, then, Shakespeare was known as an actor and as a playwright. There has been much speculation as to what he had written by this time, and the dating of his earlier plays is both difficult and somewhat controversial, not least because some plays may have been revised at a later date. *Greene's Groatsworth* parodies a line from *3 Henry VI*: "O tiger's heart wrapped in a woman's hide" (I.iv.137), so this play was known by 1592, although it was not printed until 1595. The first and second parts of *Henry VI* had also been written by this time; Philip Henslowe records that *1 Henry VI* was performed by Lord Strange's Men on 3 March 1592. At this time, Shakespeare may have been acting with Lord Strange's Men or with the Earl of Pembroke's Men, who went bankrupt in 1593. Exactly how his stage career began is not known; anecdotes of his beginning by looking after the patrons' horses outside the playhouse door cannot be substantiated. It was not, however, a prosperous time for the theatre in London, since plague and civic disorder were so widespread that the playhouses hardly opened between June 1592 and the summer of 1594. The chief companies toured the provinces during this time, but Shakespeare may have stayed in London to write, since in 1593 he appeared for the first time in print with his erotic narrative poem *Venus and Adonis*, following it the next year with *The Rape of Lucrece*. Both were dedicated to Henry Wriothesley, Earl of Southampton, a wealthy young nobleman who was a favourite with the Queen. If Shakespeare did not know Southampton when he wrote the first poem it is possible that the two men became acquainted in the year that passed before the second, as the dedication to that mentions the patron's favour. Both poems were popular; *Venus and Adonis* went through nine editions in Shakespeare's lifetime, *The Rape of Lucrece* six. From this time on Shakespeare's name began to appear in print more and more frequently.

It is possible that he also began to write his sonnets at this time (although they were not published until 1609), since this was the great decade of the English sonnet, with sequences by Sir Philip Sidney (*Astrophel and Stella*, published in 1591, though probably written in 1582), Samuel Daniel (*Delia*, 1592), Henry Constable (*Diana*, 1592), and Edmund Spenser (*Amoretti*, 1595), among others. If, as many have thought, Southampton was "Mr. W.H." to whom the sonnets seem to have been dedicated, then this period is all the more likely for their composition. But again there is no proof of when they were written, although it is known that some of the sonnets had circulated privately among Shakespeare's friends by 1598.

When the theatres reopened in 1594, there was a general regrouping of the members of the chief companies, from which emerged two companies that were to exist as rivals for some time to come: the Lord Admiral's Men, headed by Edward Alleyn, and the Lord Chamberlain's Men, whom Shakespeare joined as a shareholder (possibly one of the original ones) in 1594. He remained with them as actor and playwright for the rest of his London career, and after joining them he wrote for no other company. The Lord Chamberlain's Men was a closely knit group that continued to prosper during the time that Shakespeare was part of it. In 1594 the company included Richard Burbage, the great tragedian, Will Kemp, the clown, John Heminges, later to become one of the editors of Shakespeare's first folio, Thomas Pope, Augustine Phillips, and George Bryan. Kemp was replaced by Robert Armin in 1599, but Burbage, Heminges, and Henry Condell, who joined in about 1598, were still with the company when Shakespeare retired from it in 1610 or 1611, and he commemorated the long friendship with bequests to them in his will. In the ten years from 1599 to 1609 only five new actor-shareholders joined the company, two coming as replacements for actors who had died. During Elizabeth's reign they were to give thirty-two performances at court, as against twenty by the Lord Admiral's Company. When James I came to the throne, royal favour continued, and the company then (1603) became the King's Men.

In the winter of 1594 the Lord Chamberlain's Men performed twice for the Queen at court, and a warrant for payment for these performances, issued on 15 May 1595, names Shakespeare, Richard Burbage, and Will Kemp as the payees for the company. From this it can be assumed that by 1595 he had an assured status in the theatre and in his company, and a certain financial security. He had written historical plays and comedies, including *The Comedy of Errors*, *The Taming of the Shrew*, *The Two Gentlemen of Verona*, and *Love's Labour's Lost*, as well as narrative poems and at least one tragedy, *Titus Andronicus*. *Romeo and Juliet* probably dates from this period too.

Shakespeare and His Company, 1595–1603

The years from 1595 to 1600 were eventful ones for Shakespeare. In August of 1596 his son Hamnet died. In the same year John Shakespeare, apparently recovered from his earlier financial straits, successfully applied to the College of Heralds for a grant of arms to the family and was assigned a golden shield with the design of "a Bend Sables, a Speare of the first steeled argent. And for his crest or cognizaunce a falcon his winges displayed Argent standing on a wrethe of his coullers" (*WS*, ii, 19). With this, the Shakespeare family officially became members of the gentry.

In 1597 Shakespeare bought a residence to suit this advance in rank, New Place, a decayed but elegant house in Stratford, restored by him and his family to such magnificence that Queen Henrietta Maria later stayed there when she came to Stratford during the Civil War. In London he was fast becoming the foremost playwright. Francis Meres, an otherwise obscure man of letters, wrote in his *Palladis Tamia, Wit's Treasury* (1598) that not only was Ovid reborn in "mellifluous & hony-tongued" Shakespeare but also that "among the English" Shakespeare was the most excellent in both comedy and tragedy. Meres cites specifically the comedies *The Two Gentlemen of Verona*, *The Comedy of Errors*, *Love's Labour's Lost*, *A Midsummer Night's Dream*, *The Merchant of Venice*, and the ever mysterious *Love's Labour's Won*, and the tragedies *Richard II*, *Richard III*, *Henry IV*, *King John*, *Titus Andronicus*, and *Romeo and Juliet* (*WS*, ii, 194). This comprises a complete list of all that Shakespeare is thought to have written up to that time, with the exception of *Henry VI*, *The Taming of the Shrew*, and perhaps *The Merry Wives of Windsor*.

During this time the Lord Chamberlain's Men were engaged in finding themselves a new playhouse. They had been performing for some years at the Theatre, a building erected in Finsbury Fields in 1576 by James Burbage, the father of the tragedian. The site was held on a 21-year lease due to expire in April 1597. The Burbages had hoped to move the company to a more fashionable neighbourhood inside the city limits, to Blackfriars, an indoor theatre that James Burbage had refurbished before his death in February 1597. Men of the theatre might be prosperous gentlemen, but at that time theirs was still not a respectable profession, and the residents of the Blackfriars area successfully petitioned the Privy Council to prevent the Lord Chamberlain's Men from moving in. Meanwhile, Giles Alleyn, who owned the lease of the ground on which the Theatre stood, was procrastinating about a renewal, and the company was performing in the nearby Curtain, an old and shabby building. At the end of 1598 Richard Burbage and his brother Cuthbert, realizing that Alleyn hoped to acquire for himself the Theatre building, pulled it down themselves, carried the timbers across the frozen Thames, and began to build their new playhouse, the Globe, on a site they had bought in Southwark. To provide the necessary capital, Cuthbert Burbage devised a scheme that was new in his day; he formed a stock company for the theatre consisting of ten shares, five for himself and his brother Richard, and one each for five members of the company— Heminges, Phillips, Pope, Kemp, and Shakespeare. This meant that Shakespeare owned a tenth part of the new playhouse as well as his own share in the company and had now three sources of revenue—the plays that he wrote for the company, his pay as an actor plus a share of all the profits made by the company, and also a tenth of the rent that the company as a whole paid to the owners of the playhouse. The Globe opened in the summer of 1599. Among Shakespeare's first plays to be performed there were *Julius Caesar, As You Like It,* and *Twelfth Night. Hamlet* was to follow around the turn of the century, about the time when Shakespeare's own father died.

The company became, probably unwittingly, involved in affairs of state when the Earl of Essex commissioned them to perform Shakespeare's *Richard II* on 7 February 1601. In the judicial examination of the players that followed the event, Augustine Phillips, the company's spokesman, said that they had not wanted to play *Richard II* because it was "so old & so long out of vse as that they shold have small or no Company at yt" (*WS*, ii, 325). However, the Earl's representative, Sir Gelly Meyrick, offered them £2 as an inducement, and so the show went on. It was intended as a prelude to a rebellion against the throne, but the real event was much less well-planned and successful than the one in the play. On 8 February, Essex and his friend and follower, the young Earl of Southampton, having returned from a disastrous expedition to quell the unrest in Ireland and out of favour with Elizabeth, rode into London at the head of a body of 200 men, determined to raise the city against the old queen. At this stage of her reign she was much less popular than she had been a decade or so earlier, but even so the earls found no support. They never reached her palace at Whitehall where she sat waiting for them. Instead, they were arrested the same day at Essex House and brought to trial a week later. Both were condemned to death, but at the last moment Southampton was reprieved. Essex went to the block on 25 February. The Lord Chamberlain's Men were summoned by the Privy Council to account for their part in the uprising but were acquitted of any responsibility. As a result of this, however, a ban was placed, for a time, on the production of plays dealing with England's history.

At this same time, the Lord Chamberlain's Men was not without its professional problems. They were facing strong competition from the increasingly popular companies of boy actors, especially the newly formed Children of the Chapel, the "little eyases" that the players in *Hamlet* feared as rivals; the children were then performing at the Blackfriars theatre, from which the Lord Chamberlain's Men had been prohibited. Another source of competition, the Rose theatre, the home of the Admiral's Men, was in close proximity to the Globe on the Bankside location. Ben Jonson was writing for both the Admiral's and the Chamberlain's, but with his unruly temper, could keep peace with neither. He moved on to the children's company at the Blackfriars and in his comedy *The Poetaster* he satirized his fellow playwrights Marston and Dekker and poured scorn on the players and their "wormwood comedies." The Lord Chamberlain's Men retaliated by commissioning Dekker's *Satiromastix* in which Jonson is represented as an empty boaster. Shakespeare seems to have kept out of this literary in-fighting. An anonymous play put on at Cambridge in the Christmas season of 1601–02 compliments him on putting down all his rivals, especially the irascible Jonson: "Our fellow Shakespeare hath given him a purge that made him bewray his credit" (*Two Return from Parnassus*). Nonetheless, Shakespeare acted, probably for the last time, in Jonson's tragedy *Sejanus* at Christmas 1603; it was hissed off the stage by a bored audience, unimpressed by Jonson's observance of classical decorum. When the play was published, two years later, Jonson took care to note that the text was not that of the stage version, "wherein a second pen had good share," but was entirely his own. The second pen has sometimes been thought to have been Shakespeare's, but there is no evidence of this.

At Elizabeth's court the Lord Chamberlain's Men were a favourite company. Their production of *Twelfth Night* was chosen for the Christmas festivities of 1600–01 in preference to Jonson's *Cynthia's Revels*, and they played (there is no record of which play) for Elizabeth on the night in 1601 before Essex was executed. They were three times at court in the Christmas season of 1601–02, and they performed the last play Elizabeth was ever to see, in February 1603 at Richmond Palace.

London, 1603–10

Immediately after his accession, James I took Shakespeare's company under his patronage and they became known as the King's Men. Nine of them, including Shakespeare, were promoted to the rank of Grooms of the Bedchamber and as such were employed at court from time to time. In 1604 they acted as part of the Spanish ambassador's entourage when he came to negotiate for peace, and Shakespeare and his fellows, as the Master of the Great Wardrobe records, were each given four yards of red cloth, presumably to wear as the livery of the monarch's servants when James proceeded in state through London on 15 March 1604.

James was an even keener patron of the theatre than Elizabeth had been; Shakespeare's company performed at court 177 times in the period from 1603 to 1613. In the Christmas season of 1604–05 alone, James saw *The Merry Wives of Windsor*,

The Comedy of Errors, Love's Labour's Lost, Henry V, The Merchant of Venice, Othello, and *Measure for Measure,* and two plays by Jonson. James also favoured the boy players and in 1604 gave a Royal Patent to the Children of the Chapel, known as the Children of the Queen's Revels until 1605, when they lost the Queen's patronage by performing *Eastward Ho,* a comedy by Chapman, Jonson, and Marston in which the Scots were indiscreetly satirized. James also favoured extravagant and expensive masques, which Jonson readily supplied for him, though Shakespeare never did.

Shakespeare was now forty. He had apparently given up acting and all of his professional attention was directed toward writing plays. In the year of James's accession, the plague was so severe that the theatres were closed from 7 May 1603 to 9 April 1604, and the city was deserted. About a sixth of the population died. The King's Men toured the provinces, visiting Bath, Shrewsbury, Coventry, Ipswich, and Oxford, and their royal patron provided them with subsidies to supplement the diminished profits. It is not known if Shakespeare travelled with the company, but in December 1603 he was present when they performed at Wilton House, the home of Sir Philip Sidney's sister, the Countess of Pembroke, who wrote to her son urging him to solicit the King's presence at a performance of *As You Like It,* for "we have the man Shakespeare with us." Around this time Shakespeare probably wrote his "problem plays" *Troilus and Cressida, All's Well that Ends Well,* and *Measure for Measure,* and the great tragedies, *Othello, King Lear,* and *Macbeth.*

Records of Shakespeare's private affairs show that he was growing increasingly prosperous. He had inherited the Henley Street houses in Stratford after his father's death in 1601, and in 1602 he bought two more pieces of Stratford property, amounting to 107 acres of arable land, for £320. In 1605 he made his most sizeable transaction, the purchase of the lease of certain Stratford tithes for £440. He was amassing considerable personal wealth, and he preferred to spend it in putting down roots in the country rather than in bringing his family to London. During his twenty or more years in the city he had always lived in rented lodgings.

In about 1604 he was living in Cripplegate, in the heart of the City, in the house of Christopher Mountjoy, a Huguenot tire-maker (ornamental headdress maker). Legal records show that Shakespeare was involved in arranging a marriage between Mountjoy's daughter Mary and his apprentice, Stephen Belott, and also in the lawsuit that took place in 1612 when Stephen Belott sued his father-in-law for a part of the marriage portion that had not been paid.

Between 1604 and 1608, when Shakespeare was writing some of his great tragedies, little is known of his movements. The King's Men toured the provinces and performed at court as well as in the Globe theatre, but Shakespeare may not have accompanied them on their travels, since he was no longer acting. Augustine Phillips, one of the original Globe shareholders, died in 1605, leaving a 30-shilling (£1.50) piece to Shakespeare in his will, and John Heminges took over as business manager. Aubrey tells of Shakespeare making annual visits to Stratford and lodging during the trip at Oxford, in the inn of John Davenant and his wife. The Davenants' son, William, who was born in 1606 and became well-known in the

Restoration as a playwright and theatre manager, liked to encourage the rumour that Shakespeare was his natural father. Several eighteenth-century writers record the anecdote, based on an old jest, that the young William Davenant, referring to Shakespeare as his godfather, was jokingly reproved by an old man with the words, "Fie, child … why are you so superfluous? Have you not learned yet that you should not use the name of God in vain?" (*WS*, ii, 272). This rumour is now generally held to be untrue.

By 1607 Shakespeare had removed from the Mountjoys' house and was living south of the river. Meanwhile, his family group was altered. In 1607, Edward, the illegitimate infant son of Shakespeare's youngest brother Edmund, also an actor, died. Several months later, in the winter of 1607, Edmund himself died at the age of twenty-seven. Perhaps it was William who paid the twenty shilling (£1) fee for a "forenoon knell of the great bell" at Edmund's funeral in the actors' church, St Saviour's, Southwark. Earlier that year Shakespeare's elder daughter Susanna was married to John Hall, a Stratford doctor, and in February 1608, during one of the hardest winters for many years, Susanna gave birth to a daughter, Elizabeth, Shakespeare's first and only granddaughter. In September of 1608 Shakespeare's mother died.

Meanwhile, Shakespeare's professional life was also changing. In August 1608 the King's Men at last acquired the lease of the Blackfriars Theatre, from Henry Evans, the manager of the Children of the Chapel, who had fallen from royal favour by allowing the presentation of one or both of Chapman's *Byron* plays in which the French royal family were unflatteringly portrayed, thus causing severe offence to the French ambassador. The Blackfriars was an indoor theatre, and it became the winter home of the King's Men. They continued to play at the Globe in the summer, but the new playhouse brought them far more profit. Shakespeare's own income was probably considerably increased by this transaction. He still owned his share in the Globe, now about one-twelfth, and he held over one-seventh of the shares in the Blackfriars, along with Condell, Heminges, William Sly, Henry Evans, and the Burbage brothers. The venture was financially most successful; in a lawsuit of 1612 it was claimed that the King's Men "gott & as yet dothe, more in one Winter in the said great Hall by a thousand powndes than they were used to gett in the Banckside" (*WS*, ii, 69–70). The price of admission at the Blackfriars was higher than at the Globe and the audience was less mixed. Shakespeare's plays continued to be performed at both the Globe and Blackfriars, and *Antony and Cleopatra* and *Timon of Athens* belong to this period. But with the Children of the Chapel, Blackfriars audiences had been used to sophisticated plays, satire, and tragicomedy; accordingly, Shakespeare wrote for them the plays that are known as his romances, or last plays: *Pericles* (probably only in part), *Cymbeline, The Winter's Tale*, and finally *The Tempest*.

Once the company was established in the Blackfriars, Shakespeare's output decreased and he began to spend more time in Stratford. His cousin, Thomas Greene, the town clerk of Stratford, with his wife and family, had been lodging in Shakespeare's house, New Place, with Anne and the still unmarried Judith. In 1610 the Greenes moved out and it seems likely that Shakespeare, then aged forty-six, returned after more than twenty years to live in his home town.

The Last Years, 1610–16

For a time Shakespeare kept up his London contacts. He was still writing, although no longer at the rate of two plays a year, and he continued to visit London. In May 1612 he was in the city to make a deposition in the Belott–Mountjoy case. The next year he was there in March, when he bought for £140 the Blackfriars gatehouse and at once mortgaged it. In the same month he designed an *impresa*, a symbolic device with a motto, for Francis, Earl of Rutland, to display at a Royal Tournament and was paid 44 shillings (£2.20) for it. Tradition has it that he coached the actor John Lowin of the King's Men for the leading part in *Henry VIII*, and if so, he may have stayed till June for the première. His last visit was in November 1614 when he came with his son-in-law, Susanna's husband John Hall, to discuss Stratford property matters with Thomas Greene.

During 1611, *Cymbeline, The Winter's Tale,* and *The Tempest* were all performed in London, the last at court in November. If *The Tempest* was intended as Shakespeare's farewell to the stage, then somehow he was persuaded to go back on this final gesture, perhaps by John Fletcher, who with, and sometimes without, his partner Francis Beaumont, had begun to write the tragicomedies and romances that became so popular with London playgoers. *The Two Noble Kinsmen* is a collaboration between Fletcher and Shakespeare, and so too is Shakespeare's last play, *Henry VIII*, a Globe but not a Blackfriars production. The first performance of this play began with great ceremony and splendour in the afternoon of 29 June 1613, but it proceeded no further than the first act. At an entrance of the king in the play, a sound-effect cannon behind the stage fired, a small piece of burning material caught in the thatched roof over the galleries, and in no time the whole place was ablaze. The audience and actors escaped, but the entire building and probably a good part of the company's wardrobe were totally destroyed. The Globe was rebuilt and in operation a year later, but by that time Shakespeare had retired permanently from writing.

It was as a wealthy citizen and a respected gentleman that Shakespeare retired to Stratford. He had friends among the leading townspeople and the local gentry. The poet and playwright Michael Drayton, with whom he was acquainted, was a regular visitor at the home of Sir Henry and Lady Rainsford, who lived very near Stratford, and may well have found the time to call on him. Shakespeare became involved in the life of Stratford. He entertained a preacher in his home and was sent a quart of sack and a quart of claret by the town. In his garden that became famous, flourishing for over a century, he planted a mulberry tree. Family affairs, inevitably, were to the fore. His two remaining brothers, Gilbert and Richard, died in Stratford in 1612 and 1613 respectively, both unmarried. His elder daughter, Susanna, was involved in court action in the ecclesiastical court at Worcester in 1613 to clear her name from a slander put about by John Lane of Alveston Manor. Accused of mismanaging her household and committing adultery, Susanna was legally vindicated and her accuser punished by excommunication.

Two months before Shakespeare's death his second daughter, Judith, then aged thirty, was married to Thomas Quiney, a tavern-keeper. The marriage did not have an auspicious beginning. It took place in February, a prohibited season, without a special licence of the kind Shakespeare himself had obtained, and in consequence the couple were excommunicated. The next month a local girl called Margaret Wheeler died giving birth to a baby that also died, and Thomas Quiney confessed in court that he was the father. Shakespeare evidently altered the will that he had drafted in January on account of Judith's marriage. He signed the final settlement on each page (three of the six undisputed signatures of Shakespeare) on 25 March, in the month when, according to tradition, a "merry meeting" took place between Shakespeare, Drayton, and Jonson, which resulted in his death. It is possible that the three men did meet, since Drayton may well have been paying a visit to the Rainsfords and Jonson, a good friend, staying with him. The story, reported by John Ward, vicar (1662–81) of Stratford, in his notebook (c.1662), goes that Shakespeare drank too much at this "meeting" and as a result caught a fever. He died on 23 April and was buried in the chancel of the parish church.

His will was left in the form of a much-corrected draft and not a fair copy, perhaps because this was the practice of his lawyer, Francis Collins, or perhaps because of the need for haste if Shakespeare's death appeared imminent. The provisions do nothing to solve the many unanswered questions of his life. His property in Stratford and London went to his daughters, his granddaughter, and their heirs. His sister Joan and her sons were provided for. He made small bequests to the poor and to various local people, and he left twenty-eight shillings and six pence (£1.43) apiece to his old fellows Burbage, Heminges, and Condell, to buy memorial rings. To Anne, his wife, he left his second-best bed, in addition to the common law provision that entitled her to a life interest in one-third of all her husband's heritable estates. The best bed, which is not mentioned in the will, belonged in the master bedroom of New Place, and it went with the house to Susanna and her family, who lived there after Shakespeare's death. The hope that is implied in the terms of the will for the establishment and continuance of Shakespeare's family was not to be realized. When his granddaughter Elizabeth died in 1670, childless after two marriages, his direct line became extinct.

WS: E. K. Chambers, *William Shakespeare: A Study of Facts and Problems*. 2 vols. Clarendon Press: 1930

THEATRE AND PLAY PRODUCTION
IN SHAKESPEARE'S TIME

The Elizabethan theatre began to develop in the 1570s. This is not to say that before that time there had been no tradition of organized drama in England. The highly complex and conventionalized medium of Marlowe, Jonson, and Shakespeare did not spring to life from a void. The beginnings of European drama have been traced back to musical elaborations of the Mass that took place during Easter ceremonies in the tenth century, in particular to the *Quem Quaeritis* trope, a musical sequence sung by a soloist representing the angel at Christ's tomb and singers representing the three Maries. This trope became a little play in its own right, and over the years other episodes were added, including some with no biblical warrant; similar dramas evolved for other religious festivals. These were in Latin, but gradually, during the thirteenth century, drama detached itself from church worship and became secular in its organization and vernacular in its medium. From this time onward religious and moral plays were performed in public in the open air, in market places or on village greens. At Whitsuntide or Corpus Christi in England, cycles of mystery plays based on biblical stories were performed in processional manner through the streets of such towns as Chester or York by members of the various local trade or craft guilds.

Many other kinds of performances took place during these centuries, including miracle plays, based on the lives of the saints and martyrs, and moralities, didactic plays of various lengths in which the central subject is human life and destiny, often represented in terms of conflict between personified virtues and vices. One of the last of these plays, *The Summoning of Everyman*, was written at the end of the fifteenth century, but like the miracle and mystery plays, moralities continued to be performed in the sixteenth century. Folk plays or festivities connected with seasonal rites such as seed-sowing and harvest time were sometimes absorbed into the church plays and sometimes continued separately. On May Day there was dancing round the maypole and the election of a May king and May queen; at Christmas time mummers would go from house to house, sometimes disguised with costumes and blackened faces. The king and his court had their own ceremonies. Tournaments and jousts, which encouraged great displays of heraldry and special costumes for knights and their ladies, might go on for several days at a time. John Stow, the chronicler, records that in 1374, Dame Alice Perrers (the king's concubine), dressed as the Lady of the Sun, "rode from the Tower of London, through Cheape, accompanied of many Lords and Ladies, every Lady leading a Lord by his horse bridle, till they came into West Smithfield, and then began a great Just, which endured seven dayes after" (*EES*, i, 20–21). Under Henry VIII, court revels flourished, with all kinds of elaborately costumed spectacles, masques, dances, and interludes. Henry himself retained a troupe of eight players, the Lusores Regis, or Players of the King's Interludes, and paid them from the Exchequer.

Professional entertainers such as minstrels, jugglers, conjurers, and ballad-singers travelled throughout the country to perform at fairs and in market places and, by invitation, at the homes of the rich. There were street pageants and processions, especially on festival occasions or for the entertainment of royalty or nobility; decorated wagons might be pulled through the streets or platforms set up on which would be posed a *tableau vivant*, a group of people costumed and arranged to represent an idea or theme. When Margaret of York came to Bruges to marry Charles the Bold in 1468 there were a number of *tableaux vivants* showing scenes on the theme of marriage: Adam and Eve, the wedding at Cana, Cleopatra marrying King Alexander.

All these forms of theatre contributed in some way to the Elizabethan drama, but there were other more direct influences. During the sixteenth century, and probably earlier, boys in grammar schools and young men at Oxford and Cambridge and the Inns of Court acted in classical plays and also in plays, in both Latin and English, written by teachers and lawyers. Authors of such plays included Nicholas Udall, sometime headmaster of Eton, who wrote *Ralph Roister Doister*, and Sackville and Norton, the co-authors of *Gorboduc*. The companies of child actors, the "little eyases" that troubled the players in *Hamlet*, were already in existence in embryo early in the sixteenth century. The Children of the Chapel, originally choristers in the royal household, were first trained to act by their master, William Cornish, who produced pageants, interludes, and entertainments of all kinds for the court of Henry VIII. Groups of boys from this institution played before Elizabeth I and in the seventeenth century acted in plays written for them by Ben Jonson. They were rivalled by the Children of Paul's, who also played both at court and before a paying public under Elizabeth and her successor.

The court was a friend and benefactor to the drama in this period, and royal patronage was particularly important during the 1570s, the early years of the permanent playhouses. At that time, the Church and the City Fathers, as the civic authorities of London were called, took every opportunity to attack the "sumptuous Theatre houses, a continuall monument of Londons prodigalitie and folly" (*ES*, iv, 197) as well as the actors. Semi-professional companies of adult male actors began to appear in considerable numbers in the mid-sixteenth century. These companies were usually attached to the household of some nobleman or man of wealth, and they played at court and in the households of their patron and his friends, and from the 1550s, if not earlier, they travelled the countryside and also performed in London innyards. There were, as well, companies of strolling players who were not under the regular patronage of a nobleman but travelled in small groups, singing, clowning, and acting.

Legislation in the middle part of the century suggests that by then, amateur and semi-professional actors constituted a recognized element in the life of the country, especially in London. Censorship of interludes concerned with politics or religion began in 1533, and in 1543 there was a regulation that all interludes, books, and ballads that dealt with the interpretation of scripture were to be officially scrutinized. In 1553 the City Fathers issued an edict forbidding artificers and handicraftsmen to abandon their occupations and wander about singing in taverns and at weddings and feasts. But the most important legislation regulating the activities of actors came in the significant decade of the 1570s. In 1572 there was an Act of Parliament *"for the punishement of Vacabondes"* (14 Eliz. c.5) by which only those who held the rank of baron or above were allowed to license players who "wandered abroad" (*ES*, iv, 269–71). All those "Fencers Bearewardes Comon Players in Enterludes & Minstrels, not belonging to any Baron of this Realme or towardes any other honorable Personage of greater Degree" who wandered the country were liable to be "adjudged and deemed Roges Vacaboundes and Sturdy Beggers" and punished accordingly. The Act is notable in that it shows very clearly the stigma attached to the acting profession that lingered in the minds of many in this period despite the wealth and prestige that some men of the theatre obtained. Even more significant is the fact that the Act defined the actor's status and, by distinguishing between amateur and professional, encouraged the growth of a professional theatre.

One of the first companies formed in accordance with the statute was the Earl of Leicester's Men; it included Robert Wilson, famous for his wit, and James Burbage. Leicester was a great favourite of the Queen and a very wealthy man. He had maintained players in his household for several years before the statute, and his influence was available to win them many a hearing at court. In 1574 his company received a licence by royal patent.

The Elizabethan Playhouse

At this time, the players had been performing in London for some years, but without any permanent headquarters for their performances. The first performances of plays in London innyards were recorded from 1557 onwards at the Saracen's Head in Islington and the Boar's Head in Aldgate. Innkeepers encouraged visits from the players, and may have even modified their premises for their convenience, so that the inns gradually became little less than permanent theatres. References to inns such as the Bell and Cross Keys in Gracechurch Street, the Bull in Bishopsgate Street, and the Bel Savage on Ludgate Hill confirm their status as known playhouses for the rest of the century, sometimes perhaps as winter quarters for the major companies. The importance of these inns is recognized in legislation of 1574, when the City Fathers issued a regulation specifically aimed at the control of "great Innes, haveinge chambers and secrete places adioyninge to their open stagies and gallyries" where "playes, Interludes, and shewes" lured the youth of the city and gave occasion for "ffrayes and quarrelles" (*ES*, iv, 273–76). In 1595 they finally prohibited the use of City inns by players.

While there is no denying that professional theatre was very much alive in London before the first playhouse was built, James Burbage's venture in building London's first permanent playhouse was nonetheless of great significance for the theatre of his day. Burbage was a member of the Earl of Leicester's Men and perhaps the confidence provided by so powerful a patron encouraged him in his undertaking. His playhouse, the Theatre, was erected on a site in Shoreditch, outside the city limits, on land leased from Giles Alleyn for an annual rent of £14. It cost Burbage and his partner John Brayne £700 to build. Construction began in 1576, and the Theatre opened in 1577, before the work was actually complete; the last stages of the building were paid for out of the first takings. No illustrations of it have survived, but it is known that it was round in shape, like the two rings for animal-baiting that existed on the south bank of the Thames, that it was built mainly of timber, and that contemporaries thought it very fine. A second theatre, the Curtain, was built the same year in the same locality. "It is an euident token of a wicked time when plaiers wexe so riche that they can build such houses," remarked a disapproving contemporary (*ES*, iv, 269).

In Shakespeare's London there were eventually nine open-air, so-called public playhouses:

1. The Theatre, built in Shoreditch in 1576 by James Burbage. It was pulled down in 1597 when the ground lease expired.

2. The Curtain, built nearby in 1577. It was still in use in 1626.

3. A theatre at Newington Butts, built shortly after the Theatre and the Curtain. It was in use in the 1580s and early 1590s.

4. The Rose, built on the Bankside c.1587 by the financier Philip Henslowe. It was substantially rebuilt in 1592, and remained in use until about 1603.

5. The Swan, built on the Bankside in 1596 by Francis Langley, a goldsmith. It was in use as a playhouse until about 1620. It is the only Elizabethan theatre of which a contemporary interior view exists.

6. The Globe, built on the Bankside in 1599 by the Burbages, out of the fabric of the old Theatre. It burnt down in 1613 and was immediately rebuilt.

7. The Fortune, built just outside Cripplegate in 1599–1600 by Philip Henslowe and Edward Alleyn as a rival to the Globe. Its building contract has survived. It burnt down in 1621 and was rebuilt in brick in 1623.

8. The Red Bull, built about 1604 in Clerkenwell. It was later enlarged and probably roofed over, and continued in use after the Restoration, until 1663.

9. The Hope, built by Philip Henslowe and Jacob Meade in 1614 on the site of the old Bear Garden on the Bankside. The builder's contract, which survives, shows that it was designed to be used as both playhouse and bear-baiting arena, and had a removable stage. The shape was based on the Swan.

There existed also so-called private theatres consisting of the halls of existing buildings, where performances took place by candlelight and a higher price was charged. The first of these was in Blackfriars, a large old building situated between St Paul's and the river; it had once been used as a convent and later as a residence for important officials at court. In 1576, a few months after James Burbage signed the lease for the land where the Theatre was to be built, the upper story of Black-friars was rented by Richard Farrant for the Children of Windsor and the Children of the Chapel to perform before the public. But the lessor of the rooms objected to the way they were used, and in 1584 the arrangement came to an end. The Burbages purchased a part of the building in 1596 and converted it for the use of the Lord Chamberlain's Men, but were prevented from using it as a theatre for adult actors by a petition of residents who objected to a common playhouse being set up within their select locality. For a time, the Burbages leased it to the Children of the Chapel, but in 1609 the Lord Chamberlain's Men, now the King's Men, managed to acquire the lease, and the company and its successors played there until 1642. Other private theatres existed at Whitefriars in an old monastic hall and in the choir singing school near St Paul's.

The appearance and construction of these playhouses, especially of the public ones, is a matter of immense controversy. There have been a number of attempts at reconstruction, in particular of the Globe, which often differ very startlingly. Formerly, much stress was laid on the influence of the innyard on theatre design, and it was held that both auditorium and stage façade owed their characteristic features to the galleries, doors, windows, and yard that were an essential part of the sixteenth century inn. Other scholars have felt that since the Elizabethan playhouse was usually round or polygonal in shape while the traditional innyard was square or rectangular, the innyard theory cannot be satisfactory. It has also been suggested that the theatres owe much to the medieval and Tudor great halls in gentlemen's houses that were used by earlier players, and to the screens, often carved and ornate, that acted both as a shield between the guests in the main body of the hall and the doors to the kitchen, and as a background to the play. Another possible influence is the tradition of street pageantry with its use of *tableaux vivants* and monumental sculpture, from which the structure and symbolism of the Elizabethan stage façade may be derived.

Although contemporary evidence for the structure and organization of the Elizabethan theatre continues to be discovered, it is still fragmentary and not entirely consistent in its implications. This information consists of incidental references in letters, diaries, pamphlets, and so on, of the implications of the action and stage directions of plays themselves, and of documents such as the decrees of the Privy Council, the records of the Master of Revels, accounts of litigation in various courts, the contracts for the building of the Fortune and Hope theatres, and the excavations in 1989 of the remains of the Rose and part of the Globe theatres on the Bankside.

The diary of Philip Henslowe, the theatre owner and manager, who kept an account of the daily takings at the Rose theatre from February 1592 to November 1597, is a unique and invaluable source, not only of information about the theatres themselves, but also for the lives of the playwrights and actors who furnished their business. Foreigners who visited London in the period, such as Prince Lewis of Anhalt-Cöthen, Johannes de Witt, Paul Hentzner, and Thomas Platter of Basle, gave accounts of London's playhouses, sometimes contradicting one another. Pamphleteers and ministers of the church variously praised and condemned the phenomenon. Maps give interesting if unreliable testimony to the position, duration, and external appearance of the theatres. There is otherwise very little in the way of contemporary illustration to help us. There are a few title-pages and other engravings. Also extant are Inigo Jones's designs for scenery and costumes for his masques, and the drawing copied from one made by Johannes de Witt of the interior of the Swan, probably sometime after his visit to London in or about 1596.

Because of the survival of its building contract, the dimensions of the Fortune Theatre are known for certain (*ES*, ii, 436–39). The building was square, 80 feet each way outside and 55 feet within. It was constructed of timber plastered over, on a foundation of brick and piles. The stage measured 43 feet by 27 feet, large by modern standards, and is usually presumed to have been rectangular. There were three tiers of galleries in the auditorium, the lowest being 12 feet high, the next 11 feet, and the topmost 9 feet. Each was 12 feet broad, and the upper two each extended ten inches over the one beneath. Each storey contained four sections for "gentlemens roomes" and an unspecified number of "Twoe pennie roomes." In most respects the Fortune was designed, according to the contract, to resemble "the late erected Plaiehowse ... called the Globe," except that "all the princypall and maine postes of the saide fframe and Stadge forwarde [presumably the stage front] shalbe square and wroughte palasterwise [made like pilasters]." The carpenter, Peter Street, had assisted the Burbages when the Theatre was demolished and the Globe built out of its fabric, and it seems reasonable to suppose from this and from the wording of the contract itself, which constantly refers to the Globe as a model, that the two theatres were similar in design. De Witt, in the description of the Swan theatre that accompanies his drawing, said that it would take 3,000 people seated but did not mention how many could be accommodated standing in the yard.

The archaeological excavations on the site of the Rose theatre show it to have been a polygonal structure, originally with about fourteen sides, of roughly 72 feet in diameter. The yard, with a diameter of 49 feet, was covered in mortar and sloped down towards a small stage with tapered sides. Major alterations were carried out in 1592, giving the building a bulging tulip-shape. Henslowe's diary includes a list of costs for the alterations, and shows that the walls were made of lath and plaster, and that some of the ceilings were plastered, and the roof thatched. The Rose was originally considerably smaller than the other public theatres, and the enlargement was presumably carried out in part to increase audience capacity. Calculations based on the excavated groundplan, and assuming three tiers of galleries as at the Fortune, give a capacity of 2,000 prior to the enlargement and 2,400 afterwards. The enlarged stage measured only some 37 feet by 17 feet and probably still tapered towards the front, so that it was still substantially smaller than at the other amphitheatres like the Fortune. Access to the galleries appears to have been from within the yard. Although the archaeological evidence presents many puzzles, it is clear that the design of the Rose was distinctly different from that of the Fortune or the Globe.

In contrast, the excavation of the site of the Globe has only revealed a small part of the foundations of the structure, comprising part of the gallery walls and stairs. The archaeological evidence indicates that the theatre was polygonal, with perhaps twenty sides in all, and with a diameter of roughly 100 feet. The yard was about 80 feet in diameter, considerably larger than at the Rose. The evidence from the foundations reveals little about the stage itself, but it may well have compared in size with that of the Fortune, and it could have been square in shape rather than tapered as at the Rose. The requirements of plays known to have been staged at the Globe suggest that it must have had a trap and two stage doors, and provision for balcony scenes. Again, unlike the Rose, the stairs to the galleries at the Globe were located in stair turrets outside of the main structure.

The other theatres doubtless also differed in some ways, as modern theatres differ one from another. Most of the public theatres seem to have been approximately round or octagonal, and the halls at the Blackfriars and Whitefriars were rectangular, the Fortune being exceptional in being square. The roof of the Fortune was tiled, whereas that of the first Globe, like the Rose, was thatched. The contract for the Hope theatre, which was to resemble the Swan, is less specific than the Fortune contract, but apart from features such as a removable stage and the absence of pillars supporting the stage covering, designed to provide for the dual function of playhouse and bear-baiting ring, it does not differ significantly. The Hope was constructed of timber on a brick foundation, with three galleries of the same height as the Fortune's, and a tiled roof.

Elizabethan Stages and Stagecraft

On the important matter of the construction of the stage both the Fortune (except for giving dimensions) and the Hope contracts are unfortunately silent, and the inconclusive evidence that survives has led scholars to differ, often quite widely, on certain matters. That the stage projected far out into the yard is certain, and it was probably usually rectangular rather than square. Part of the audience, the "groundlings," stood round three sides of it in the yard. The evidence that exists for the stage structure of the Rose, the Swan, the Globe, the Fortune, and the Hope suggests that the construction in each case differed. It is thought that in the earlier houses, the Theatre and the Curtain, stages were built to be simple and easily removable, whereas they may have become more complex in the later theatres, when the financiers realized that permanent playhouses were no longer a risky enterprise. The stage was about level with the tops of the heads of the spectators in the yard, and was supported on posts. There seems to have been a low rail around the edge, perhaps to discourage the groundlings from climbing onto it.

The area directly beneath the stage, which had many uses, was probably hidden from the audience in some way, perhaps by oak boards, as at the Fortune, or by hangings. The Swan drawing may show the front of the stage supported on posts at either corner and the area beneath it unconcealed, or it may show the area beneath the stage concealed by hangings with gaps through which performers could emerge. There was at least one trapdoor set in the stage, through which villains might descend to death or ghosts arise from the "cellarage."

The roof of the stage, or "heavens," was high above, probably supported on wooden pillars, except at the Hope, where the contract specified that it was "to be borne or carryed without any postes or supporters to be fixed or sett vppon the saide stage" (*ES*, ii, 466–67). It may have covered all or only part of the stage. Over the heavens was built a hut, thatched at the Globe, tiled at the Fortune and the Hope, which maps and engravings usually show with windows. This is thought to have housed the machinery for raising and lowering thrones, chariots, and other such properties onto the stage, though it is a matter of dispute as to whether such machinery actually existed at the Globe. The whole structure was topped by a flagpole, and a flag was flown at times of performance.

The construction of the building, usually called the tiring-house, at the back of the stage is still more conjectural. In general, it is agreed that this part of the building was divided into two or possibly three levels, perhaps equivalent in height to and level with the spectators' galleries, although again the Swan drawing shows no such thing. At the lowest of these levels were two doors through which the actors made their exits and entrances, as are clearly indicated in the Swan drawing. Controversy exists as to whether, between these doors, there was a curtained recess used as the "inner" or "rear" stage, a wider door or porch, or simply, as in the Swan drawing, a blank wall. A recess would seem a most convenient location for those many scenes in Elizabethan plays that take place in some sort of alcove or removed place, as when Prospero reveals Miranda and Ferdinand playing chess in *The Tempest* or when Portia's caskets are discovered behind a curtain in *The Merchant of Venice*. However, such a recess would have been invisible to spectators in many areas of the theatre, and the term "inner stage," which seems the obvious way of describing it, was never used by the Elizabethans.

The use of the middle level of this tiring-house is also debatable. In the Swan drawing it seems to be shown as a spectators' gallery, divided into six compartments; but there are enough references to the "upper stage" in Elizabethan plays to indicate that at least some part of this level was sometimes used by the actors. How many scenes were played "aloft" in this gallery is a matter for conjecture. Again, it is hard to imagine that the space inside it was clearly visible to many in the audience, or that in general it would have been dramatically effective to leave the great

21

area of the main stage unused while a sustained scene was played out in this enclosure. This gallery may also have been used at times by musicians as well as by spectators who could afford to pay for the privilege of being so near to the play and so visible to the rest of the audience, as well as by the actors.

It is not known what sort of appearance the stage façade presented, but it was probably ornate and decorative. The Fortune, the Hope, and probably the Swan featured columns as part of it, and it may well have been painted. There was space backstage, between the stage façade and the outer wall of the playhouse, that was used in several ways: for dressing rooms, for the storage of costumes and properties, for actors to await their entrances, for the prompter and other attendants to carry out their offices, for the playwright to watch the enactment of his drama, for gallants and noblemen to chat with the actors. Most scholars are agreed that it is this whole backstage area behind the galleried façade that is meant by the term "tiring-house."

Shakespeare disparaged his theatre and called it a "cockpit" and "an unworthy scaffold," but others, both defenders and detractors of the stage, wondered at its splendour. John Stockwood, a preacher, called the Theatre a "gorgeous Playing place," and Philip Stubbes, a Puritan, talked of "*Venus* pallace," while Thomas Nashe, a pamphleteer, compared the English stage favourably with the Roman one: "our Sceane is more statelye furnisht than euer it was in the time of *Roscius*" (*ES*, iv, 200, 223, 239).

The actors, however, had frequently to perform in places other than their London playhouses—at court, in country barns, in the halls of great houses, in inn-yards—so that plays and styles of acting had to be adaptable. Of course there are some features of Elizabethan drama that must be related to the contemporary stage conditions. The neutrality of the stage is obviously a major point. The stage was free from any suggestion of a restricted location; at one moment it could represent Rome, at the next Egypt, without any pause in the action or change in its appearance. Neither space nor time had to be treated realistically. An actor might stand next to another and yet deliver an aside that was inaudible to him. A commentator could stand a few feet from the action that he was interpreting and yet not be observed by the other characters. The aside and the soliloquy are characteristic features of this drama. So too are various kinds of staging not possible in a realistically designed setting. For instance, in *Othello*, while Cassio and Bianca quarrel about Desdemona's handkerchief, Iago and Othello stand unobserved a little way off, misinterpreting the scene. In Shakespeare's *Troilus and Cressida* Cressida pleads with Diomede, watched separately by two different groups, the jeering Thersites to one side and the unhappy Troilus to the other. In *Richard III* the tents of the opposing leaders, Richmond and Richard, are simultaneously presented on the stage. In *King Lear*, Kent is placed in the stocks at the end of II.ii and left on stage, mute and sleeping, during the next scene while Edgar soliloquizes, until he is discovered by Lear and his followers in II.iv.

Space and time expand according to the demands of the imagination. An hour can pass in the course of a thirty-line soliloquy, as it does at the end of Marlowe's *Doctor Faustus*, or a whole night in the course of a scene, as in *Othello* II.iii. On such a stage, where representation is unhindered by the need to create the illusion of actuality, the dramatist has no need to restrict himself to a few long scenes with plausible backgrounds. He can use as many scenes and locations as he likes and move back and forth from interior to exterior, from one country to another, without any slowing of the pace of the action, since there were no breaks between scenes. Location boards may have been used to help the audience follow the changes of scene where this was important. Sometimes the text makes the scene change clear, with lines such as "This is Illyria, lady," in *Twelfth Night*, or "Barkloughly Castle call they this at hand" in *Richard II*, but not always.

On this kind of stage, and in a theatre where sightlines were by no means perfect, much emphasis fell on the spoken word. At the same time, note should be taken of the Elizabethans' great love of stage spectacle and the prominence of dumb-shows, tableaux, processions, swordfights, and ceremonial dances. Colourful and expensive costumes added to the brilliance and visual appeal of the stage. Puritan critics were censorious of players who earned a mere "vi s. by the weeke" being able to "jet under gentlemens noses in sutes of silk" (*ES*, iv, 204) (it was said to be customary for the rich clothing of lords and noblemen to be handed on after their deaths to the actors). Henslowe's diary contains an inventory of costumes owned by the Lord Admiral's Men that included cloaks in scarlet and black velvet, gowns, caps, suits and jerkins, and doublets in silk, satin, and damask, with trimmings of gold and silver tinsel and lace. Henslowe records paying £7 for "a dublet of whitt satten layd thicke with gowld lace, and a payer of rowne pande hosses [hose] of cloth of sylver, the panes layd with gowld lace" (*Diary*, 325). Colours were often used symbolically on the stage, as for instance the white, red, and black tents in Marlowe's *Tamburlaine*, the sable suit worn by Hamlet, and the yellow stockings that signified Malvolio's role as a lover in *Twelfth Night*.

Properties, too, were often elaborate. Henslowe provides a useful list, including such intriguing items as "the sittie of Rome" and "the clothe of the Sone & Mone," which were perhaps painted hangings, and "i Hell mought [mouth]" and "i dragon in fostes [Faustus]," which come directly from the trappings of medieval drama, as well as the tombs, crowns, and mossy banks that we know to have been standard properties (*Diary*, 319–20). Despite the fact that the Elizabethans did not use movable scenery as such, there is much evidence that the stage was frequently decked out to represent certain conventional settings; an arbour or garden, a cave, a castle, or a tomb.

But, obviously, the dramatist did have to rely very much on the words to create atmosphere and setting. In *A Midsummer Night's Dream* the evocation of moonlight and enchanted woods in the language of the fairies and the lovers makes a very deliberate contrast with the efforts of Bottom and his company to provide a moon-lit setting for their play with such mechanical and symbolic aids as the man in the moon and his dog. The soldiers in the opening scene of *Hamlet* must evoke the eerie midnight atmosphere with their edgy dialogue, since they can have no assistance from lighting. It is, in fact, not so much the lack of scenery that the dramatist must compensate for, as the lack of lighting. In the public theatres plays were performed in the afternoon, and while the use of candles or tapers may have suggested night-time scenes, there was no way of providing darkness or moonlight.

This lack of blackout and also of curtaining created another difficulty, that of the management of violence and climaxes; dead bodies had to be disposed of and the ending of the play had to be so contrived that the players all walked or were carried off. There was no chance to end with a final tableau. Shakespeare's tragedies *Hamlet* and *King Lear* present contrasting ways of dealing with this problem. In the last scene of *Hamlet*, five characters die on stage, with Hamlet himself last; Shakespeare cannot end with Hamlet's "the rest is silence," or yet with Horatio's epitaph, for the stage is piled with corpses—so Fortinbras enters and ends the play with the arrangements for the disposal of the bodies. In *King Lear* most of the deaths take place before the final scene or else offstage; this makes the disposal easier but also leaves the stage free for Lear and his lamentations over Cordelia's body, so that attention is centred on the sight of father and daughter reunited in death, before Albany gives the order, "Bear them from hence."

One feature of Elizabethan stagecraft that does seem to result directly from the construction of the stage is the use of vertical movement. The upper stage could serve as a balcony or platform to which characters might climb (Romeo) or be conveyed (Antony); it might be an upper room, a city wall, a battlement, where characters could watch and comment on the action taking place below on the main stage. Richard II descends symbolically from the walls of his castle to the courtyard below where Bolingbroke awaits him. Richard III appears "aloft" in the company of two bishops. In *The Taming of the Shrew* Christopher Sly watches the whole play from the upper room, here representing the lord's bedroom in an inn. The action on the upper stage was, however, usually brief and restricted to a limited number of actors. It could easily have been played, as required, in an above-stage gallery area normally given over to spectators. The trap door on the main stage provided for downward movement. Hamlet and Laertes could jump into it in their scuffle at Ophelia's funeral; the Jew of Malta might plunge down it into his burning cauldron. Devils, ghosts, and furies could arise from and descend into it. Just as the stage canopy was painted to represent heaven so the area below stage could represent hell.

The Elizabethan Audience

There is no doubt that the nobility and the uneducated alike attended the theatre, along with artisans, apprentices, students, foreign visitors, and pickpockets and prostitutes; the audience could not have been so dissimilar to that at a bear-baiting, and among those who were mentioned as present when Paris Garden, the bear-baiting arena, collapsed in 1583 were a baker, a clerk, several servants, a fell-monger, and several women. Plays had to appeal to a very heterogeneous crowd and undoubtedly this influenced their character. To this factor we can partly ascribe the variety of Elizabethan drama—the mixture of sophisticated wit and rhetoric, dazzling poetry, high comedy, clowning, farce, and all manner of spectacle. There were duels and fencing matches, dumbshows, conjuring, supernatural characters, music and songs, dancing, and much bloodshed. Shakespeare rejected some of these elements; there is very little conjuring, few magic tricks, few dumb-shows, and after the excesses of *Titus Andronicus*, not much bloodshed in his plays. But he never ceased to mix high and low comedy and to introduce fools and clowns at moments of the greatest dramatic tension, and his use of music and dancing does not diminish but grows increasingly subtle and refined. Later, under the Stuart kings the drama narrowed its scope and ceased to attract so wide and varied an audience.

Plays were advertised by bills posted in the city or distributed by hand. Since seats were not reserved, the audience would need to assemble early for a new or popular production, perhaps gathering fairly soon after the midday meal, as the performances started at 2 p.m. The performance lasted at least two hours, according to references such as that in the Prologue to *Romeo and Juliet* to the "two hours traffic of our stage," and longer, if it was followed, as was customary, by a jig. On dull days in winter the last act must have been played in the falling dusk.

During Shakespeare's time the cheapest price of admission to the public theatre was 1d. (roughly half of 1p) which bought standing room out in the open in the yard. In days when a quart of ale cost 4d. (2p), and a small pipe of tobacco or a very cheap meal 3d.(1p), such a price was not expensive. For the payment of a second penny the spectator might sit in the topmost gallery or one of the twopenny rooms. Pamphleteers and satirists made little distinction in their scorn between the "Twopeny Clients and Peny Stinkards" (*ES*, ii, 533). Thomas Platter, a visitor to London from Basle in 1599, said that for 3d. one of the best seats, with a cushion, might be bought. In the hall playhouses admission cost 6d. (2½p) and a stool on the stage itself a further 6d., while boxes at the side of the stage were more expensive. At the turn of the century the London artisan earned between 10d. (4p) and 16d. (6p) a day, and so prices in the theatre were comparatively affordable.

For the richest and most fashionable playgoer the place to sit was in one of the boxes over the stage, or on a stool on the stage itself. Apparently it became most fashionable to sit on the stage, and by 1609 the lords' room over the stage was being referred to as the haunt of the less reputable patrons. It is clear that those who sat on the stage made their presence felt to actors and audience alike. They blew smoke from their pipes onto the stage. They obstructed the actors. If they disliked the play or its author they might leave very conspicuously at some important point. Ben Jonson particularly objected to those capricious gallants who "have taken such a habit of dislike in all things, that they will approue nothing, be it neuer so conceited or elaborate, but sit disperst, making faces, and spitting, wagging their vpright eares, and cry filthy, filthy" (*The Case Is Altered* II.vii).

The gallants who sat on the stage were most obtrusive at the hall playhouses, which tended to attract a more socially exclusive audience. It is harder to judge the behaviour of the majority of the audience at the public theatres. The players regularly complained about the noise of the cracking of the nuts the audiences ate during performances, and occasionally remarked on the hiss of bottled ale being opened. Recent archaeological evidence confirms that large quantities of nuts were indeed consumed in the theatres. Complaints about violent, criminal, or immoral behaviour in the theatres describe the potential consequences of any large crowd of people gathered together. Prostitutes and cutpurses did frequent the theatres, and occasionally there were affrays and other interruptions to the proceedings. In 1617 the London apprentices attacked the Cockpit theatre, apparently out of anger that plays from this public theatre had been transferred to a newly opened and more expensive hall playhouse. Other accounts indicate that the audiences could be forthright in expressing their opinions of the play. They clapped at what they liked, but they also booed, hissed, and "mewed." They wept without inhibition, and they roared with laughter and delight: "Player is much out of countenance, if fooles do not laugh at them, boyes clappe their hands, pesants ope their throates, and the rude raskal rabble cry excellent, excellent" (*Playgoing*, 230).

Elizabethan Actors and Theatrical Companies

An enthusiastic theatregoer might go several afternoons a week to the same playhouse and see a different production each time, for the repertory system was a characteristic feature of the Elizabethan theatre. It was also a necessary feature, for the potential audience of the London playhouses was not large. In 1600 London itself had between 200,000 and 250,000 inhabitants; it has been calculated that perhaps 13 per cent of these Londoners went once a week to the theatre. At times, three or even four public theatres might be in operation, and the rebirth of the children's companies at the turn of the century provided a serious source of competition for the adult companies. The repertory system was so arranged that over a period of two weeks the patron of a particular theatre might see a different play almost every day. During the period from 25 August 1595 to 28 February 1596, 150 performances of thirty different plays were given at the Rose, where the Lord Admiral's Men performed. Of these plays, fourteen were new that season, and there were eighty-seven performances of these; eight plays were less than a year old and there were forty-six performances of these; the remaining eight that were more than a year old accounted for only seventeen performances, five of these being of Marlowe's *The Jew of Malta*, newly revived that season. This account illustrates the extent to which the theatre depended on new plays. It also shows what enormous demands were made of the Elizabethan actor. The system was such that every member of a theatrical company appeared in each production, sometimes in more than one part. Thus a leading actor in the Lord Admiral's company for that period would have had at least thirty roles at his command, nearly half of them newly learned. He would be also expected to retain a part over a long period, since he might have to wait several weeks or months between performances of the play.

Whenever the theatres were not closed on account of plague, civic disturbance, or Lent, there must have been at least two or three companies active simultaneously in the capital. The adult companies usually consisted of eight to twelve sharehold-ers and from six to thirty hired men, plus boy apprentices, stagehands, and musi-cians. The Earl of Leicester's Men consisted of six actors in 1572, when they wrote to their patron to ask for appointment as his household servants in order to meet the terms of the Act of Parliament that regulated the licensing of players. Queen Elizabeth's Men, formed in 1583, had twelve men and was the largest troupe. Some of these companies stayed together with very little change of personnel over long periods, continuing as a group under a succession of patrons; others played together for a short period, broke up, and re-formed under another name.

Conditions in the theatre were not stable for very long during the 1580s, espe-cially since opposition to the development of the drama came from several fronts and the City Fathers did all they could to inhibit its growth. In 1583 a company was formed under the patronage of the Queen herself. This became the leading group of the day until the death of Richard Tarlton, the great clown, in 1588, and the rise of the Lord Admiral's Men. Allied with the Lord Strange's Men, the Ad-miral's Men became the leading group in 1590. During 1594 there was a major reshuffle in which some minor or declining companies disappeared; the allied Strange's and Admiral's groups broke up, and two new companies were formed: the Lord Admiral's Men and the Lord Chamberlain's Men. Together, these two com-panies dominated the London stage for the next forty years. On his accession, James I became patron of the company to which Shakespeare belonged, the Lord Cham-berlain's Men, which then became known as the King's Men. Royal patronage does not seem to have conferred any special benefits; Elizabeth did not save her men from financial loss or professional eclipse, and James's men had to defend themselves be-fore the Privy Council for playing in the prohibited season of Lent. James himself exerted strong control over the theatre, and while on the one hand this was a pro-tective measure and effectively silenced opposition from the City Fathers and from the Church during his reign, on the other it could be said that his influence was ultimately repressive and served to divorce the theatre from the popular audi-ence that had given it life.

The Lord Chamberlain's Men were financially the most successful and also the most stable group of their time. They formed in 1594 and moved into their own new playhouse, the Globe, in 1599; there were then nine sharers: Thomas Pope, John Heminges, Augustine Phillips, Richard Cowley, Richard Burbage, William Sly, Henry Condell, Robert Armin, and William Shakespeare. A company had three types of member: the sharers, who bought, for a down payment of perhaps £50, the right to a portion of the company's profits and usually, though not always, took the leading parts; the hired men, who were not permanent members of the company but worked with them for a time in whatsoever capacity was required and received a regular, if not very substantial, wage; and the apprentices, boys or young men who played the women's parts and meanwhile received dramatic training, apprenticed to one of the sharers. By no means all actors began as apprentices; many—perhaps Shakespeare himself—went directly into the theatre from some trade or profession. James Burbage, who "by occupacion a joyner and reaping but a small lyving by the same, gave it over and became a commen player in playes" (*ES*, ii, 305), was untypical not in his change of career but in the success he made of it. Robert Armin, the clown, was said to have once been a goldsmith's apprentice. John Heminges called himself in his will a citizen and grocer.

There is some disagreement as to how far the actors specialized in roles, but it does seem fairly clear that the same actors constantly took the main parts. At the Globe, Burbage was always the straight lead, Robert Armin the comic lead, and Richard Cowley took secondary parts. Cast-lists for plays performed by the King's Men survive from 1623–32, and the implications of these are that characters could be roughly categorized into types—the hero, the foil for the hero, the smooth villain, the dignitary or old king, the young man or lover, and the comic figure—and that the actors usually specialized in a particular type of role. A kind of star system was in operation, but actors cannot have been rigidly type-cast. Some doubling of parts was called for, and of course an actor had to be prepared to take over another's role in emergencies. Playwrights at times wrote on the assumption that certain players would take certain parts. Shakespeare may well have written *Richard III*, *Hamlet*, *Othello*, and *King Lear* in the knowledge that Richard Burbage would play the lead, but this, of course, only proves how far Burbage was from being type-cast.

The Elizabethan actor had to be versatile: he was above all an entertainer. Actors could sing, dance, fence, and perform acrobatic tricks; comic actors were expected to be able to improvise (which according to Hamlet they sometimes did too readily). Tarlton, whose quips were preserved in print, was apparently so noted for his extempore wit that it was customary at the end of a play in which he appeared for the audience to shout out "themes" in rhyme for him to answer on the spot.

As the account of the repertory system shows, the actors had to work very hard for their money, retaining a large number of parts in their minds while constantly learning new ones. Some actors became very prosperous and sought to win respectability. Some of them, like Tarlton, who had Sir Philip Sidney as a godfather to his son, and Burbage, whose death in 1619 left his friend the Earl of Pembroke disconsolate, were on familiar terms with the great men of the realm. Shakespeare became a prosperous man and a property owner, but Edward Alleyn (of the rival Lord Admiral's Men), who took for his third wife a daughter of the poet John Donne, by that time Dean of St Paul's, was probably six times more wealthy. He was able to buy the manor of Dulwich for about £10,000 and found a college there, as well as becoming in old age a patron of writers and actors. But these were exceptional cases, and for the most part acting was a precarious profession, which in certain quarters at least was held in disrepute. Pamphleteers and even playwrights themselves attacked the actors, perhaps jealous of their fame and success. The writer Robert Greene said they were "base minded ... in their corse of life, for they care not how they get crowns, ... how basely so they haue them" (*ES*, iv, 240). Plays were commonly said to be "a speaciall cause of corrupting their Youth, conteninge nothinge but vnchast matters, lascivious devices, shiftes of Coozenage, & other lewd & vngodly practizes" (*ES*, iv, 322). Players were called "the worste and daungerousest people in the world" and "Schoole-masters in bawderie, and in idlenes" (*ES*, iv, 207, 212).

A study of the legislation concerning the theatre during this period shows the desire of citizens and civil authorities to repress the theatre growing all the stronger for its resilience. Some new law, some petition from powerful citizens against the actors was a constant threat in Elizabeth's reign; James's efficient appropriation into his own hands of control over the theatres regulated their activities no less than before. During Shakespeare's time the plague was rarely long absent from London, and whenever plague deaths amounted to more than thirty (later forty) a week the authorities were only too glad to close down the playhouses and send the actors off to exile in the country. Prolonged closures were occasioned by the plague in 1581–82, 1592–93, and a great many times between 1603 and 1610, perhaps for almost thirty months. Players and playwrights disliked these excursions; profits were lower and the companies had to reduce their establishments and dismiss hired men. Sometimes groups broke up as a result. Moreover the loss of dignity was great. In the city the more prominent actors were men of wealth and substance, but in the country all were reduced to the level of the wandering minstrel. "Players, by reason they shal have a hard winter, and must travell on the hoofe, will lye sucking there for pence and twopences, like young pigges at a sowe newly farrowed" prophesied Thomas Dekker in 1609 (*ES*, i, 332).

If the system was sometimes hard on the players, at least there were profits to be had by some; those who owned shares in a company, or better still, were "housekeepers" (that is, had a right to a percentage of all the company's takings, not merely those from certain sections of the house) had a good steady income, and there were sometimes bonuses of £10, £20, or more for a performance at court. Playwrights in general fared less well. At any rate Robert Greene, according to the famous passage in his pamphlet *Greene's Groatsworth of Wit*, seems to have thought that playwrights had the worst of it, denouncing the players as "those Puppits ... that speake from our mouths, those Anticks garnisht in our colours" (*ES*, iv, 241). Plays were sold outright to theatrical companies or their managers. Some playwrights were contracted to individual companies and paid a fixed wage in return for writing a specified number of plays a year, while others sold their plays to whoever would buy them.

Philip Henslowe, who financed one of the two main companies between 1594 and 1602 and had dealings with many playwrights of his time, paid them about £6 for a play in the 1590s. Often he paid by installments of £1 or so as a batch of sheets came in, an arrangement that was much more advantageous to himself than to the authors. A number of entries in Henslowe's diary record him bailing playwrights out of debtors' prisons: "Lent [paid] ... to discharge Mr. Dicker [Thomas Dekker] owt of the cownter in the powltrey the some of fortie shillinges"; "vnto harey chettel [Henry Chettle] to paye his charges in the marshallsey the some of xxxs"; "Lent vnto .. w^m harton [William Haughton] to releace hime owt of the clyncke [Clink prison] the some of xs" (*Diary*, 86, 103, 131).

Playwrights received no royalties for their work, and a play once sold became the property of the company to do with as it liked. The company was usually reluctant to allow its plays to be published, since there was no system of limiting acting rights and the plays could be appropriated for performance by another company. The Earl of Pembroke's Men only sold their playbooks to the printers in time of financial difficulties, in 1593. Plays were not generally regarded as of the same order of literature as poetry, and Ben Jonson was much ridiculed when he saw his collected plays through the press in 1616, calling them his "works." Playwrights supplemented their income from their own individual plays by hackwork or collaboration. During periods of theatrical prosperity, the demand for new plays was very great, and the Admiral's Men, between 1594 and 1600, needed one almost every two weeks. Often four or five authors would contribute to a single work. Thomas Heywood, who wrote for Queen Anne's Men at the Red Bull Theatre from 1605/6 to 1619, claimed to have worked on some 220 plays. Other occasional sources of income were court performances, for which a playwright might be paid between £15 and £30, or benefit performances, for which there is a little evidence. Conditions for playwrights did improve in the seventeenth century, especially as a result of Ben Jonson's efforts to raise the standing of the dramatist, but it may be noted that greater stability and larger payments did not in general produce better plays.

Diary: *Henslowe's Diary*, Ed. R. A. Foakes and R. T. Rickert. Cambridge University Press: 1961

EES: Glynne Wickham, *Early English Stages 1300–1600*. 2 vols. Routledge and Kegan Paul: 1963, 1972

ES: E. K. Chambers, *The Elizabethan Stage*. 4 vols. Clarendon Press: 1923

Playgoing: Andrew Gurr, *Playgoing in Shakespeare's London*. Cambridge University Press: 1987

A SELECTED BIBLIOGRAPHY

This bibliography, which has been compiled with the needs of students in mind, is divided into the following sections:

1. Editions of Shakespeare's Works
2. Reference Books
3. Background Reading
4. Critical Studies
5. Theatres and Stagecraft
6. Shakespeare in Performance: Stage and Screen
7. Shakespeare's Reputation

1. Editions of Shakespeare's Works

Brockbank, P., general editor. *The New Cambridge Shakespeare*. Cambridge University Press: 1984– . (Separately edited volumes with illustrations, notes, and appendices. Particular attention is paid to the plays as realized on stage, and to their social and cultural settings.)

Brooks, H.F., Jenkins, H., and Morris B., eds., *The Arden Shakespeare*. Methuen: 1955– . (Individual volumes, separately edited, with very full scholarly notes and substantial introductions, but becoming superseded the Arden Shakespeare Third Series.)

Evans, G. Blakemore, textual editor, *The Riverside Shakespeare*. Houghton Mifflin: 1974. (Contains illustrations, excellent brief introductions to each play, footnotes, and useful appendices.)

Greenblatt, S., general editor, with Cohen, W., Howard, J. E., and Maus, K.A. *The Norton Shakespeare*. Norton and co.: 1997. (Single volume edition, based on the text of the Oxford Shakespeare, though with independent critical introductions to each play. Lively and informative.)

Mulryne, J. R., and Bulman, J. C., eds. *Shakespeare in Performance Series*. Manchester University Press: 1982– . (Individual volumes, with detailed accounts of specific performances.)

Proudfoot, G. R., Thompson, A., and Kastan, D., general editors. *Arden Shakespeare Third Series*. Routledge: 1995– . (Individual volumes, separately edited, with full annotation incorporating the latest scholarship.)

Spencer, T.J.B., general editor, and Wells, S., associate editor. *The New Penguin Shakespeare.* Penguin: 1971–   . (Individual volumes, separately edited, with helpful notes and introductions.)

Wells, S., general editor. *The Oxford Shakespeare.* Oxford University Press: 1982–   . (Individual volumes, separately edited. Good notes, introductions, and glossaries.)

Wells, S., and Taylor, G., general editors. *William Shakespeare: The Complete Works.* Oxford University Press: 1986; compact edn., 1988. (Incorporates new theories about Shakespeare's texts, and arranges the plays in hypothetical order of composition.)

2. Reference Books

Bergeron, D.M. *Shakespeare. A Study and Research Guide.* Macmillan: 1975. (A handy, practical guide to the study of Shakespeare, designed for the student or general reader.)

Blayney, P. *The First Folio of Shakespeare.* Washington, DC: 1991

Campbell, O. J., and Quinn, E. G., eds. *A Shakespeare Encyclopaedia.* London: 1966

McDonald, R. *The Bedford Companion to Shakespeare: An Introduction with Documents.* Boston, 1996

McManaway, J.G., and Roberts, J.A. *A Selective Bibliography of Shakespeare. Editions, Textual Studies, Commentary.* The Folger Shakespeare Library: 1975. (A bibliography of 4,500 entries, mostly of books and articles published since 1930. Designed for the research student or scholar.)

Onions, C.T. *A Shakespeare Glossary*, revised and enlarged by R.D. Eagleson. Oxford University Press: 1986. (A dictionary of Shakespearean language.)

Partridge, E. *Shakespeare's Bawdy: A Literary and Psychological Essay and a Comprehensive Glossary.* Routledge: 1947, revised and enlarged, 1968. (Informative glossary of Shakespeare's extensive sexual vocabulary.)

Rubinstein, F. *A Dictionary of Shakespeare's Sexual Puns and their Significance.* 2nd edn. Macmillan: 1989. (More attentive to wordplay than Partridge, but sometimes very speculative.)

Spevack, M. *A Complete and Systematic Concordance to the Works of Shakespeare*, 9 vols. Olms: 1968–80. (Complete computerised concordance.)

Spevack, M. *The Harvard Concordance to Shakespeare.* Belknap Press of Harvard University Press: 1973. (The standard one-volume concordance.)

Wells, S. ed. *Shakespeare: A Bibliographical Guide*, new edition. Clarendon Press: 1990. (Selective guide to the best scholarship and criticism in all major areas of Shakespeare study.)

Wells, S., Taylor, G., with J. Jowett and W. Montgomery. *William Shakespeare: A Textual Companion.* Oxford University Press: 1987.

3. Background Reading

Baldwin, T.W. *William Shakespeare's Small Latine and Lesse Greeke*, 2 vols. University of Illinois Press: 1944. (Long scholarly account of education in Shakespeare's day with detailed discussion of school curricula.)

Bate, J. *Shakespeare and Ovid*. Oxford University Press: 1993. (Definitive account of Shakespeare's creative relationship with Ovid.)

Bradbrook, M.C. *The Growth and Structure of Elizabethan Comedy*. Chatto and Windus: 1955; Peregrine Books: 1963. (A study of the development of Elizabethan comedy from medieval origins to about 1610, including sections on Shakespeare.)

Bradbrook, M.C. *Themes and Conventions of Elizabethan Tragedy*. Cambridge University Press: 1935; paperback edn.: 1960. (A study of Elizabethan tragedy with special emphasis on conventions of acting and characterization, and separate chapters on Marlowe, Tourneur, Webster, and Middleton.)

Cohen, W. *Drama of a Nation: Public Theater in Renaissance England and Spain*. Cornell University Press: 1985. (Densely written comparative study of drama in the political context of an absolutist state.)

Dollimore, J. *Radical Tragedy: Religion, Ideology and Power in the Drama of Shakespeare and his Contemporaries*. 2nd ed. Harvester Press: 1989. (Marxist-influenced account which challenges traditional humanist readings.)

Doran, M. *Endeavors of Art: A Study of Form in Elizabethan Drama*. University of Wisconsin Press: 1954. (Wide-ranging and scholarly study of form and genre in Elizabethan drama with useful material on the theoretical background.)

Farnham, W. *The Medieval Heritage of Elizabethan Tragedy*. Reprinted Basil Blackwell: 1956. (A study of the medieval philosophical and dramatic background to Elizabethan tragedy.)

Ferguson, M.W., Quilligan, M., and Vickers, N.J. *Rewriting the Renaissance: The Discourses of Sexual Difference in Early Modern Europe*. University of Chicago Press: 1986. (Collection of important articles relating widely to issues of sexual difference, including influential accounts of *The Tempest* by Orgel, and of *A Midsummer Night's Dream* by Montrose.)

Greenblatt, S. *Renaissance Self-Fashioning: From More to Shakespeare*. Chicago and London: 1981 (Seminal new historicist study of the social self in early modern England, with chapter on *Othello*.)

Jardine, L. *Still Harping on Daughters: Women and Drama in the Age of Shakespeare*. 2nd ed. Harvester Press: 1989. (Carefully researched studies of separate aspects of the presentation of women in Elizabethan drama, with close attention to the socio-historical background.)

Lanham, R.A. *The Motives of Eloquence. Literary Rhetoric in the Renaissance.* Yale University Press: 1976. (Provocative study of the rhetoric of self-presentation in Renaissance literature, with chapters on *Hamlet* and *Venus and Adonis*.)

Lever, J.W. *The Tragedy of State. A Study of Jacobean Drama.* New edn. Methuen: 1987. (Pioneering account of Jacobean drama in the context of contemporary political issues.)

Smith, H.D. *Elizabethan Poetry: A Study in Conventions, Meaning, and Expression.* Harvard University Press: 1952. (Detailed account of form, genre and convention in Elizabethan poetry including Shakespeare, whose sonnets and narrative poems are helpfully located in a contemporary context.)

Spenser, T.J.B. ed. *Shakespeare's Plutarch.* Penguin Shakespeare Library, Penguin Books: 1968. (Anthology of extracts from Plutarch's *Lives* on which Shakespeare based his plays.)

Welsford, E. *The Fool: His Social and Literary History.* Faber and Faber: 1935. (Well-documented account of origins of the Fool in English and European literature and folklore.)

Wiles, D. *Shakespeare's Clown, Actor and Text in the Elizabethan Playhouse.* Cambridge University Press: 1987. (Illuminating account of Shakespeare's clown roles in relation to traditions of performance.)

Woodbridge, L. *Women and the English Renaissance: Literature and the Nature of Womankind, 1540–1620.* Harvester Press: 1984. (Wide-ranging exploration of controversies about the literary representation of gender.)

Wright, L.B. *Middle Class Culture in Elizabethan England.* University of North Carolina Press: 1935. (Extensive survey of minor literature of Shakespeare's day, useful for any study of the social background to the drama.)

4. Critical Studies

Adelman, J. *The Common Liar: An Essay on 'Antony and Cleopatra'.* Yale University Press: 1973. (Important account of identity and selfhood in the play.)

Auden, W. H. *The Dyer's Hand and other essays.* Faber and Faber: 1963. (Includes brilliant essays on Falstaff, *The Merchant of Venice*, Iago, and music in Shakespeare.)

Barber, C.L. *Shakespeare's Festive Comedy: A Study of Dramatic Form and its Relation to Social Custom.* Princeton University Press: 1972. (Influential book relating Shakespeare's comedy to a background of popular native festivity.)

Berry E. *Shakespeare's Comic Rites.* Cambridge University Press: 1984. (Relates the comedies to anthropological theory and the rites of passage from adolescence to maturity in Elizabethan social practice.)

Bethell, S.L. *The Winter's Tale: A Study.* Staples Press: 1947. (A Christian interpretation of the play which pays close attention to stage presentation.)

Blake, N.F. *Shakespeare's Language. An Introduction.* The Macmillan Press: 1983. (Clearly written introductory account of the Elizabethan aspects of Shakespeare's language.)

Booth, S. *An Essay on Shakespeare's Sonnets.* Yale University Press: 1969. (Close and detailed analysis of language and structure.)

Bradbrook, M.C. *Shakespeare and Elizabethan Poetry.* Cambridge University Press, paperback edn.: 1976. (Study of Shakespeare's art focused on his non-dramatic poetry in relation to the poetry of contemporaries.)

Bradley, A.C. *Shakespearian Tragedy*, 1904. Macmillan Student Editions, reprinted: 1985. (Immensely influential account of Shakespearean tragedy, focusing especially on the characters of the tragic heroes.)

———. *Oxford Lectures on Poetry.* Macmillan: 1909, 1950. (Includes essays on *Antony and Cleopatra* and the famous 'The Rejection of Falstaff'.)

Bullough, G. ed. *Narrative and Dramatic Sources of Shakespeare*, 7 vols. Routledge and Kegan Paul: 1957. (Immensely useful work, containing substantial accounts of Shakespeare's treatment of his source-material in each play, as well as extensive extracts from sources and analogues.)

Chambers, Sir E.K. *William Shakespeare: A Study of Facts and Problems*, 2 vols. Clarendon Press: 1930. (The most thorough and scholarly account of Shakespeare's life and theatrical career, abridged by C. Williams as *A Short Life of Shakespeare with the Sources*, Clarendon Press: 1933.)

Clemen, W.H. *A Commentary on Shakespeare's 'Richard III'.* Methuen: 1968. (Detailed, scene-by-scene account of the play with attention both to patterns of language and to stage presentation.)

———. *The Development of Shakespeare's Imagery.* 2nd edn. Methuen, University Paperback edn.: 1977. (A consideration of the dramatic function of imagery in the plays.)

Coleridge, S.T. *Coleridge's Shakespearian Criticism*, ed. T.M. Raysor, 2 vols. Revised edn., Everyman's Library. J M Dent: 1960. (Useful collection of Coleridge's imaginative and brilliant Shakespeare criticism.)

Danby, J.F. *Shakespeare's Doctrine of Nature.* Faber and Faber, paperback edn.: 1975. (A study of the radically contrasting ideas of nature in Shakespeare's time, especially illuminating on *King Lear*.)

Dollimore, J., and Sinfield, A., eds. *Political Shakespeare: New Essays in Cultural Materialism.* Manchester University Press: 1985. (Influential collection of essays by different authors, demonstrating a variety of political readings of Shakespeare.)

Dubrow, H. *Captive Victors: Shakespeare's Narrative Poems and Sonnets.* Ithaca and London: 1987. (Study of themes and language derived from close readings of the texts.)

Dusinberre, J. *Shakespeare and the Nature of Women.* Macmillan Press, paperback edn.: 1979. (Detailed study tracing proto-feminist sympathies in Shakespeare's presentation of women.)

Elam, K. *Shakespeare's Universe of Discourse: Language Games in the Comedies*. Cambridge University Press: 1984. (Detailed account of dramatic rhetoric, particularly in *Love's Labour's Lost*, in a context of modern linguistics.)

Eliot, T.S. *Selected Essays*. Faber and Faber: 1932. (Contains his famous essay on *Hamlet* and an influential view of *Othello* in 'Shakespeare and the Stoicism of Seneca'.)

Felperin, H. *Shakespearian Romance*. Princeton University Press: 1972. (Stimulating study of *Pericles*, *Cymbeline*, *The Winter's Tale*, and *The Tempest*, especially interesting on their structure.)

Frye, N. *A Natural Perspective: The Development of Shakespearian Comedy and Romance*. Columbia University Press: 1965. (Highly influential account of the genres of comedy and romance as practised by Shakespeare.)

Granville-Barker, H. *Prefaces to Shakespeare*, 6 vols. Batsford: 1971–74. (A series of introductory essays, stressing practical aspects of Shakespeare's stagecraft.)

Greenblatt, S. *Shakespearean Negotiations: The Circulation of Social Energy in Renaissance England*. Clarendon Press: 1988. (Important essays by one of the foremost new historicist critics.)

Heilman, R.B. *This Great Stage: Image and Structure in 'King Lear'*. Louisiana State University Press: 1948. (Account of language and poetic structure in the play.)

———. *Magic in the Web: Action and Language in 'Othello'*. University of Kentucky Press: 1956. (Account of language and poetic structures in the play, especially illuminating about Iago.)

Honigmann, E.A. *Shakespeare: The 'Lost Years'*. Manchester University Press: 1985. (Makes a case for Shakespeare's Roman Catholic background.)

Howard, J., and Rackin, P. *Engendering a Nation. A Feminist Account of Shakespeare's English Histories*. London and New York: 1997. (Illuminating account of the role of gender in representations of nationhood in the English history plays.)

James, D.G. *The Dream of Prospero*. Clarendon Press: 1967. (An account of *The Tempest* with a useful chapter on Shakespeare's use of contemporary literature of colonization.)

Jenkins, H. *The Structural Problem in Shakespeare's 'Henry the Fourth'*. Methuen: 1956. (Carefully argued theory of the relationship between Parts I and II of *Henry IV*.)

Jones, Emrys. *The Origins of Shakespeare*. Oxford University Press: 1977. (A study of Shakespeare's early histories in the light of their origins in medieval and humanist thought.)

———. *Scenic Form in Shakespeare*. Oxford University Press, paperback: reissued (with corrections) 1985. (Treats the conception and realization of the scene as a unit and as part of a sequence.)

Jones, Ernest. *Hamlet and Oedipus*. Victor Gollancz: 1949. (Study of *Hamlet* in terms of Freudian theory.)

Knight, G. Wilson. *The Imperial Theme*. Methuen University Paperback: reprinted 1985. (Influential study of kingship in Shakespeare.)

———. *The Shakespearian Tempest*. Oxford University Press: 1932, 1960. (An analysis of Shakespeare's dramatic use of tempest imagery throughout his work.)

——. *The Sovereign Flower*. Methuen: 1958. (A study of Shakespeare as the poet of royalism, containing indexes to occurrences of major themes throughout his work.)

——. *The Wheel of Fire*. Methuen University Paperback: 1988. (Study of Shakespeare's major tragedies in terms of imagery and symbolic themes. Important chapter on *King Lear*.)

Leavis, F.R. *The Common Pursuit*. 1952. Hogarth Press paperback: reissued 1984. (Contains his well-known essay on *Othello* 'The Diabolic Intellect and the Noble Hero'.)

Leggatt, A. *Shakespeare's Comedy of Love*. Methuen: 1974. (Account of romantic and moral themes in Shakespeare's great comedies.)

Lenz, C., Greene, G., and Neely, C., eds. *The Woman's Part: Feminist Criticism of Shakespeare*. University of Illinois Press: 1980. (Useful collection of articles, mostly by American feminists, on issues of gender in Shakespeare.)

Long, M. *The Unnatural Scene: A Study in Shakespearian Tragedy*. Methuen: 1976. (Considers the tragedies in relation to the social worlds in which they are set.)

Mahood, M.M. *Shakespeare's Wordplay*. Methuen: 1957. (Stimulating study of punning, innuendo, etc. in the plays and poems.)

Melchiori, G., *Shakespeare's Dramatic Meditations: An Experiment in Criticism*. Oxford University Press: 1976. (Microscopically detailed analyses of five specific sonnets.)

Muir, K. *The Sources of Shakespeare's Plays*. Methuen: 1977. (A study of the relationship between Shakespeare's reading and his plays, which illuminates his working methods.)

Nevo, R. *Comic Transformations in Shakespeare*. Methuen: 1980. (Stimulating study of the comedies, especially on themes of metamorphosis and identity.)

Parker, P., and Hartman, G., eds. *Shakespeare and the Question of Theory*. Methuen: 1985. (Represents a wide range of theoretical approaches. See especially N.J. Vickers on *The Rape of Lucrece*.)

Patterson, A. *Shakespeare and the Popular Voice*. Blackwell: 1989. (Provocative accounts of seven plays which challenge the view of Shakespeare as conservative and undemocratic.)

Paul, H.N. *The Royal Play of 'Macbeth'*. Macmillan (New York): 1950. (A study of the play's contemporary background and its connections with King James I.)

Prosser, E. *Hamlet and Revenge*. Stanford University Press: 1972. (A study of Shakespeare's treatment of the dramatic and ethical aspects of revenge.)

Reese, M.M. *The Cease of Majesty: A Study of Shakespeare's History Plays*. E. Arnold: 1961. (Basic account of the history plays and their relation to Tudor political thought.)

Righter, A. *Shakespeare and the Idea of the Play*. Chatto and Windus: 1962. (Fascinating study of the conceptions of the actor and the play as expressed within Shakespeare's work.)

Rosenberg, M. *The Masks of Othello*. University of California Press: 1981. (An account of stage interpretations of *Othello*.)

Salingar, L. *Shakespeare and the Traditions of Comedy.* Cambridge University Press, paperback edn.: 1976. (Detailed account of the comedies in relation to their background in European comic literature.)

Slater, A.P. *Shakespeare the Director.* Harvester Press, paperback edn.: 1984. (Illuminating study of internalized stage-directions within Shakespeare's plays.)

Spivack, B. *Shakespeare and the Allegory of Evil.* Oxford University Press: 1959. (A consideration of the relation of Shakespeare's villains to the medieval figure of the Vice.)

Taylor, G., and Warren, M., eds. *The Division of the Kingdoms.* Clarendon Press: 1986. (Theories as to the nature and relationships of the Quarto and Folio texts of *King Lear.* A major addition to the new bibliography.)

Tillyard, E.M.W. *Shakespeare's History Plays.* Penguin Books: 1962. (Argues for the history plays as vehicles of Tudor political propaganda.)

Vickers, B. *The Artistry of Shakespeare's Prose.* Methuen: 1968. (Detailed, illuminating account of Shakespeare's uses of prose speech.)

Weimann, R. *Shakespeare and the Popular Tradition in the Theatre,* ed. R. Schwartz. Johns Hopkins University Press: 1978. (Wide-ranging study of the disparate sources in popular art that went to form Shakespeare's drama, written from a Marxist perspective.)

Wilders, J. *The Lost Garden: A View of Shakespeare's English and Roman History Plays.* Macmillan: 1978. (Account of the history plays, which is critical of the view of them as propaganda.)

5. Theatres and Stagecraft

Bentley, G.E. *The Jacobean and Caroline Stage,* 7 vols. Clarendon Press: 1941–68. (Seminal work of scholarship and reference, a mine of facts and information on playhouse buildings, theatre companies, players and playwrights, performances, etc.)

——. *The Profession of Dramatist in Shakespeare's Time, 1590–1642.* Princeton University Press: 1971. (Closely documented study of the professional circumstances of Shakespeare and his fellow playwrights.)

——. *The Profession of Player in Shakespeare's Time, 1590–1642.* Princeton: 1984.

Bradbrook, M.C. *The Rise of the Common Player.* Chatto and Windus: 1962; Cambridge University Press, paperback: 1979. (Study of the actor and society in Elizabethan times.)

Chambers, E.K. *The Elizabethan Stage,* 4 vols. Clarendon Press: 1923. (Like Bentley's *The Jacobean and Caroline Stage,* a huge work of scholarship, still the authority on its subject.)

Cook, A. J. *The Privileged Playgoers of Shakespeare's London* (1576–1642). Princeton University Press: 1982. (Exhaustively documented study of Elizabethan playgoers, arguing that they represented a privileged elite in their society.)

Dessen, A. C. *Elizabethan Stage Conventions and Modern Interpreters*. Cambridge University Press: 1984.

Eccles, C. *The Rose Theatre*. Routledge: 1990. (Account of the history and significance of this theatre in the light of recent archaeological finds.)

Foakes, R. A., and Rickert, R. T., eds. *Henslowe's Diary*. Cambridge University Press: 1961.

Gurr, A. *Playgoing in Shakespeare's London*. Cambridge University Press: 1987. (Important study of audiences and tastes.)

——. *The Shakespearian Stage, 1574–1642*. Cambridge University Press: 3rd edn. 1992. (A redaction of the multi-volume works by Chambers and Bentley, and a lucid summary of accepted facts and modern scholarly opinion on players, playhouses, staging, audiences, etc., in the period.)

——. *The Shakespearian Playing Companies*. Clarendon Press: 1996. (Comprehensive history and documentation of the players.)

Hattaway, M. *Elizabethan Popular Theatre: Plays in Performance*. Theatre Production Studies. Routledge and Kegan Paul: 1982. (Contains a detailed account of Elizabethan theatre practice in general, and a useful chapter on *Titus Andronicus*.)

Hodges, C. W. *The Globe Restored*. 2nd edn. Oxford University Press: 1968. (Handsomely illustrated account of Hodge's theory of the Globe theatre's structure and origins.)

King, T. J. *Shakespearean Staging 1599–1642*. Harvard University Press: 1971. (Comprehensive, authoritative account of stage structures and staging in this period.)

Orrell, J. *The Human Stage. English Theatre Design, 1567–1640*. Cambridge University Press: 1988. (Sees theatre of the period as embodying the architectural principles of the age of humanism.)

Thomson, P. *Shakespeare's Theatre*. Theatre Production Studies. Routledge and Kegan Paul: 1983. (Account of playhouse practice and play production at the Globe theatre 1599–1608, with chapters on *Twelfth Night, Hamlet*, and *Macbeth*.)

Wickham, G. W. G. *Early English Stages 1300–1600*, Vol. 2, Parts 1 and 2. Routledge and Kegan Paul: 1963, 1972. (A fully documented account, with some illustrations, of stages and stage practice, their history and development, in this period.)

6. Shakespeare in Performance: Stage and Screen

Bate, J., and Jackson, R., eds. *Shakespeare: An Illustrated Stage History*. Oxford University Press: 1996. (Separate articles on aspects of the performance of Shakespeare from his own day to the present.)

Burt, R., and Boose, L., eds. *Shakespeare the Movie: Popularizing the Plays on Film, TV, and Video*. Routledge: 1997. (Collection of articles exploring the cultural impact of Shakespeare in media other than the theatre.)

Collick, J. *Shakespeare, Cinema and Society*. Manchester University Press: 1989. (On the cultural issues raised by Shakespeare on film.)

Holland, P. *English Shakespeares: Shakespeare on the English Stage in the 1990s.* New York: 1997.

Kennedy, D., ed. *Foreign Shakespeare: Contemporary Performance.* Cambridge University Press: 1993. (Articles on Shakespeare productions in Europe and the Far East.)

——. *Looking at Shakespeare: A Visual History of Twentieth-Century Performance.* Cambridge University Press: 1993. (Usefully illustrated account of major trends in Shakespeare production worldwide.)

Odell, G. C. D. *Shakespeare from Betterton to Irving,* 2 vols. Scribner: 1920. (Standard history of Shakespeare on stage, usually in adapted forms, from the Restoration to the end of the nineteenth century.)

7. Shakespeare's Reputation

Bate, J. *The Genius of Shakespeare.* Picador: 1997. (Learned but also very readable account of Shakespeare's place in English culture, and why he has earned it.)

——. *Shakespearean Constitutions: Politics, Theatre, Criticism, 1730–1830.* Oxford University Press: 1989. (Account of the changing cultural role of Shakespeare during this period.)

Dobson, M. *The Making of the National Poet. Shakespeare, Adaptation, and Authorship, 1660–1769.* Oxford University Press: 1992. (Traces the history of Shakespeare's reputation through an account of adaptations of his work on stage.)

Grady, H. *The Modernist Shakespeare. Critical Texts in a Material World.* Oxford University Press: 1991. (Study of the construction of Shakespeare in modernist terms, 1930–70, and of the context for post-modernist Shakespeare.)

Schoenbaum, S. *Shakespeare's Lives.* Oxford University Press: 1970, revised 1991. (Full and lively account of biographies and biographical traditions of Shakespeare from his own time to the 1960s.)

Taylor, G. *Reinventing Shakespeare. A Cultural History from the Restoration to the Present.* Hogarth Press: 1990. (Argues that Shakespeare's cultural dominance is an effect of the different interests his work and status have been called upon to serve.)

Vickers, B., ed., *Shakespeare: The Critical Heritage,* 6 vols. Routledge and Kegan Paul: 1974–81. (Extracts, with introduction and commentary, from critical accounts of Shakespeare, organized chronologically, from 1632–1801.)

——. *Appropriating Shakespeare. Contemporary Critical Quarrels.* Yale University Press: 1993. (Polemical survey of recent trends in Shakespeare criticism, arguing that many of them misrepresent Shakespeare in the service of their own interests.)

Woudhuysen, H., ed., *Samuel Johnson on Shakespeare.* Penguin: 1989. (Modernized texts of all Johnson's major pieces of Shakespeare criticism, including critical notes.)

ALPHABETICAL LISTING

A

Aaron In *Titus Andronicus*, the Moorish lover of the Gothic queen, Tamora. He arranges the elaborate murders of Bassianus, Quintus, and Martius, and the mutilation of Titus and Lavinia. He is punished by Lucius, the new emperor, for his treachery and cruelty on behalf of Tamora against Titus's family. His devotion to evil-doing recalls Barabas in ➤Marlowe's near-contemporary *The Jew of Malta*.

Abergavenny, Lord In *Henry VIII*, a baron who adheres to Buckingham's cause against Wolsey and is sent to the Tower with Buckingham.

Abhorson In *Measure for Measure*, an executioner who thinks of his job as a "mystery" (i.e., a skilled craft).

Abigail In ➤Marlowe's play *The Jew of Malta*, the daughter of Barabas. The relationship of father and daughter bears resemblances to that of Shylock and Jessica in *The Merchant of Venice*.

Abram In *Romeo and Juliet*, a servant of Montague.

Achilles In *Troilus and Cressida*, a Greek commander who is aroused from his moody inactivity in the war by the death in battle of his friend Patroclus. To avenge his friend, Achilles attacks Hector (who is resting unarmed) and has him slaughtered by his Myrmidons.

Adam In *As You Like It*, the old servant who faithfully follows the exiled Orlando, leaving the service of Orlando's elder brother, Oliver. There is a late tradition, based on a statement (1750) of William Oldys, that Shakespeare himself acted this part.

Admiral's Men ➤Lord Admiral's Men.

Adrian In *Coriolanus*, a Volscian.

Adrian In *The Tempest*, a lord who attends Alonso and is shipwrecked with him.

Adriana In *The Comedy of Errors*, the wife of Antipholus of Ephesus. She confuses her husband with his twin, Antipholus of Syracuse.

Aegeon In *The Comedy of Errors*, a merchant of Syracuse, husband of Aemilia, and the father of the Antipholus twins.

Aemilia In *The Comedy of Errors*, the wife of Aegeon and mother of the Antipholus twins. When she is separated from her family she becomes an abbess at the convent of Ephesus, where she later harbours Antipholus of Syracuse when he is thought to be a lunatic.

Aemilius In *Titus Andronicus*, a Roman who asks Titus's brother Marcus to present Lucius as emperor in the final scene.

Aeneas In *Troilus and Cressida*, a Trojan commander who informs Troilus of the exchange of Cressida for the Trojan warrior Antenor, a prisoner of the Greeks.

Agamemnon In *Troilus and Cressida*, the Greek general. He opens the discussion with Nestor, Ulysses, and Menelaus on the ill fortunes of the Greeks in the war with Troy (I.iii), and is present in many of the following scenes.

Agincourt A village in northern France, near which the English bowmen under Henry V defeated (1415) a very much larger force of heavily armed French knights. This battle forms the background of some of the principal scenes in *Henry V*.

Agrippa In *Antony and Cleopatra*, a friend of Octavius who suggests that Antony marry Octavia, the sister of Octavius.

Aguecheek, Sir Andrew In *Twelfth Night*, a foolish and effeminate country squire. He is the friend of Sir Toby Belch.

Ajax In *Troilus and Cressida*, a Greek commander who is praised beyond his worth by the other leaders in order that Achilles, who has refused to go to battle, will become indignant and return to the wars.

Alarbus In *Titus Andronicus*, the eldest son of Tamora. When he is sacrificed by the sons of Titus, Tamora is provided with the motive for her acts of vengeance.

Albany, Duke of In *King Lear*, the husband of Goneril, Lear's eldest daughter. At first he is apparently a nonentity, but the play reveals him as an honourable man who accuses Goneril and Regan of being unnatural in their treatment of Lear. At the death of Lear, the kingdom becomes his.

Alcibiades In *Timon of Athens*, an Athenian captain who is banished for speaking hotly before the Senate when its members refuse to pardon one of his friends. Timon aids him toward the capture of Athens and thus they get revenge on their common enemy.

Alençon, Duke of In *Henry V*, a French nobleman, the father of the Duke of Alençon in *1 Henry VI*, who is mentioned as having been killed in battle by Henry. Henry gives William's glove to Fluellen, saying it is Alençon's, in order to be amused by the two men challenging and attacking each other.

Alençon, Duke of In *1 Henry VI*, a French nobleman who speaks contemptuously of Englishmen's habits, but admires their bravery in battle; he also praises Joan of Arc.

Alexander In *Troilus and Cressida*, a servant of Cressida.

Alexas In *Antony and Cleopatra*, an attendant of Cleopatra who, as Enobarbus relates, deserts Antony, only to be hanged by Octavius.

Alice In *Henry V*, a lady in attendance on Princess Katherine. She gives the Princess a lesson in English which allows for bawdy punning (III.iv).

Aliena In *As You Like It*, the name assumed by Celia when, disguised as a shepherdess, she accompanies Rosalind (disguised as Ganymede) to the forest.

Alinda A character in ►Lodge's *Rosalynde*, the source of *As You Like It*. She corresponds to Celia.

All is True ►*Henry VIII*.

Alleyn, Edward [Also, Alleyne; sometimes called Ned Allen] (1566–1626) With Richard ►Burbage, one of the two leading actors of Shakespeare's day; son-in-law of Philip ►Henslowe and later, by a second marriage, of John Donne. He was the founder (1613) and director (1619–26) of Dulwich College (the College of God's Gift), at London. Rated by ►Jonson, ►Nashe, and others as the foremost actor, especially of tragedy, of his time, he was a member of the Earl of Worcester's Men (1586 *et seq.*), head of the ►Lord Admiral's (Earl of Nottingham's) Men (*c.* 1592), and owner-manager, with Henslowe, of various London theatres, including the ►Rose and the ►Fortune, and of a bear-baiting house at Paris Garden (1594–1626). He played leads in ►Marlowe's *The Jew of Malta*, *Tamburlaine*, and *Doctor Faustus*. His last known appearance was at a reception address to James I (*c.* 1604).

All's Well That Ends Well A comedy by Shakespeare, probably written in large part in the period 1603–04. It was first printed in the first folio of 1623. The main source for the plot is the story of Giletta of Narbonne from Boccaccio's *Decameron* (Day 3, Story 9), which Shakespeare probably knew in the translation by William Painter in *The ►Palace of Pleasure* (1566–67, 1575). Giletta, unlike Shakespeare's heroine Helena, is a rich heiress who has refused many suitors; otherwise her situation is very similar. She too wins the right to choose a husband after curing the King of a mysterious illness, is rejected by the man she chooses, Bertram, son of the Countess of Roussillion, and finally wins him after performing the seemingly impossible task of conceiving a son by him and gaining possession of a ring from his finger in his absence. Shakespeare alters Boccaccio's story chiefly by adding the characters of the Countess, Bertram's mother, Lafew, the old courtier, and Parolles, the boastful coward. In Boccaccio and Painter, the King is unwilling for the heroine to marry the man of her choice because he is of higher rank than she; Shakespeare not only widens the social gulf between Helena and Bertram but also gives the King a significant speech on the worth of true virtue over high birth, an important theme in the play.

Dramatis Personae

King of France	Countess of Roussillion, *mother of*
Duke of Florence	*Bertram*
Bertram, Count of Roussillion	Helena, *a gentlewoman protected by the*
Lafew, *an old Lord*	*Countess*
Parolles, *a follower of Bertram*	*A Widow of Florence*
Steward to the Countess of Roussillion	Diana, *daughter of the Widow*
Clown, in her household	Mariana, *friend of the Widow*
A Page	*Lords, Officers, Soldiers*

The Story. Helena, the daughter of a famous physician, Gerard de Narbon, cures the King of France of a supposedly incurable disease and as a reward asks that Bertram, the young Count of Roussillion, marry her. This Bertram does reluctantly, and leaves immediately for the wars, at the suggestion of the coward and braggart Parolles. Bertram sends a message to Helena that "When thou canst get the ring upon my finger which never shall come off, and show me a child begotten of thy body that I am father to, then call me husband" (III.ii). Passing through Florence on a pilgrimage, Helena discovers that Bertram is attempting to seduce Diana, the daughter of her hostess. She arranges to have Bertram informed that she (Helena) is dead, and to replace Diana in his bed. Bertram gets her with child and she exchanges her ring (which the King had given her) for Bertram's. When Bertram returns home, the King notices the ring and accuses Bertram of killing Helena. Helena arrives in time to explain and to demand that Bertram accept her as his wife now that the conditions in his letter have been met.

Alonso   In *The Tempest*, the King of Naples, who has helped Antonio to usurp Prospero's dukedom. On a return voyage from Tunis he is shipwrecked on Prospero's island and is made to repent his action. His son, Ferdinand, marries Miranda.

Amiens   In *As You Like It*, one of the lords attending the banished father of Rosalind. He sings the well-known "Under the greenwood tree" (II.v) and "Blow, blow, thou winter wind" (II.vii).

Andromache   In *Troilus and Cressida*, the wife of Hector. She, the prophetess Cassandra, and Hector's father Priam, the King of Troy, plead with Hector not to go into battle, because they feel certain that he will be killed, as he is.

Angelo   In *The Comedy of Errors*, a goldsmith.

Angelo   In *Measure for Measure*, the Duke's deputy who is granted full administrative powers in Vienna when the Duke pretends to leave. He condemns Claudio, brother of Isabella, to death for unchastity, but agrees to pardon him in exchange for Isabella's virginity. Isabella changes place in Angelo's bed with Mariana, to whom he has been betrothed. When the Duke resumes his own guise, Angelo is punished and is forced to marry Mariana.

Angus   In *Macbeth*, a Scottish thane who eventually supports Malcolm against Macbeth.

Anne, Lady   In *Richard III*, the historical Anne Neville, daughter of Warwick "the Kingmaker" and widow of Edward, Prince of Wales. She curses Richard for the murder of her husband but she is won over by his powers of speech and marries him. Later, Richard has her put away when he plans to marry Elizabeth, and she dies under unexplained circumstances. Her ghost appears to Richard before the battle of Bosworth.

Antenor   In *Troilus and Cressida*, a Trojan commander who is captured by the Greeks and exchanged for Cressida.

Antigonus   In *The Winter's Tale*, a lord of Sicilia and husband of Paulina. He is sent by Leontes to abandon the baby Perdita in a "desert place" (II.iii), takes her to the "seacoast of Bohemia" (III.iii) and there is killed by a bear.

Antiochus   In *Pericles*, the King of Antioch. He tries to poison Pericles, who has discovered his incestuous relationship with his daughter. Fire from heaven finally destroys him.

Antipholus of Ephesus and **Antipholus of Syracuse**   In *The Comedy of Errors*, twin brothers, sons of Aegeon, a merchant of Syracuse, and his wife, Aemilia. The arrival of Antipholus of Syracuse in Ephesus creates the plot complications, when he is mistaken for his wilder brother.

Antonio   In *The Merchant of Venice*, the merchant who gives the play its name. He borrows money from Shylock, the Jew, in order to meet the needs of his beloved friend Bassanio, and is induced to sign a bond agreeing to forfeit a pound of flesh if he does not repay the money within a specified time. Not being able to pay, he nearly loses his life to satisfy the demands of Shylock, but is saved by Portia who, disguised as a lawyer, points out to Shylock the impossibility of taking the flesh— his legal right—without spilling a drop of blood—a criminal act.

Antonio   In *Much Ado About Nothing*, the aged brother of Leonato, Governor of Messina. When Leonato's daughter Hero has her reputation impugned by Claudio, he tries to comfort Leonato and himself challenges Claudio.

Antonio   In *The Tempest*, the usurping Duke of Milan, and Prospero's wicked brother, who is wrecked on the island where Prospero landed twelve years before. By Prospero's use of magic he is made to restore the dukedom to its rightful ruler.

Antonio   In *Twelfth Night*, a sea captain devoted to Sebastian. He lends his purse to Sebastian and later (upon arriving in Illyria) mistakes Viola for Sebastian. Upon being arrested by the officers of Duke Orsino for fighting in defence of the supposed Sebastian, he demands the purse from her.

Antonio   In *The Two Gentlemen of Verona*, the father of Proteus.

Antonio   The chief character of John ➤Marston's plays *Antonio and Mellida* and *Antonio's Revenge*. *Antonio's Revenge* (*c.* 1600) bears many resemblances to *Hamlet*.

Antony   In *Antony and Cleopatra,* the hero. ➤Mark Antony.

Antony and Cleopatra [Full title, *The Tragedy of Antony and Cleopatra*]   A tragedy by Shakespeare, written *c.* 1606, entered on the Stationers' Register in 1608 and printed in the first folio of 1623. The events dramatized in the play took place between 40 BC and 30 BC, very soon after those of *Julius Caesar*. The main source was North's translation of the life of Antony from Plutarch's *Lives of the Noble Grecians and Romans*, which Shakespeare followed very closely, for instance in Enobarbus's famous speech about Cleopatra on the river Cydnus. As well as following North's wording, he also made some use of almost every incident in Plutarch's account of Antony's later years, except for the long Parthian campaign merely alluded to in III.i. Shakespeare's one addition is the character of Enobarbus, which he created from a few sentences in Plutarch. In the later scenes of the play the time sequence is shortened; in particular, Shakespeare leaves no interval between the battle of Actium and the events that follow it, whereas in Plutarch there is a long space of time between Antony's defeat and his embassy to Caesar. Hints for Caesar's character may have come from Simon Goulart's *Life of Octavius Caesar Augustus*, which was published in North's translation in the 1603 edition of Plutarch, although this added nothing to the account of the life of Antony. Shakespeare supplemented Plutarch's account of the military background with *The Roman Civil Wars* of Appian of Alexandria, Book V, in a translation of 1578; this gave details of the wars of Fulvia, Lucius Antonius (Antony's brother), and Pompey. The story of Antony and Cleopatra appealed to the Renaissance, and there were several dramatic versions of it. Some verbal echoes suggest that Shakespeare may have consulted the Countess of Pembroke's translation of Garnier's *Marc Antoine* (1592), a moral play with a simple, sincere Cleopatra. It is more likely that he used Samuel ➤Daniel's play *Cleopatra*, which was first published in 1594 and considerably remodelled before its reappearance in 1607 after Daniel had seen another stage version, possibly the Countess of Pembroke's *The Tragedie of Antonie*, less possibly *Antony and Cleopatra*. Daniel's play and Shakespeare's share certain features not found elsewhere, for instance Cleopatra's fear of Octavia's scorn as one of the motives for her actions after Antony's death, and the reminiscence of Cydnus as Cleopatra prepares for death. Shakespeare may also have used Daniel's poem "A Letter from Octavia to Marcus Antonius," which was published in his *Poeticall Essayes* (1599). The subject was used by John ➤Dryden in *All for Love* (1678), and by John ➤Fletcher and Philip Massinger in *The False One*. Dryden's play, with its nobler and less complex protagonists, was acted more often than Shakespeare's for a century. It was not until 1849 that the Shakespeare play was produced in its original form, being mixed with scenes from Dryden until that time.

Dramatis Personae

Mark Antony, *triumvir*	Varrius, *friend of Pompey*
Octavius Caesar, *triumvir*	Taurus, *lieutenant-general*
M. Aemilius Lepidus, *triumvir*	Canidius, *lieutenant-general*
Sextus Pompeius (Pompey)	Silius, *officer*
Enobarbus, *friend of Antony*	Euphronius, *ambassador*
Ventidius, *friend of Antony*	Alexas, *attendant on Cleopatra*
Eros, *friend of Antony*	Mardian, *eunuch attendant on*
Scarus, *friend of Antony*	*Cleopatra*
Dercetas, *friend of Antony*	Seleucus, *attendant on Cleopatra*
Demetrius, *friend of Antony*	Diomedes, *attendant on Cleopatra*
Philo, *friend of Antony*	A *Soothsayer*
Maecenas, *friend of Caesar*	A *Clown*
Agrippa, *friend of Caesar*	Cleopatra, Queen of Egypt
Dolabella, *friend of Caesar*	Octavia, *sister to Caesar and wife to*
Proculeius, *friend of Caesar*	*Antony*
Thyreus, *friend of Caesar*	Charmian, *attendant on Cleopatra*
Gallus, *friend of Caesar*	Iras, *attendant on Cleopatra*
Menas, *friend of Pompey*	*Officers, Soldiers, Messengers, and other*
Menecrates, *friend of Pompey*	*Attendants*

The Story. In Alexandria, Antony luxuriates in the love of Cleopatra and the sybaritic life of the Egyptian court, but hearing of the death of his wife Fulvia and Pompey's uprising, he reluctantly departs for Rome. There he quarrels with Octavius, one of the Triumvirate with Lepidus and Antony, and in order to heal the breach between them Antony agrees to marry Octavius's sister, Octavia. Cleopatra, meanwhile, longs for Antony, and when the news of his marriage reaches her she almost kills the messenger in jealous wrath. In Rome the antagonism between the two men resumes, and unable to stay away from Cleopatra longer, Antony returns to Egypt. Octavius imprisons Lepidus, renews the war against Pompey, and begins a campaign against Antony. In Egypt, Octavius challenges Antony to a sea battle and Antony accepts, although his forces would have proved superior on land. During the battle at Actium, Cleopatra suddenly orders her fleet to retreat and Antony follows, thus losing both the battle and his military reputation. He tries to make peace with Octavius, requesting to be allowed to live in Rome, but Octavius refuses and sends a messenger to try to persuade Cleopatra to renounce Antony. Antony's followers, including his friend Enobarbus, desert him; Antony sends his friend's belongings after him, and Enobarbus, doubly stricken by his own betrayal in the face of this magnanimity on the part of Antony, dies of a broken heart. A land battle commences, but once more Cleopatra's retreat decides the victory in favour of Octavius. Antony determines to kill Cleopatra for her supposed treachery, and she, in terror, flees to her tomb and sends word to Antony that she has killed herself. Antony, believing the news, falls on his own sword, but lives long enough to be carried to Cleopatra, and the two reaffirm their eternal love. Cleopatra tricks Caesar, and procures a triumphant suicide from the bite of an asp, her attendants Charmian and Iras choosing to die with her.

Apemantus   In *Timon of Athens*, a cynical and churlish philosopher who warns Timon about his false friends. When Timon becomes a recluse, and even more misanthropic, he drives even Apemantus away from his cave.

Aragon, Prince of   In *The Merchant of Venice*, the second of Portia's suitors. He chooses the silver casket as the one containing her portrait; it does not and he thus fails to win her.

Archibald, Earl of Douglas   ➤Douglas, Archibald, (4th) Earl of.

Archidamus   In *The Winter's Tale*, a Bohemian lord.

Arcite   In *The Two Noble Kinsmen*, one of the principal characters, the cousin of Palamon and his rival for the love of Emilia. Originally a character in Chaucer's *The Knight's Tale*.

Arden, Forest of   An English forest that in former times extended through Warwickshire and other midland counties of England. The Forest of Arden of *As You Like It* may well have been intended for the Forest of Ardennes in French Flanders.

Arden of Faversham, Tragedy of Mr   A domestic tragedy first printed (anonymously) in 1592, sometimes attributed to Shakespeare, and dramatized from Holinshed's account of the murder of a leading citizen of Faversham in Kent in 1551 (➤Holinshed's *Chronicles*). Alice Arden, who conspired with several others including her lower-born lover, Mosby, to murder her husband, was notorious for many years afterwards.

Ariel   "An airy spirit" in *The Tempest*, employed by Prospero as agent of his magic. Ariel has been imprisoned by the witch, Sycorax, in a cloven pine, from which Prospero frees him on condition that he assist his plans. At the close of the play, after Ariel presents a masque before the lovers, Ferdinand and Miranda, Prospero reluctantly allows him to go. The well-known lyrics "Come unto these yellow sands" (I.ii), "Full fathom five" (I.ii), and "Where the bee sucks" (V.i), are sung by Ariel.

Armado, Don Adriano de   In *Love's Labour's Lost*, a fantastical Spaniard who speaks with elaborate language and contends with Costard for Jaquenetta. He may be intended as a caricature of Sir Walter Raleigh.

Armin, Robert   (*c.* 1568–1615) English actor, who joined the ➤Lord Chamberlain's Men as a comedian in 1599, probably as a replacement for William

►Kemp. He probably played singing roles such as Feste and Lear's Fool. He was also a writer, and produced the jestbook *Foole upon Foole* (1600), and the play *Two Maids of Moreclacke* (1607–08?).

Arne, Thomas Augustine (1710–78) English composer of songs, especially for Shakespearean plays, and of oratorios and operas. He wrote music for "Under the greenwood tree" and other songs in *As You Like It* and for "Where the bee sucks," among others, from *The Tempest*.

Arragon, Prince of ►Pedro, Don.

Artemidorus In *Julius Caesar*, a teacher of rhetoric who tries to save Caesar by a note of warning. Unfortunately, Caesar refuses to read the note.

Artesius In *The Two Noble Kinsmen*, an Athenian captain.

Arthur, Duke of Britain In *King John*, the historical Arthur of Brittany, son of Constance of Brittany and (posthumously) of Geoffrey Plantagenet, John's elder brother. Arthur should have been king, but John was chosen by the Great Council. Arthur serves as a rallying point for the discontented English nobles and John orders him put to death. In a pathetic scene, Arthur begs the chamberlain, Hubert de Burgh, for his life. He then escapes, but in doing so falls to his death in such a way as to make it appear that murder has been committed.

Arviragus In *Cymbeline*, the son of Cymbeline, brought up in exile as Cadwal, the son of Belarius, a banished lord, who is disguised as Morgan.

Ashcroft, Dame Peggy (1907–91) British actress well known for her roles with the ►Royal Shakespeare Company, especially Margaret of Anjou in *The Wars of the Roses* (1963), a trilogy composed from the three parts of *Henry VI* and *Richard III*. Her debut in Shakespeare was as Desdemona (1930) and other roles included Imogen, Rosalind, Portia, Viola (in the 1930s); Miranda, Ophelia, Titania, Beatrice (in the 1940s); and Mistress Page, Portia, Cleopatra, Rosalind, and Imogen (in the 1950s).

As You Like It A comedy by Shakespeare entered on the Stationers' Register in 1600, but not printed until the first folio of 1623. The play was based on the prose romance *Rosalynde* by Thomas ►Lodge, published in 1590. Lodge's tale derived from a medieval poem, the *Tale of Gamelyn*, once attributed to Chaucer, which contained the basic situation of the three brothers, the youngest hated by the eldest and forced into exile in the forest where he lived with a band of outlaws until restored to his rightful position. There are a few resemblances of detail between *As You Like It* and the *Tale of Gamelyn* that are not found in *Rosalynde*, and it has been argued that Shakespeare did know the unpublished poem. He followed *Rosalynde* quite closely, both in detail and in general conception, though he did make certain alterations. The names of almost all Lodge's characters, with the exception of the heroine's, are changed and made less exotic; the brothers Oliver, Jaques, and Orlando were

Saladyne, Fernadyne, and Rosader in Lodge, Celia's name was Alinda, and Duke Frederick was King Torismund. Shakespeare added the characters of Le Beau, Touchstone, and the melancholy Jaques, who give to the play a satirical tone lacking in *Rosalynde*, and also Audrey and William, whose earthy realism forms a contrast with the pastoralism and artifice of the shepherdess Phebe and her lover Silvius. Some of Shakespeare's alterations were made in the interests of symmetry; for instance, Celia's father, the usurping Duke, is made brother to Rosalind's father, the rightful Duke, so that a parallel is formed with the brothers Oliver and Orlando, where again one is mistreated and deprived of his rights by the other. Shakespeare takes over Lodge's theme of the opposition between court and country, nature and artifice, but whereas Lodge's romance is basically a study of the escape from cruel society to an idyllic pastoral world, Shakespeare's play treats the pastoral world more critically and many of its themes reappear in *King Lear*.

Dramatis Personae

Duke Senior

Frederick, *his brother, usurper of his dominions*

Amiens, *lord attending the Duke*

Jaques, *lord attending the Duke*

Le Beau, *a courtier*

Charles, *a wrestler*

Oliver, *son of de Boys*

Jaques, *son of de Boys*

Orlando, *son of de Boys*

Adam, *Oliver's servant*

Dennis, *Oliver's servant*

Touchstone, *a clown*

Sir Oliver Martext, *a vicar*

Corin, *shepherd*

Silvius, *shepherd*

William, *in love with Audrey*

A person presenting Hymen

Rosalind, *daughter of the Duke*

Celia, *daughter of Frederick*

Phebe, *a shepherdess*

Audrey, *a country wench*

Lords, Pages, Foresters, and Attendants

The Story. Orlando, the son of the late Rowland de Boys, objects to cruel treatment by his brother, Oliver, in whose charge he has been left, whereupon Oliver plans that Orlando will be killed during a wrestling match sponsored by Frederick, usurper of the dukedom of his elder brother, the Duke Senior. The latter has had to flee with his followers, including the melancholy Jaques, to the Forest of Arden, leaving behind his daughter Rosalind with her cousin and friend, Celia, the daughter of Frederick. During the wrestling match, Orlando and Rosalind fall in love, and when Orlando defeats his opponent he escapes from Oliver to the Forest of Arden, accompanied by the old family servant, Adam. There they fall in with the banished Duke and his attendants. Frederick, meanwhile, banishes Rosalind. She disguises herself as a boy, calling herself Ganymede, and with Celia (posing as Aliena, sister of the supposed boy Ganymede) also seeks refuge in the Forest of Arden. Their jester Touchstone goes with them. There Rosalind meets Orlando, who, thinking she is the boy Ganymede, accepts her suggestion that he should court her as if she were his beloved Rosalind. Oliver arrives in pursuit of Orlando, but is saved from a lion and, repentant, falls in love with Celia. Ganymede promises Orlando that by magic Rosalind will appear in time for the wedding the following day, and at that time Rosalind reveals herself. These two couples, plus two more (Audrey and Touchstone, Phebe and Silvius), are gathered for the ceremonies, when Orlando's second brother, Jaques de Boys, arrives with the news that Frederick has left for a monastery and restored the dukedom to his elder brother.

Athens, Duke of ➤Theseus.

Aubrey, John (1626–97) English antiquary. Reduced to poverty by various lawsuits and amorous adventures, he was commissioned (1671) to make surveys of antiquities, which he described in *Perambulation of Surrey* and other manuscripts published after his death. Supported mainly by wealthy friends, he collected anecdotes of such notables as Francis ➤Bacon, John Milton, Thomas Hobbes, Sir Walter ➤Raleigh, and Shakespeare, which he contributed to the historian Anthony à Wood, as *Minutes of Lives* (first published separately in 1813; called *Brief Lives* in twentieth-century editions), for his *Athenae Oxonienses* (1690). Author also of *Miscellanies* (1696), a collection of ghost stories and dreams.

Audrey In *As You Like It*, an awkward country girl. Touchstone discovers her in the Forest of Arden and eventually marries her.

Aufidius, Tullus In *Coriolanus*, the general of the Volscians and rival to Coriolanus. He accepts the offer of Coriolanus, who has been banished from Rome, to lead the Volscian army against Rome. When Coriolanus spares Rome, the Volscians kill him.

Aumerle, Duke of ➤York, (2nd) Duke of.

Austria, Duke of [Also, Lymoges] In *King John*, an ally of Philip and the Dauphin, supposed to have killed Richard I (the Lion-Hearted). The Bastard, Philip Faulconbridge, kills him in battle (III.ii).

authorship theories Although doubts had been cast on the authorship of parts of some of the weaker plays, such as *Titus Andronicus* and *Pericles*, since the late seventeenth century, Shakespeare's authorship of the works attributed to him was not otherwise questioned until the late eighteenth century. Probably in the 1780s a certain Rev. James Wilmot concluded that Shakespeare's plays were in fact written by Francis ➤Bacon but did not publish his view. In 1848 Joseph C. Hart put it in print for the first time in *The Romance of Yachting*, and soon after, Delia Bacon, who was to become the best known proponent of this theory, took it up in *The Philosophy of the Plays of Shakespere Unfolded* (1857). Her ideas were largely substantiated by the use of elaborate cryptograms. The "authorship question" became significant in Victorian Shakespeare scholarship, and an "Anti-Stratfordian" movement of those who did not believe in Shakespeare's authorship of the plays gathered strength. Because Shakespeare was thought too uneducated to have been capable of writing them, more learned and also socially elite candidates were sought. The main rival to Bacon has been the Earl of Oxford, Edward de Vere, proposed in the 1920s by T. J. Looney and accepted by Freud, among others. Other suggested authors have included Elizabeth I, the Earl of ➤Essex, the Earl of Rutland, the Earl of Derby, and Christopher ➤Marlowe. Although the authorship question continues to surface from time to time, no specialist has ever been seriously persuaded by the claims advanced for alternative candidates.

Autolycus   In *The Winters Tale*, a witty thieving pedlar, a "snapper up of unconsidered trifles" (IV.iii). He uses the kind of trickery described in the cony-catching pamphlets of Greene and Dekker to deceive the innocent Clown, and the simple Bohemian country folk. He sings the song "When daffodils begin to peer" (IV.iii).

Auvergne, Countess of   In *1 Henry VI*, a French noblewoman. She tries but fails to trap Talbot. He shows her that his power lies in his army, not himself.

Avisa [Full title, *Willobie his Avisa, or the True Picture of a Modest Maid and of a Chast and Constant Wife*]   A poem by an English writer named Henry Willoughby (or Willobie). It was first printed in 1594, and prefixed to the second edition in 1596 are some verses that allude to Shakespeare's *Rape of Lucrece*:

> Yet Tarquin plucked his glistering grape,
> And Shakespeare paints poor Lucrece' rape.

This is the earliest known work to make printed mention of Shakespeare's name. The poem refers to a Mr "W.S.," friend to "Henrico Willobeog," who has been rejected as a lover by Avisa. This Mr W.S. has sometimes been identified with Shakespeare.

B

Bacon, Sir Francis (1561–1626) Writer and statesman, who published a number of scientific and philosophical works, and became Lord Chancellor in 1618. He was charged with bribery and corruption soon after, and died in disgrace. Largely on the basis of cryptographic clues, he has been regarded as a possible author of the works ascribed to Shakespeare (►authorship theories).

Bagot In *Richard II*, a parasitic follower of King Richard. He is imprisoned after Richard's deposition and informs against Aumerle.

Balthasar In *The Merchant of Venice*, a servant of Portia. The name is assumed by Portia in her guise as a lawyer.

Balthasar In *Much Ado About Nothing*, a servant of Don Pedro. He sings the song "Sigh no more, ladies" (II.iii).

Balthasar In *Romeo and Juliet*, Romeo's servant who bears word to Romeo in Mantua of Juliet's supposed death and returns with him to Verona. When Romeo enters the tomb, he threatens Balthasar with death if he follows or watches.

Balthazar [Also, Balthasar] In *The Comedy of Errors* (III.i), a merchant who is accompanying Antipholus of Ephesus to dinner when the latter's wife has locked him out. He convinces Antipholus that to break down the door would reflect on the character of his wife.

Bankside The south bank of the Thames between the Blackfriars and Waterloo bridges, London. In the time of the Tudors it consisted of a single row of houses, built on a dike, or levee, higher both than the river at high tide and the ground behind the bank. At one end of "Bank Side" (as it was then spelled) stood the Clink Prison, Winchester House, and St Mary Overies Church (now Southwark Cathedral). Numerous theatres were located in this district, including the ►Globe (a little to the west of the Clink and behind the houses), the ►Swan, the ►Rose, and the ►Hope. It was an area of ill reputation in Shakespeare's day.

Banquo In *Macbeth*, the Thane of Lochaber. He is a general in the King's army, with the same rank as Macbeth. Macbeth has him murdered because the Witches prophesy that his offspring shall be kings, and his ghost appears at Macbeth's banquet to taunt and horrify the murderer. Although Holinshed mentions him, Banquo is not a historical figure, but was included as a compliment to King James I, and regarded by the King as his ancestor.

Baptista Minola   In *The Taming of the Shrew*, a rich gentleman of Padua, the father of Katherina (the "Shrew") and Bianca. He will not allow the latter to wed until Katherina has a husband.

Bardolph   In *1* and *2 Henry IV*, one of Falstaff's companions, called the "Knight of the Burning Lamp" by Falstaff on account of his red face. He is characterized also in *Henry V* as "white livered and red-faced, by means whereof a' faces it out and fights not" (III.ii). As a military man his exploits in *Henry V* are limited to robbing a church, on account of which he is hanged, unjustly as Pistol sees it. In *The Merry Wives of Windsor*, he is a tapster (bartender) at the Garter Inn, having been cast off by Falstaff.

Bardolph, Lord   In *2 Henry IV*, a supporter of Northumberland who brings false news of Hotspur's victory over Prince Hal at Shrewsbury. He discusses the uprising with Archbishop Scroop, and Lords Hastings and Mowbray, and later (IV.iv) news is brought to the King that he has been defeated with Northumberland.

Barnardine   In *Measure for Measure*, a savage and sullen prisoner who torpidly "apprehends death no more dreadfully but as a drunken sleep." He is ordered to be executed by the Duke of Vienna in place of Claudio. Barnardine refuses, however, to die on that particular day and eventually is pardoned.

Barnardo   In *Hamlet*, a Danish officer. It is he, with Marcellus, who first sees the murdered king's Ghost.

Barry, Elizabeth   (1658–1713) English actress of the Restoration era. Regarded as the first great actress on the English stage, she was trained by ►Davenant and the Earl of Rochester. Among others, the role of Cordelia in the revision of *King Lear* by Nahum ►Tate was written for her. She also played Lavinia (Juliet) in Thomas Otway's adaptation of *Romeo and Juliet*, *Caius Marius* (1679).

Barton, John   (1928–   ) British director of a large number of Shakespeare productions (over fifty between 1960 and 1990) who has been associated with the work of the ►Royal Shakespeare Company since 1964. He is particularly known for adaptations of the history plays, including *The Wars of the Roses*, a trilogy based on the three parts of *Henry VI* and *Richard III*.

Bassanio   In *The Merchant of Venice*, a Venetian nobleman, close friend of Antonio, and Portia's successful suitor. It is on Bassanio's account that Antonio obligates himself to Shylock, since Bassanio needs money to woo Portia.

Basset   In *1 Henry VI*, a supporter of the Lancastrian (or Red Rose) faction, who quarrels with Vernon, who is on the Yorkist (or White Rose) side.

Bassianus   In *Titus Andronicus*, a brother of Saturninus and son of the late emperor of Rome. He marries Lavinia, but is murdered by Tamora's sons.

Bastard of Orléans In *1 Henry VI*, the historical Jean Dunois, bastard son of Louis Duc d'Orléans. Persuaded that Joan of Arc may be able to save France from the English, he arranges a meeting between her and the Dauphin (I.ii).

Bates, John In *Henry V*, an English soldier who talks with the disguised King before the battle of Agincourt. Although wishing he were at home in England, he determines to fight bravely for the King.

Bawd In *Pericles*, the wife of the Pander who keeps the brothel in Mytilene.

Beatrice In *Much Ado About Nothing*, the witty and outspoken niece of Leonato, cousin of Hero, and initially reluctant lover of Benedick. Her relationship with Benedick is actually a subplot, but one whose interest overshadows the main action, particularly in the scene (IV.i) where, having previously revealed her love for him to the audience, Beatrice encounters Benedick and they admit their love for each other. She is the only one to recognize at once the falseness of Claudio's accusation of Hero, and she tests Benedick's love by demanding that he challenge Claudio to a duel.

Beaufort, John ➤Somerset, Earl of.

Beaufort, Henry ➤Winchester, Bishop of.

Beaufort, Thomas ➤Exeter, Duke of.

Beaumont In *Henry V*, a French lord.

Beaumont, Francis (*c.* 1584–1616) Playwright and collaborator with John ➤Fletcher. His erotic Ovidian poem, *Salmacis and Hermaphroditus*, was published anonymously in 1602. His earliest work for the theatre may have been in collaboration with Fletcher on *Love's Cure* (*c.* 1605). He uses a quotation from *Hamlet* in *The Woman-Hater* (*c.* 1606), and may allude to *Macbeth* in *The Knight of the Burning Pestle* (*c.* 1607), his best-known work. His play *The Maid's Tragedy* (*c.* 1609), written in collaboration with Fletcher, shows considerable influence from *Hamlet*.

Bedford, Duke of ➤Lancaster, Prince John of.

Belarius In *Cymbeline*, a banished lord disguised under the name of Morgan. He steals Arviragus and Guiderius, Cymbeline's sons, out of revenge, passing them off under false names as his own sons. When Cymbeline is made prisoner by the Roman general, Belarius comes to his rescue, is reconciled, and restores the princes.

Belch, Sir Toby In *Twelfth Night*, the uncle of Olivia. He is a roistering knight, fond of drinking and singing and exploiter of the wealthy Sir Andrew Aguecheek. In his enjoyment of Maria's plot against Malvolio, he decides to marry her.

Bellaria The wife of Pandosto in Robert ➤Greene's *Pandosto*. She is the character on which Hermione in *The Winter's Tale* is based.

Bellario, Dr   In *The Merchant of Venice*, an erudite lawyer of Padua, as whose substitute Portia appears in the trial scene. He makes no stage appearance.

Belmont   In *The Merchant of Venice*, Portia's estate.

Benedick   In *Much Ado About Nothing*, a witty and sophisticated gentleman of Padua, who ridicules love. He engages in witty verbal duelling with Beatrice, adopting the pose of a confirmed bachelor, but is easily manoeuvered by Claudio and Don Pedro into falling in love with her. He proves his love by agreeing to fight Claudio, formerly his friend.

Benfield, Robert   English actor. He is listed in the 1623 folio of Shakespeare's plays as a principal actor, and probably joined the King's Men as a shareholder in 1615.

Benvolio   In *Romeo and Juliet*, a friend of Romeo and nephew of Montague. His actions contribute to the tragic outcome of the play, for it is his fight with Tybalt in the opening scene that leads to the decree that street brawling is a capital offence, and it is he who persuades Romeo to attend Capulet's ball, where Romeo meets Juliet. He is present at Mercutio's death and at the time of Romeo's revenge against Tybalt for this.

Berkeley   In *Richard III*, a gentleman attendant on the Lady Anne.

Berkeley, Lord   In *Richard II*, a minor character who appears once to ask Bolingbroke why he has returned, armed, to England.

Bernhardt, Sarah   (1834–1923) French actress, often considered the greatest of the 19th century. She played Cordelia in *King Lear*, Desdemona (1878), Macbeth (1884), and Hamlet (1899). She was the first woman to play Hamlet on film (*Hamlet's Duel*, 1900).

Berowne [Also, Biron]   In *Love's Labour's Lost*, the chief of the three lords attending the King of Navarre at his rural academy. In order to get wisdom they swear to study at the academy for three years and to avoid the sight of women. Berowne is a somewhat unwilling partner to the agreement because he realizes the folly of it. Shortly after the Princess of France and her three ladies, including the volatile Rosaline, appear on the scene, each of the lords and the King find that the vow has been broken by their falling in love. Berowne confesses his love for Rosaline in a speech designed to prove that love is the best form of learning (IV.iii).

Bertram   In *All's Well That Ends Well*, the young Count of Roussillion, who is loved by Helena and forced to marry her. He refuses to treat her as his wife unless she fulfils certain apparently impossible conditions; these she meets by means of a ruse, and Bertram agrees to live with her.

Betterton, Thomas   (1635–1710) Leading actor in the Restoration theatre, who played Hamlet first in 1661, and continued to do so until he was over seventy. His other Shakespearean roles included Mercutio (1662), Henry VIII (1663), Macbeth (1664), Timon (1678), Troilus (1679), King Lear (1680–81), and many more.

Bevis, George   In *2 Henry VI*, a supporter of Jack Cade.

Bianca   In *Othello*, a prostitute of Cyprus and the mistress of Cassio, whom she loves. He asks her to copy the embroidery of Othello's fatal handkerchief.

Bianca   In *The Taming of the Shrew*, the sister of Katherina (the "Shrew"). She is wooed by Hortensio and Gremio, but is won by Lucentio with whom she elopes.

Bigot, Lord   In *King John*, a noble who joins the French after Arthur's death but later returns to England.

Biondello   In *The Taming of the Shrew*, a servant to Lucentio.

Birnam Wood   In *Macbeth*, a forest near Dunsinane, the seat of the Scottish kings. The Witches prophesy that Macbeth will not be vanquished until Birnam Wood shall come to Dunsinane Hill against him. The prophecy is fulfilled when Macduff's army takes branches from the woods for concealment as they march against Macbeth.

Blackfriars   The name of two private playhouses situated near the north bank of the Thames in London. The first Blackfriars was an indoor theatre in use from 1576 to 1584, so-called because it was formed from a Dominican priory originally built in 1275. One portion of this priory passed to the Master of the Revels on the suppression of the monasteries in 1538 and then to Sir William More in 1559. This part of the priory was a series of two-storey buildings along the west side of the cloisters. A chamber in the priory 125 feet by 25 feet was leased in 1576 to Richard Farrant, Master of the ►Children of the Chapel, for public performances by the Children preceding their court appearances. After Farrant's death the performances continued under William Hunnis and Henry Evans. The Children of the Chapel and of Paul's performed ►Lyly's plays there (1582– 84). More recovered the chamber in 1584. The second theatre was formed nearby from buildings bought by James ►Burbage in 1596. A hall 66 feet by 46 feet, it had a stage, galleries, and seats. Like the first Blackfriars, it was located within the City walls, but not under the City's jurisdiction, being in a 'liberty', a former religious precinct. It was leased (1600) to Henry ►Evans and Nathaniel Giles for performances by the Children of the Chapel, who were not competing with adult companies. The ►King's Men obtained the theatre in 1608 when a syndicate was formed of Richard ►Burbage, Cuthbert ►Burbage, Shakespeare, ►Heminges, ►Condell, ►Sly, and Thomas Evans. Since it was an enclosed theatre with somewhat different arrangements from the public playhouses, the style of acting was different and the price of admission was dearer. Shakespeare's late romances with their masques and scenic requirements may have been written for this theatre or ones like it, and musical interludes between the acts were a feature of its productions. The building was torn down in 1655.

Blanche of Spain   In *King John*, the historical Blanche of Castile, daughter of the King of Castile and the niece of John. She is married to the French Dauphin to seal the truce between John and the French, but her loyalties are soon strained when Pandulph excommunicates John and the French fight him. She follows the Dauphin.

Blunt   In *2 Henry IV*, an officer in the royal army who is ordered by John to Lancaster to guard the rebel, Colevile (IV.iii).

Blunt, Sir James   In *Richard III*, a supporter of Richmond.

Blunt, Sir Walter   In *1 Henry IV*, the historical Sir Walter Blount, a supporter of King Henry. He acts as intermediary between the King and the rebels before the battle of Shrewsbury. Later Douglas kills him thinking he is King Henry.

Boar's Head   A tavern in Eastcheap, London, celebrated by Shakespeare as the scene of Falstaff's carousals in *1* and *2 Henry IV*. It did not exist in the time of the historical Henry IV. The tavern is not explicitly mentioned in the original text, but is inferred from remarks made by Falstaff and others. It was destroyed in the great fire of London (September 1666), afterwards rebuilt, and again demolished to make room for one of the approaches to London Bridge.

Boar's Head theatre   The innyard of the Boar's Head Inn, east of Aldgate, where, from the late 1550s on, plays were enacted.

Bogdanov, Michael   (1938–   ) British theatre director who worked with the ►Royal Shakespeare Company and at the Royal National Theatre before he established his own company, the ►English Shakespeare Company, with Michael ►Pennington in 1985. He is known for his radical and political productions. In 1989 he became Director of the Deutsches Schauspielhaus in Hamburg.

Bohemia, seacoast of   In *The Winter's Tale*, the place where Antigonus abandons Perdita. Since Bohemia (now part of the Czech Republic) has no coast, this has been often cited as an example of a mistake on Shakespeare's part. Bohemia was known in the period as a site of fabulous adventures.

Bolingbroke, Henry   In *Richard II*, the usurper of the throne; in *1* and *2 Henry IV*, the King of England (i.e., Henry IV himself). He is the Duke of Hereford, son of John of Gaunt, and, after the latter's death, Duke of Lancaster. In *Richard II*, Bolingbroke replaces the weak Richard on the throne. In *1 Henry IV*, he is a less successful figure. Factions around the kingdom are in rebellion, and he grieves for his wild son, Prince Hal, wishing him more like the gallant Hotspur. In *2 Henry IV*, he has become yet more weary and anxious about the fate of his kingdom. He recognizes his insecurity as the price of his usurpation.

Bolingbroke, Roger In *2 Henry VI*, a conjurer. He summons a prophetic spirit for Eleanor, Duchess of Gloucester, who aspires to the throne. York discovers them and arrests them as traitors.

Bona In *3 Henry VI*, the sister of the Queen of France who has agreed to marry Edward IV at Warwick's suggestion but finds that he has taken Lady Grey instead. She urges King Lewis (Louis) to support Margaret in her fight against Edward and is joined by Warwick, who has been made a fool by the secret marriage.

Borachio In *Much Ado About Nothing*, a follower of Don John. He has the incriminating conversation with Margaret (who pretends to be Hero) that persuades Claudio of Hero's infidelity. He is arrested and confesses the scheme under Dogberry's cross-examination. The name also is used by other Elizabethan dramatists for a drunkard, alluding to the Spanish word for a large leather bag used for wine.

Bottom, Nick In *A Midsummer Night's Dream*, an Athenian weaver who plays the part of Pyramus in the interpolated play. He is ambitious and enthusiastic, and in his eagerness wants to take all the parts in the play. While rehearsing the play in the forest, he has an ass's head put on him by Puck. In this guise he meets Titania, who has been put under a spell by Oberon to love the first person she sees on waking; when this is Bottom with his ass's head, she is deluded into thinking him beautiful, until Oberon releases her from the magic. He is the only one of the mortal characters to see the fairies.

Bottom the Weaver, The Merry Conceited Humours of Farce made from the comic scenes of *A Midsummer Night's Dream*, published in 1672. It was attributed to Robert Cox, a comedian of the time of King Charles II.

Boult In *Pericles*, a servant to the Pander in Mytilene.

Bourbon, Duke of In *Henry V*, a leader in the French army who is captured at Agincourt after urging on the French forces to the attack.

Bourchier, Cardinal In *Richard III*, the Archbishop of Canterbury. Gloucester persuades him to take the young Duke of York from his mother, Queen Elizabeth, so that Gloucester can imprison him, with his brother Edward, Prince of Wales, in the Tower, on the pretext that they there await the coronation.

Boyet In *Love's Labour's Lost*, a mocking lord attending on the Princess of France. He informs the Princess and her ladies that the Muscovite masquers are the King of Navarre and his lords.

Brabantio In *Othello*, a Venetian senator, father of Desdemona. He violently denounces Othello for his marriage with her. He is reported in the last scene to have died.

Brakenbury, Sir Robert   In *Richard III*, the Lieutenant of the Tower who surrenders Clarence to the two murderers sent by Gloucester. He presumably surrenders the two young Princes later to Tyrrel.

Branagh, Kenneth   (1960–   ) British actor and director of Shakespeare for the stage and the cinema. He has worked with the ➤Royal Shakespeare Company and with his own company, the Renaissance Theatre Company. He has directed films of *Henry V* (1989), *Much Ado About Nothing* (1993), and *Hamlet* (1996), playing the lead role in each case.

Brandon   In *Henry VIII*, an officer who arrives with the sergeant-at-arms to arrest Buckingham and Abergavenny on charges of high treason.

Brandon, Sir William   In *Richard III*, a follower of the Earl of Richmond. He is the father of Charles Brandon, Duke of Suffolk, who appears in *Henry VIII*.

Brook, Master   In *The Merry Wives of Windsor*, the name assumed by Ford for the purpose of fooling Falstaff, who is seeking an affair with Ford's wife. Falstaff, unaware of Brook's true identity, boasts to him of progress in his pursuit of Mistress Ford.

Brook, Peter   (1925–   ) British theatre director who directed Shakespeare for many years at the ➤Shakespeare Memorial Theatre, Stratford-upon-Avon. His productions, some of the most original and influential of the postwar era, include *Titus Andronicus* (1955), *King Lear* (1962, filmed 1970), *A Midsummer Night's Dream* (1970), and *Antony and Cleopatra* (1978). Since 1971 he has worked mainly for the International Centre of Theatre Research in Paris, which he founded, directing *Timon of Athens* (1974), *Measure for Measure* (1990), and *The Tempest* (1995).

Brooke, Arthur   [Also, Broke]   (d. 1563) English translator who wrote *The Tragicall Historye of Romeus and Juliet* (1562), one of the first English versions of the famous tragedy of love. This is the principal source of *Romeo and Juliet*. Brooke translated freely from the French version of Matteo Bandello's Italian version of the story, published in the *Histoires Tragiques* (Paris, 1559).

Brutus, Decius   In *Julius Caesar*, one of the conspirators who succeeds in bringing Caesar to the Capitol by interpreting Calphurnia's dreams in a hopeful fashion. This is probably the historical Decimus Junius Brutus, who was put to death by Antony in 43 BC.

Brutus, Junius   In *Coriolanus*, a tribune who, together with Sicinius, so arouses the Romans against Coriolanus that the latter is banished. Upon Coriolanus's return with the Volscian army, they deny responsibility and ask Menenius to stop his advance.

Brutus, Marcus   In *Julius Caesar*, the historical Marcus Junius Brutus, the chief assassin. The conspirators appeal to his love of Rome and its traditional freedoms in order to obtain his aid in their plot against Caesar as the embodiment of tyranny. Brutus is Caesar's friend, and at the assassination his presence calls forth the words "*Et tu Brute*, Then die Caesar" from the fallen Caesar (III.i). Brutus is a man of honour, who falls because of an inability to understand the practical aspects of politics and war. In spite of Cassius's warning, he permits Antony to make his inflammatory address to the people over Caesar's body; he nearly alienates Cassius by censuring his levy of funds from their supporters; and finally he loses the struggle with Antony and Octavius by choosing to fight on the plains of Philippi instead of withdrawing as Cassius advises. When the battle is lost, he kills himself. In the Renaissance he was equivocally regarded, sometimes as a traitor, sometimes as a champion of freedom over tyranny.

Bryan, George   (*fl. c.* 1586–98) English actor. He is first recorded as acting at Elsinore, Denmark, in 1580. He is listed as a principal actor in the first folio (1623) of Shakespeare's plays and was probably an original member of the ➤Lord Chamberlain's Men (formed 1594).

Buckingham, Duke of   In *2 Henry VI*, the historical Humphrey Stafford, one of the nobles who cause Gloucester's downfall. He persuades the followers of the rebel, Jack Cade, to disperse and later supports Henry in the war with the Yorkists. In *3 Henry VI*, his death is reported at the battle of St Albans (1455); Shakespeare was compressing history to fit his play, since the historical personage was killed at Northampton in 1460.

Buckingham, (2nd) Duke of   In *Richard III*, the historical Henry Stafford, the accomplice of Richard (Gloucester) in his conspiracy and crime. He assists Richard in his rise to power, but hesitates when asked to murder the two princes in the Tower. He attempts to desert to Richmond, but is executed before he can do so. His ghost appears to Richard on the night before the battle of Bosworth.

Buckingham, (3rd) Duke of   In *Henry VIII*, the historical Edward Stafford, son of the Buckingham who was executed by Richard III. He is an enemy of Wolsey, whom he sees as dangerous to England. Arrested by Wolsey on a charge of threatening Henry's life, he defends himself at the place of execution in a speech probably written by Fletcher.

Bullcalf, Peter   In *2 Henry IV*, a recruit to Falstaff's troop.

Bullen, Anne   In *Henry VIII*, the historical Anne Boleyn, second wife of the King and former lady-in-waiting of Katherine, his first wife. Wolsey's downfall is brought about by the discovery of his plan to prevent the King from divorcing Katherine and marrying Anne. She is the mother of Elizabeth I.

Burbage, Cuthbert   (*c.* 1566–1636) English theatre manager. He was the elder son of James ➤Burbage and the brother of Richard ➤Burbage, the actor, with whom he built the ➤Globe theatre. He held interests in several theatres, and developed the "stock company" system, in which shareholders owned a part of the company.

Burbage, James (d. 1597) English actor and the first builder of a theatre in England; father of Richard and Cuthbert ►Burbage. He was originally a joiner. In the period 1576–77 he erected the first English building specifically intended for plays. It was between Finsbury Fields and the public road from Bishopsgate and Shoreditch, in what is now part of London. It was of wood, and was called simply "the Theatre." The material was removed to the ►Bankside in 1598 and was rebuilt as the ►Globe theatre. The ►Curtain theatre was put up near the ►Theatre soon after the latter was opened, and Burbage was instrumental in the conversion of a large house at ►Blackfriars into a theatre, probably in November 1596.

Burbage, Richard (b. *c.* 1567; d. 1619) With Edward ►Alleyn, one of the two leading actors of Shakespeare's day; son of James ►Burbage. With his brother Cuthbert he was proprietor of the ►Theatre and later of the ►Globe, as well as of the ►Blackfriars theatre. He already had some acting experience when he joined with Shakespeare and others in forming the ►Lord Chamberlain's Men in 1594, but he went on to make his fame as an actor with this company (which became the King's Men in 1603). He apparently played the leading parts in most of the plays produced by this company, and seems to have been the original Richard III, Hamlet, Lear, and Othello as well as playing the heroes in many other of Shakespeare's plays. His ability and style of acting may have had some influence on the kinds of leading roles Shakespeare created for his plays. Burbage excelled in tragedy and was held in high esteem by playwrights as well as by the public; he was sometimes even introduced into plays in his own person as in the Induction to John ►Marston's *The Malcontent* (1603). Besides his fame as an actor he was known as a painter and is traditionally held to be the painter of one of the extant Shakespeare portraits. At his death, many poems and tributes were written in his memory. William ►Herbert, 3rd Earl of Pembroke, was his friend.

Burgundy, Duke of In *Henry V*, the French noble who arranges the terms of peace between the French and the English. In a long speech (V.ii) he compares war-torn France to a dying and uncared-for garden. In *1 Henry VI*, he fights at first on the English side, but in a speech much like his own in *Henry V*, Joan of Arc persuades him to return to the French (III.iii).

Burgundy, Duke of In *King Lear*, a rival of the King of France for the hand of Cordelia. He refuses to marry her when she is left without a dowry.

Bushy In *Richard II*, a follower of the King.

Butts, Dr In *Henry VIII*, the King's physician, the historical Sir William Butts.

C

Cade, Jack In *2 Henry VI*, the rebel leader, the historical John Cade. York, planning to usurp the throne, encourages Cade to stir up a rebellion in England. Cade assumes the name Mortimer and claims the throne himself. He captures London Bridge, but his followers desert him; he flees and is killed by Alexander Iden.

Cadwal In *Cymbeline*, the name under which Arviragus is raised from infancy. As Cadwal, Arviragus believes himself to be the son of Morgan (who is actually Belarius).

Caesar, Julius In *Julius Caesar*, the dictator of Rome, whom the conspirators, led by Brutus and Cassius, assassinate (on the part of Brutus solely, and on the part of Cassius at least partly, for fear that he would abridge the traditional Roman freedoms). Shakespeare's presentation of him is ambiguous: he is noble but an egoist, over-insistent on his personal integrity and fearlessness. He is arrogant, yet also physically weak, superstitious, yet acute in his understanding of men. Caesar's reputation in Renaissance England was ambiguous; as in medieval times, he was still seen by some as an epic hero and mighty conqueror, but by others as a tyrant and dictator.

Caesar, Octavius ➤Octavius Caesar.

Caithness In *Macbeth*, a Scottish thane.

Caius In *King Lear*, the assumed name of Kent.

Caius In *Titus Andronicus*, a kinsman of Titus.

Caius, Doctor In The *Merry Wives of Windsor*, a comic French doctor in love with Anne Page. Despite an arrangement with Mistress Page to carry off Anne and marry her, he loses her through a substitution arranged by Fenton and the Host of the Garter Inn.

Caius Lucius ➤Lucius, Caius.

Caius Marcius ➤Coriolanus.

Calchas In *Troilus and Cressida*, a Trojan priest who becomes a traitor to his native city and joins the Greeks. He requests that his daughter Cressida (whom he has left in Troy) be exchanged for Antenor, a Trojan held prisoner by the Greeks. He does not object to Diomedes's seduction of his daughter.

Caliban   In *The Tempest*, a "savage and deformed" slave. The son of the witch Sycorax, who ruled the island before Prospero's shipwreck on it, he becomes a reluctant captive to Prospero's magic powers and regards himself as rightful ruler of the island. He readily subjects himself to the drunken Stephano, with whom he plots Prospero's murder. In the later twentieth century, he is regularly seen as a colonized subject.

Calphurnia   In *Julius Caesar*, the historical Calpurnia, wife of Caesar. She is fearful for her husband's safety because of dreams she has had and tries to persuade him not to go to the Capitol.

Cambridge, Earl of   In *Henry V*, the historical Richard, Earl of Cambridge, a conspirator who plots with Scroop and Grey to murder the King. The plot is discovered and the King hands them death warrants in place of the expected commissions for his French campaign. In *Richard II*, he is a son of the Duke of York and brother of Aumerle. His son is the York appearing in *1*, *2*, and *3 Henry VI*.

Camillo   In *The Winter's Tale*, a Sicilian noble who saves Polixenes and accompanies him to Bohemia. He later induces Leontes to protect Florizel and Perdita and at the end of the play is urged to marry Pauline.

Campeius, Cardinal   In *Henry VIII*, a papal legate who, with Wolsey, considers the question of the King's divorce from Katherine.

Canidius   In *Antony and Cleopatra*, the chief lieutenant of Antony. He withholds his forces from the sea battle and, when he sees that Antony is losing, joins Octavius.

Canterbury, Archbishop of   In *Henry V*, a counsellor to the King who, in hopes that a war with France will deter the King from confiscating church property, proves at length that the old Salic Law, forbidding the succession of women and their descendants to the throne, would not apply to France, and that Henry's genealogy entitles him to claim French lands.

Canterbury, Archbishop of   ➤Bourchier, Cardinal; ➤Cranmer.

Caphis   In *Timon of Athens*, a servant of one of Timon's creditors.

Capucius   In *Henry VIII*, an ambassador from Charles V to the dying Katherine.

Capulet   In *Romeo and Juliet*, the irascible father of Juliet. Ignorant of her marriage to Romeo, he insists that she take Paris as her husband.

Capulet, Lady   In *Romeo and Juliet*, Juliet's mother. She urges her daughter to marry Paris and, in an elaborate figure of speech, likens him to a beautiful book (I.iii).

Cardenio, The History of   A play of this name was entered on the Stationers' Register in 1653 as by John ➤Fletcher and Shakespeare. It was based on a story in *Don Quixote* (translated into English in 1612) of Cardenio, who is driven mad by the loss of his love, Lucinda. He has intervals of sanity and recovers completely when Lucinda is restored to him. Scholars are not certain beyond any possible doubt that Shakespeare did not have a hand in the play, which is now lost: a play called *Cardenno* or *Cardenna* was performed at court by the ►King's Men in 1613, at the time when Shakespeare and Fletcher were collaborating. Lewis Theobald, the Shakespearean editor, published a play based on the story called *Double Falsehood or the Distrest Lovers* in 1728, which he claimed to have "revised and adapted" from Shakespeare.

Carlisle, Bishop of In *Richard II*, a loyal supporter of Richard. He strenuously protests against Bolingbroke's ascension to the throne and direly predicts that "The blood of English shall manure the ground and future ages groan for this foul act" (IV.i.). He is arrested for treason, but pardoned by Bolingbroke.

Casca In *Julius Caesar*, a conspirator against Caesar who describes him having an epileptic fit.

Cassandra In *Troilus and Cressida*, a prophetess, daughter of King Priam of Troy, who foretells Troy's destruction and Hector's death.

Cassibelan In *Cymbeline*, the historical Cassivellaunus, a British prince captured by Caesar, mentioned in the play.

Cassio, Michael In *Othello*, successful rival to Iago for the post of Othello's lieutenant. He becomes, by the devices of Iago, the innocent object of Othello's jealousy, believed by the Moor to be Desdemona's lover.

Cassius In *Julius Caesar*, the historical Gaius Cassius Longinus, one of the chief members of the conspiracy against Caesar, motivated partly by fear of the threat to Rome's traditional freedoms, but also by jealousy and admiration for Brutus. After the Battle of Philippi, believing that Brutus has already been captured, he kills himself. It is he whom Caesar describes as having "a lean and hungry look, / He thinks too much" (I.ii).

Catesby, Sir William In *Richard III*, a follower of Richard.

Catherine and Petruchio A play condensed and adapted from *The Taming of the Shrew* by David ►Garrick, produced in 1756.

Cato, Young In *Julius Caesar*, a friend of Brutus and Cassius who appears briefly at the Battle of Philippi.

Cawdor, Thane of In *Macbeth*, a prosperous gentleman whose rank was promised to Macbeth by the Witches. No sooner had the prophecy been made than Macbeth learned that Cawdor was to be executed by order of Duncan for treason. He dies nobly—"nothing in his life became him like the leaving it" (I.iv)—and Macbeth succeeds to his rank.

Celia In *As You Like It*, the cousin and devoted friend of Rosalind, and daughter of Frederick, the usurping duke. She is the companion of Rosalind in the Forest of Arden, in the disguise of Aliena, a shepherdess. She falls in love with and marries Oliver, older brother to Orlando.

Ceres In *The Tempest*, a character in the masque devised by Prospero to celebrate the vows of Ferdinand and Miranda. In classical mythology, she was the goddess of fertility.

Cerimon In *Pericles*, a lord of Ephesus and healer who revives Thaisa. He sends her to the temple of Diana, where she becomes one of the vestals.

Cesario In *Twelfth Night*, the name Viola takes when in male disguise.

Chamberlain In *1 Henry IV*, an attendant at the inn at Rochester who tells Gadshill about some wealthy guests and is promised a share in the plunder.

Chamberlain, Lord ►Lord Chamberlain.

Chamberlain's Men ►Lord Chamberlain's Men.

Chancellor, Lord ►Lord Chancellor.

Chapman, George (*c.* 1559–1634) English poet and dramatist, chiefly celebrated for his translation of Homer. He was intimate with Ben ►Jonson, John ►Fletcher, and other prominent figures of the time and is sometimes thought to have been the "rival poet" referred to in Shakespeare's Sonnets.

Charles In *As You Like It*, a wrestler hired by Duke Frederick and defeated by Orlando.

Charles VI In *Henry V*, the King of France. He makes the Treaty of Troyes whereby his daughter Katherine is to marry Henry and the latter to inherit France after his death. This follows an episode in the life of the real Charles (1368–1422).

Charles, the Dauphin In *1 Henry VI*, the son of Charles VI (historically not, as Shakespeare makes him, the Dauphin). When Joan of Arc arrives to request troops, she impresses him with her prowess by overcoming him in a duel and he falls in love with her. He attributes the French victories to her, and when she is captured, he becomes viceroy under Henry.

Charmian In *Antony and Cleopatra*, Cleopatra's waiting-woman. She kills herself after Cleopatra's death.

Chatillon In *King John*, an ambassador from France sent by Philip to demand that John give up the throne to Arthur.

Chettle, Henry (*c.* 1560–*c.* 1607) English playwright and pamphleteer, also a stationer by trade. He wrote the pamphlet ►*Kind-Hart's Dream* (1592), in which he refers to Shakespeare (not by name) in flattering terms: "Myself have seen his demeanour no less civil than he excellent in the quality he professes. Besides, divers of worship have reported his uprightness of dealing, which argues his honesty, and his facetious grace in writing, that approves his art."

Chief Justice   ➤Lord Chief Justice.

Children of the Chapel [Also, at various times: Children of the Revels, Children of Blackfriars, Children of the Queen's Revels]   An Elizabethan and Jacobean company of child actors, comprising the choir boys of the Chapel (or Chapel Royal), a part of the royal household that presented interludes with adult actors in the early sixteenth century. William Cornish was Master of the Children from 1509 until 1523 and formed the acting company. The company continued during the rest of the century under such masters as Edwards, Farrant, Hunnis, and Giles, and played, at various times, at the ➤Blackfriars theatre. The Children of the Chapel, and a similar group, Paul's Boys, competed with adult companies, and are disparaged by Hamlet in II.ii. They had become established at the Blackfriars theatre in 1600, which provides a dating reference for *Hamlet*. A number of the ➤King's Men were once child actors with this company. The children's company lost favour at court, became the Children of the Revels, and finally, in 1606, the Children of Blackfriars. In 1608, they left the Blackfriars theatre and moved to ➤Whitefriars, where they remained until 1610, when they again came under royal patronage, as the Children of the Queen's Revels. When Nathan ➤Field left them about 1616, the company fell into obscurity.

Children of the Revels   ➤Children of the Chapel.

Chiron   In *Titus Andronicus*, a son of Tamora. He and his brother Demetrius are guilty of various crimes; Titus kills both by cutting their throats and then bakes them in a pie to serve to their mother.

Chronicles of England, Scotland, and Ireland, The   ➤Holinshed's *Chronicles*.

Cibber, Colley   (1671–1757) British actor and playwright who took the main role in his own adaptation of *Richard III*, which held the stage until the 1870s. He became Poet Laureate in 1730 and wrote his autobiography, *An Apology for the Life of Colley Cibber*, published in 1740.

Cicero   In *Julius Caesar*, Roman senator who is not asked to join the conspiracy. He is one of a number of senators put to death by Antony, Octavius, and Lepidus.

Cimber, Metellus   In *Julius Caesar*, one of the conspirators. His suit to Caesar (to recall his brother, Publius, from banishment) is the pretext for the gathering of the conspirators around Caesar to assassinate him.

Cinna   In *Julius Caesar*, the historical Gaius Helvius Cinna, a poet. He is mistaken for the other Cinna and is mobbed and murdered.

Cinna In *Julius Caesar*, the historical Lucius Cornelius Cinna (the younger), one of the conspirators against Caesar. He places tracts so that Brutus will find them and join in the conspiracy.

Clarence, George, Duke of In *3 Henry VI*, the historical George Plantagenet, brother of Edward IV, who creates him Duke of Clarence. He deserts the King in anger at his marriage with Lady Grey, but rejoins him later. In *Richard III*, he is imprisoned by Edward IV and ordered to his death. The reprieve that the Queen has persuaded Edward to give him is intercepted by Gloucester (Richard) and he is murdered by being drowned in a butt of malmsey.

Clarence, Thomas of In *2 Henry IV*, the Duke of Clarence, second son of the King and brother of Prince Hal. The King asks Clarence to advise Hal and keep him from his wild companions when he becomes king. In *Henry V*, he is asked by Henry to help arrange the peace terms with the French King (V.ii).

Claudio In *Measure for Measure*, the brother of Isabella, condemned to death for his sexual relationship with Juliet. Through Isabella, Angelo offers him his life, in exchange for Isabella becoming his (Angelo's) mistress. In a dramatic scene Claudio begs Isabella to yield to Angelo's wishes, but is refused. Later his death is ordered by Angelo, but the Provost of the prison prevents the execution.

Claudio In *Much Ado About Nothing*, a young Florentine in love with Hero. He is persuaded by a trick to believe Hero unfaithful, but later recognizes his mistake and is finally married to her.

Claudius In *Hamlet*, the King of Denmark and uncle of Hamlet married to Hamlet's mother, Gertrude. When he realizes that Hamlet has discovered that he is a murderer, he plots to get rid of his nephew. When his attempt to send Hamlet to England fails, he contrives a duel between Hamlet and Laertes in which Laertes is to fence with a poisoned and unbaited foil. Hamlet, stabbed and dying, kills Claudius in the final scene with the same poisoned foil.

Claudius In *Julius Caesar*, a servant of Brutus.

Cleomenes In *The Winter's Tale*, a Sicilian noble who, with Dion, is sent by Leontes to the oracle at Delphi to ask if Hermione is chaste. They return with an affirmative answer.

Cleon In *Pericles*, the governor of Tharsus (Tarsus) who is burned to death to avenge the supposed murder of Marina.

Cleopatra In *Antony and Cleopatra*, the heroine, Queen of Egypt, a paradoxical and fascinating character, of whom Enobarbus says: "Age cannot wither her, nor custom stale her infinite variety" (II.ii). She is a woman of constantly changing moods who enrages Antony but still enslaves him. At several crucial points in the play the motives for her actions appear ambiguous. After Antony's death by suicide in

Act IV, the whole final act is devoted to the ending of Cleopatra's life, her outwitting of Caesar, and her triumphant death. Shakespeare based the character closely on that in Plutarch's life of Antony from *Lives of the Noble Grecians and Romans*.

Clerk of Chatham   In *2 Henry VI*, a clerk, assaulted by the mob led by Jack Cade because he can read and write.

Clifford, Lord   In *2 Henry VI*, a Lancastrian and supporter of the King's party. With Buckingham, he persuades the rebellious mob to desert their leader Cade. He is killed by York at the battle of St Albans.

Clifford, Lord   In *2 Henry VI*, Young Clifford, the son of the elder Lord Clifford. In *3 Henry VI*, he is a member of the Lancastrian faction and stabs York at the battle of Wakefield, after first killing York's son, Rutland, both deeds having been done to avenge his father's death (I.iii, iv). He himself is wounded in battle at Towton and dies despairing of the Lancastrian cause (II.vi).

Clitus   In *Julius Caesar*, a servant of Brutus.

Cloten   In *Cymbeline*, the queen's son by a former husband, a foolish braggart. He is rejected by Imogen but pursues her to Wales, and is there challenged to fight and killed by Guiderius.

Clown   In *The Winter's Tale*, a rustic countryman, the son of the Old Shepherd. He reports the death of Antigonus (III.iii) and later is forced to go to Sicilia, where he is honoured with his father by Polixenes and Leontes.

Clowns   In *Hamlet*, the two Grave-diggers who are jesting and singing when Hamlet comes upon them as they dig Ophelia's grave (V.i). There are also unnamed clowns making brief appearances in *Othello*, *Titus Andronicus*, and *Antony and Cleopatra*. The professional jesters Touchstone, Feste, and Lavatch are identified in the Dramatis Personae as clowns, meaning they were played by the principal comedian in the company. In the Elizabethan theatre, the clown was a skilled professional actor. In general use, the term referred to a rustic or countryman. See also under *Fool*.

Cobweb   In *A Midsummer Night's Dream*, a fairy.

Cockpit, the   ►Phoenix.

Colevile, Sir John   In *2 Henry IV*, a "famous rebel" who yields to Falstaff in Gaultree Forest and is sent to his execution at York.

Comedy of Errors, The   A play by Shakespeare, possibly acted at Gray's Inn, in London, on 28 December 1594. It is likely to have been one of the playwright's earliest works (most modern scholars believe 1592 or 1593 to be the years that may most probably be assigned to it). It is sometimes thought to be the play listed by Francis ►Meres in his *Palladis Tamia* as *Love's Labour's Won*. The main plot is taken from Plautus's comedy, the *Menaechmi*, a play much edited and adapted in the Renaissance, in which the action is based on the confusions between identical twin brothers. One brother arranges to dine with a courtesan but the other turns up instead; the wife of the first brother is informed and becomes outraged, but finally all is explained. Shakespeare enlarged this very short play with material from another of Plautus's comedies, *Amphitruo*, in which the god Jupiter disguises himself as Amphitruo and takes his place in his wife's bed, while the god Mercury adds to the confusion by disguising himself as Amphitruo's slave Sosia. Shakespeare added the notion of identical twin slaves to the plot of *Menaechmi*, thereby immensely increasing the opportunities for confusion, and developed more fully the situation of one spouse being excluded while a double dines with the other. He also changed the characterization of the wife, who in Plautus is a very cynically treated shrew, making her more important in the play and also more sympathetic, gave her a sister, Luciana, as a bride for the other brother, and considerably deepened the treatment of marriage. As a frame for the comic action, he added the non-farcical story of his twins' father, Aegeon, doomed to death for no fault of his own, and his recovery of his lost wife Aemilia in a scene that probably derives from a version of the story of Apollonius of Tyre, retold by John Gower in *Confessio Amantis*. He changed the setting from Epidamnum to Ephesus, partly perhaps because Ephesus figures strongly in the Apollonius of Tyre story but also, it is thought, because of St Paul's visit to Ephesus, described in Acts xix as a city of exorcists, evil spirits, and strange arts; in Ephesians St Paul urges the people to seek marital unity, and talks of the relationships between children and parents, masters and servants, all of which are important ideas in *The Comedy of Errors*. No English translation of the *Menaechmi* is known to have been published before 1595 (and of the *Amphitruo* for about a hundred years after that), so Shakespeare must have worked from Latin sources available at the time (indeed, there is much internal evidence that Shakespeare was influenced by Latin turns of phrase, although his use of the Latin is at no point close to translation). However, if the play was written in 1593, Shakespeare may have seen Warner's translation of the *Menaechmi* in manuscript.

Dramatis Personae

Solinus, Duke of Ephesus

Aegeon, *a merchant of Syracuse*

Antipholus of Ephesus, *son of Aegeon and Aemilia, twin of:*

Antipholus of Syracuse

Dromio of Ephesus, *twin of:*

Dromio of Syracuse, *attendants of the two Antipholuses*

Balthazar, *a merchant*

Angelo, *a goldsmith*

A Merchant, *friend to Antipholus of Syracuse*

A merchant trading with Angelo

Pinch, *a schoolmaster*

Aemilia, *wife to Aegeon, an abbess at Ephesus*

Adriana, *wife to Antipholus of Ephesus*

Luciana, *her sister*

Luce, *servant to Adriana*

A Courtesan

Jailers, Officers, *and other Attendants*

The Story. Aegeon, a Syracusan merchant, had been shipwrecked with his wife, Aemilia, their twin sons, both named Antipholus, and twin slaves, both named Dromio. One of each pair of twins remained with Aegeon, but the others disappeared with Aemilia. At eighteen, one of the twins, Antipholus of Syracuse, had been allowed by his father to go and search for his lost twin brother. When he did not return in five years, his father set out in search of him. The action of the play commences when Aegeon is arrested at Ephesus and sentenced to death because of the enmity between that city and Syracuse. His story moves Solinus, the Duke of Ephesus, to allow him until nightfall to obtain his ransom money. Meanwhile, Antipholus of Syracuse has arrived in Ephesus where, unknown to him, live his brother and his brother's wife Adriana, and their Dromio. From this situation arise the complications—the comedy of errors—because everyone confuses the two sets of twins, including themselves. Antipholus of Syracuse beats Dromio of Ephesus for insisting he go home to dinner; Antipholus of Syracuse does, however, dine at Adriana's house, from which the Ephesian twin is locked out, Adriana believing her husband to be within; Antipholus of Ephesus is arrested for not paying for a gold chain that was mistakenly given to Antipholus of Syracuse. Everyone is convinced of the insanity of the others. At length, the Syracusans take refuge in an abbey. When Aegeon is led to his execution the Ephesian twins arrive to demand justice from the Duke. They, of course, do not recognize Aegeon; they deny receiving the gold chain; and after considerably more confusion, the abbess arrives with the Syracusans. With the presence of everyone, the errors are solved, Antipholus of Syracuse marries Luciana, sister of Adriana, and the pardoned Aegeon discovers the abbess to be his lost wife.

Cominius   In *Coriolanus*, a Roman general. He tries to persuade the people of Rome not to banish Coriolanus, and later, when Coriolanus has joined the Volscian forces, undertakes to persuade him to spare Rome.

Condell, Henry   [Also, Cundell]   (d. 1627) English actor, and editor with ►Heminges of the first folio edition of Shakespeare's plays, published in 1623. He was a member of the ►Lord Chamberlain's Men, to which Shakespeare was also admitted, probably in 1594. A share of the company was given him in 1604 and in 1608 he, along with Shakespeare, received a share in the ►Blackfriars theatre owned by the ►Burbages. He is mentioned in Shakespeare's will. By 1612 he had acquired a portion also of the ►Globe theatre.

Conrade   In *Much Ado About Nothing*, a follower of Don John, the bastard brother of Don Pedro.

Constable of France   In *Henry V*, one of the chief French lords and military leaders. He is killed at Agincourt.

Constance   In *King John*, the mother of Arthur, Duke of Britain (Brittany). Her part is expanded from the sources, and in II.i she strikingly confronts the Queen

Mother, Elinor, on behalf of Arthur, whom she regards as the true heir to the kingdom.

Cooke, Alexander (*fl.* 1603–13) English actor. He is listed in the first folio edition of Shakespeare's works (1623) and was a member of the ►Lord Chamberlain's Men. He presumably appeared in their plays until 1613. It is known that he played the principal tragic role in ►Jonson's *Sejanus*.

Corambis The name of Polonius in the first quarto *Hamlet* (1603).

Cordelia In *King Lear*, the youngest daughter of Lear. She offends him by the seeming coolness of her protestations of love for him, and he disinherits her. When he is ill-treated and turned out by his elder daughters, to whom he has given everything, and driven mad, she comes with an army to oust them. She is taken captive, however, and is killed in prison. Lear, in a last outburst, kills the slave who hanged her and dies holding her body.

Corin In *As You Like It*, a shepherd.

Coriolanus In *Coriolanus*, the name given to Caius Marcius when he captures the city of Corioles. He is a Roman soldier aristocrat, contemptuous of the common people; his insistence on his personal integrity and his inability to make compromises bring about his downfall.

Coriolanus [Full title, *The Tragedy of Coriolanus*] Tragedy by Shakespeare, written 1607–08 and first printed in the first folio of 1623. The principal source for the play was Plutarch's *Life of Caius Marcius Coriolanus*, which Shakespeare read in North's translation of Plutarch's *Lives* (1579), probably supplemented by Livy's history *Ab Urbe Condita*, translated by Philemon Holland in 1600, and L. Annaeus Florus's *Epitome* of Livy. As usual when using North's Plutarch, Shakespeare modified some parts extensively but elsewhere followed North's wording very closely. Events are telescoped and rearranged, but the scene of Coriolanus's attack on the tribunes and the distribution of free corn (III.i), his speech introducing himself to Aufidius (IV.i), and Volumnia's appeal to her son (V.iii) are adapted directly from North's prose with very few changes. Shakespeare's purpose was not only to re-create the characters of Coriolanus and his associates, but also to interpret the political situation in Rome in terms appropriate to England of 1607–08, when there had recently been uprisings by the poor against farmers and landlords on account of the scarcity of food and high prices. In the play he minimizes the grievances of the plebeians and emphasizes from the start the enmity between them and Coriolanus, which in Plutarch does not begin to be important until a third of the way through the narrative. Shakespeare also makes Coriolanus, after his banishment, long to destroy Rome completely, whereas in Plutarch he wants only to harm the common people. Menenius and Volumnia are considerably developed from Plutarch. Volumnia's influence on her son is evident from the citizen's talk in the first scene and her first appearance before her embassy of peace. Her admiration for bloodshed and military glory is Shakespeare's invention. Several sources for Menenius's fable of the belly and the members (I.i.) have been suggested; in particular, Shakespeare seems to have used the versions in William Camden's *Remaines of a greater worke concerning Britaine* (1605), and a pamphlet by William Averell called *A Meruailous Combat of Contrarieties* (1588). In 1705 John Dennis produced a play founded on *Coriolanus*, which he called *The Invader of His Country, or the Fatal Resentment*, and two decades earlier Nahum ►Tate had adapted the Shakespeare play for political purposes with the additional title, *The Ingratitude of a Commonwealth* (1682).

Dramatis Personae

Caius Marcius, *afterwards Caius Marcius Coriolanus*	Conspirators with Aufidius
	A Citizen of Antium
Titus Lartius	Two Volscian Guards
Cominius	Volumnia, *mother of Coriolanus*
Menenius Agrippa	Virgilia, *wife of Coriolanus*
Sicinius Velutus	Valeria, *friend to Virgilia*
Junius Brutus	Gentlewoman, *attending on Virgilia*
Young Marcius	Roman and Volscian Senators,
A Roman Herald	Patricians, Aediles, Lictors, Soldiers,
Tullus Aufidius	Citizens, Messengers, Servants to
Lieutenant to Aufidius	Aufidius, and other Attendants

The Story. Caius Marcius, having captured the Volscian city, Corioles, returns to Rome and is given the surname Coriolanus in honour of his great accomplishments. The Senate offers him the consulship, but he must first, according to custom, appear before the people of Rome, show them his wounds, and humbly ask for their support. Despite his contempt for the people, he does this, and the people agree to vote for him. However, two tribunes, Sicinius and Brutus, convince the mob that Coriolanus would rule as a tyrant, and the people of Rome reverse their decision. Coriolanus's outspoken rage at their behaviour infuriates the crowd and they attack him. Once more, at the persuasion of his friend Menenius, and particularly of his mother, Volumnia, he approaches the people, prepared to conceal his contempt for them. But because of the accusations of the tribunes, he again loses his temper and this time is banished from Rome. Bent on revenge, he offers his services as leader of the Volscian army to his old enemy, Tullus Aufidius. Under the leadership of Coriolanus the Volscians successfully advance on Rome. His old friends, Menenius and Cominius, meet him outside the gates and plead with him to spare the city. He is deaf to all entreaties until his wife Virgilia, his young son, and his mother plead with him. He returns to the Volscians and tells them that he will not capture Rome, but has arranged a treaty favourable to the Volscians. Aufidius, already jealous of Coriolanus's military talent and popularity, calls him a traitor, and with the angry support of the commoners of Corioles, Aufidius's followers stab him.

Cornelius   In *Cymbeline*, a physician. He recognizes the Queen's evil designs and gives her, not the poison she intends to use, but a sleep-inducing drug and thus saves Imogen's life.

Cornelius   In *Hamlet*, a courtier. He and Voltemand are sent on an embassy to Norway by Claudius.

Cornwall, Duke of   In *King Lear*, the husband of Regan. He puts out Glouces-ter's eyes and is then killed by one of his servants.

Costard   In *Love's Labour's Lost*, a clownish peasant who aspires to be a learned wit. He is the speaker of Shakespeare's longest word "honorificabilitudinitatibus" (V.i). He acts as messenger from Berowne to Rosaline and from Armado to Jaquenetta, confusing the two letters.

Court, Alexander   In *Henry V*, a soldier in the King's army.

Cowley, Richard   (d. 1619) English actor, listed as a principal actor in the first folio (1623) of Shakespeare's plays. He is believed to have been an original member of the ➤Lord Chamberlain's Men.

Crab   In *The Two Gentlemen of Verona*, the dog of Launce who appears on stage.

Cranmer   In *Henry VIII*, the historical Thomas Cranmer, Archbishop of Canterbury. He obtains the divorce of Henry from Katherine and remains a favourite of the King, although nobles try to convict him of heresy. The King names him godfather of Princess Elizabeth, and at her christening Cranmer predicts the glory she will bring England as Queen.

Cressida   [Also, Cressid]   Daughter of the Trojan priest Calchas, whose supposed infidelities have made her name a byword for female faithlessness. Ulysses refers to her as a "daughter of the game" (IV.v) but the play also presents her as a victim of the circumstances of war.

Cromwell   In *Henry VIII*, the historical Thomas Cromwell. He appears initially as one of Wolsey's servants and is the audience for Wolsey's speech bidding farewell to his greatness. As Secretary of the Council he defends Cranmer against Gardiner's attack. The historical Cromwell (*c.* 1485–1540) rose to become Henry VIII's chief adviser and the principal architect of the English Reformation. He was executed.

Crosse, Samuel   (d. *c.* 1605) English actor. He is listed as a principal actor in the first folio (1623) of Shakespeare's plays and was probably a member of the ➤King's Men (1604).

Cumberland, Prince of   A title formerly bestowed on the successor to the crown of Scotland when succession was declared in the king's lifetime (the crown was originally not hereditary). In *Macbeth* the title is given to Malcolm by his father Duncan.

Cupid In *Timon of Athens*, a character in the masque presented to Timon in his home. In Roman mythology, the son of Venus and god of love.

Curan In *King Lear*, Gloucester's retainer.

Curio In *Twelfth Night*, a gentleman in attendance on Orsino, Duke of Illyria.

Curtain, the A London playhouse established (*c.* 1576) in Shoreditch, off Holywell Lane. It is thought that Shakespeare acted here in his own plays as a member of the ►Lord Chamberlain's Men. It remained open as late as 1627, but was not used on a regular basis after 1600. It was associated, under James ►Burbage's management, with the ►Theatre, which stood nearby. Henry Laneman had an agreement to pool profits from the two theatres with Burbage. It took its name not from any theatrical apparatus but because the land upon which it was built was called Curtain Close.

Curtis In *The Taming of the Shrew*, a servant in Petruchio's household.

Cymbeline In *Cymbeline*, the King of Britain, dominated by his crafty Queen. After her death he is, according to the prophecy, a "lofty cedar." At the end of the play he is reunited with his two lost sons and his daughter Imogen.

Cymbeline A romance by Shakespeare, produced probably *c.* 1610 and referred to by the astrologer Simon ►Forman who saw a performance shortly before his death in 1611. No main source is known for the whole plot of Cymbeline, but each of the play's three main strands has a different origin. The story of Imogen, her love for the orphan Posthumus Leonatus and his banishment from court, her boorish stepbrother Cloten, the exiled Belarius, a former courtier living in a cave, and the providential intervention of the god Jupiter, all come from an anonymous play called *The Rare Triumphs of Love and Fortune*, published in 1589. The vision scene in *Cymbeline* particularly resembles the intervention of the gods in this play. Shakespeare took the name of the heroine, Princess Fidelia, for the name Imogen assumes in male disguise, Fidele, and he used the name of her lover, Hermione, for a female character in *The Winter's Tale*. The play provided Shakespeare with his opening, his pastoral scenes, and his last act. The setting, the early legendary period of British history, seems to derive principally from the additions to *A Mirrour for Magistrates* made by Thomas Blennerhasset and John Higgins, in 1578 and 1587 and to ►Holinshed's *Chronicles* (second edition, 1587), and from "The chronicle of Briton Kings" in ►Spenser's *The Faerie Queene* (1590), Book II Canto X, although other chronicles and plays available to Shakespeare contained accounts of this period. But *A Mirrour for Magistrates*, Holinshed, and Spenser presented conflicting stories of Cymbeline's reign, and Shakespeare's decision to make Cymbeline rather than one of his sons refuse to pay the Roman tribute seems to have been motivated by dramatic necessity rather than adherence to historical fact. The third element of the plot, the story of Iachimo's wager with Posthumus and his misrepresentation of Imogen's chastity comes from two sources, a story in Boccaccio's *Decameron* (Day 2 Tale 9), which Shakespeare must have read either in the original or in a French translation, or else from an English version of the story called *Frederyke of Jennen* (originally published in 1518 but reprinted in 1560). In both tales the heroine's husband extols her virtue and is challenged by a companion who bets that he can seduce her. The challenger meets the lady and realizes that he cannot win his bet but contrives instead to conceal himself in a chest in a bedroom so that he can observe her asleep. He gathers enough information to convince the husband that he has slept with her; the husband is enraged and tries to kill her, but she escapes and lives in male disguise. Finally, the slanderer is exposed and put to death, and the couple is reunited. The combination of elements from Roman history, Italian Renaissance fabliau, and Elizabethan romantic drama produces a mixed play, an experimental fantasy. The play resembles ►Beaumont and ►Fletcher's *Philaster*, but it is not known which was first. It was first published in the folio of 1623. It was adapted as *The Injured Princess or the Fatal Wager* by Thomas D'Urfey in 1682. Shaw wrote a new fifth act in 1937, and the play as thus amended was produced in that same year.

Dramatis Personae

Cymbeline, King of Britain
Cloten, *son to the Queen*
Posthumus Leonatus, *husband to Imogen*
Belarius, *a banished Lord, disguised under the name of Morgan*
Guiderius
Arviragus
Philario
Iachimo
Caius Lucius
Pisanio
Cornelius
A French Gentleman, friend to Philario
A Roman Captain

Two British Captains
Two Lords of Cymbeline's court
Two Gentlemen of the same
Two Jailers
Queen, *wife to Cymbeline*
Imogen, *daughter to Cymbeline by a former Queen*
Lords, Ladies, Roman Senators, Tribunes, a Soothsayer, a Dutch Gentleman, a Spanish Gentleman, Musicians, Officers, Captains, Soldiers, Messengers, and other Attendants
Apparitions

The Story. Imogen, the daughter of Cymbeline, King of Britain, has secretly married Posthumus Leonatus, a gentleman at court who is banished when Imogen's stepmother, the Queen (angry that Imogen did not marry her son Cloten), tells the King about the marriage. In Rome, Posthumus brags of the virtue of his wife and makes a wager with Iachimo, a crafty Roman, that Iachimo cannot seduce her. By the terms of the wager, if Iachimo wins Posthumus will give him a diamond ring, which he has as a gift from Imogen. In Britain, Iachimo is scorned by Imogen, but by hiding in a chest in Imogen's room one night he is enabled to describe a fictitious seduction with such a background of detail, backed up by a bracelet that he has stolen, as to convince Posthumus that Imogen has been unfaithful: Posthumus thereupon writes to his servant Pisanio instructing him to kill Imogen. Instead, Pisanio disguises Imogen as a page and suggests she flee the court and join the invading Roman forces under Lucius. However, she loses her way and instead of joining the Romans, joins Belarius, a banished nobleman who twenty years before had kidnapped Cymbeline's two sons, Guiderius and Arviragus, and is living with them in Wales. The Queen's son, Cloten, dressed in the clothes of Posthumus and in pursuit of Imogen, is killed by Guiderius. The two sons then come upon Imogen, apparently dead, and lay her beside the beheaded Cloten, whom Imogen mistakes for her husband when she revives. Finally, Lucius finds her and accepts her in his entourage as a page, but the Romans, with Iachimo, are defeated and taken prisoners as a result of the heroic fighting of Belarius, Cymbeline's two sons, and Posthumus (who has meanwhile returned to Britain). Imogen (still in the guise of a page) is granted a favour by the King and demands to know how Iachimo obtained the diamond ring. When he explains, and her identity is revealed, she is happily reunited with Posthumus. The King also discovers his sons and makes peace with the Romans, reinstating the tribute money he had previously refused to pay.

D

Daniel, Samuel (1562–1619) English poet and dramatist, some of whose works may have been used as sources by Shakespeare, for example *The Civil Warres between the Two Houses of Lancaster and York* (1595), a verse history in four books, expanded in 1609 to eight books. He is said to have been Poet Laureate for a short period in 1599, but to have resigned the post in Ben ➤Jonson's favour. He was appointed (1603) Master of the Revels, and between 1604 and 1615 (when he seems to have retired to his Wiltshire farm) he wrote court masques.

Dardanius In *Julius Caesar*, one of the servants of Brutus. He refuses his master's request to kill him.

Dark Lady The subject of most of Shakespeare's later Sonnets (127 *et seq.*), a woman variously thought to be an abstract antithesis of the conventions of courtly Elizabethan sonnets, a composite image of sensuality and infidelity, or an actual person with whom Shakespeare was involved. The speculation concerning this third possibility has produced a number of suggested identities, including both women of the court and of London. At various times scholars have proposed Mary Fitton (a maid of honour to Queen Elizabeth and mistress of William ➤Herbert, Earl of Pembroke), Penelope Devereux, Lady Rich, the ➤Avisa of *Willobie his Avisa*, Luce Morgan (a brothel keeper), and Emilia Bassano, member of a family of court musicians. The case against each of these candidates is as strong as, if not stronger than, the case in favour.

Dauphin, Charles the ➤Charles, the Dauphin.

Dauphin, Lewis the ➤Lewis, the Dauphin.

Davenant, Sir William (1606–68) English playwright, poet, and theatre manager who began his theatrical career in the reign of Charles I. He adapted several of Shakespeare's plays for the Restoration theatre, in particular *Macbeth* (1663) and *The Tempest* (1667). He is said (by John Aubrey, in *Brief Lives*) to have claimed to have been Shakespeare's illegitimate son.

Davy In *2 Henry IV*, a servant of Shallow. He asks his master to judge his friend leniently because "an honest man is able to speak for himself when a knave is not" (V.i).

Deiphobus In *Troilus and Cressida*, a son of King Priam of Troy.

Dekker, Thomas [Also, Decker] (*c.* 1572–1632) English dramatist, at various times a collaborator of ➤Middleton, Webster, Massinger, ➤Rowley, and others. He is a possible collaborator with Shakespeare and others on ➤*Sir Thomas More*. He had a hand in over forty plays, eight of which are probably his solo work. He was attacked by ➤Jonson in *Poetaster* (1601) as ignorant and pretentious, and responded in *Satiromastix* (1602). With Jonson he produced a pageant to celebrate James I's entry into London after his accession (1604). From 1613 to 1619 he seems to have been imprisoned in the King's Bench prison because of debt. He wrote many pamphlets, some in the cony-catching tradition of ➤Greene, others centring on the plague, or satirizing the vices and follies of the times. In the plays written with others he excelled in shop scenes and those laid in inns, taverns, and suburban pleasure-houses.

Demetrius In *Antony and Cleopatra*, a friend of Antony.

Demetrius In *A Midsummer Night's Dream*, a Grecian gentleman in love with Hermia. He is very little distinguished from his friend and rival Lysander.

Demetrius In *Titus Andronicus*, a son of Tamora, Queen of the Goths, and brother of Chiron.

Dench, Dame Judi (1934–) British actress who has worked for all the major theatre companies of her time and performed most of Shakespeare's leading female roles. Her first was Ophelia (Old Vic, 1957). She gave a record one hundred performances as Cleopatra at the ➤National Theatre (1987). She has also directed several Shakespeare plays, including *Much Ado About Nothing* (1988) and *Romeo and Juliet* (1993).

Dennis In *As You Like It*, a servant to Oliver.

Denny, Sir Anthony In *Henry VIII*, a gentleman of the court who appears once (V.i) to present Cranmer to the King.

Derby, Earl of ➤Stanley, Lord.

Derby's Men ➤Lord Chamberlain's Men.

Dercetas [Also, Dercetus] In *Antony and Cleopatra*, a friend of Antony who, bearing the sword on which Antony died, informs Octavius of his death.

Desdemona In *Othello*, the wife of Othello the Moor, and the daughter of Brabantio, a Venetian senator. She marries Othello in secret, against her father's wishes. Othello smothers her in an outburst of rage produced by a mistaken belief in her unfaithfulness, a belief instilled in him by Iago. As she lies dying, she still asserts Othello's innocence of the murder.

Devereux, Robert ➤Essex, (2nd) Earl of.

Diana   In *All's Well That Ends Well*, the daughter of the Florentine widow with whom Helena lodges. She makes possible the reconciliation of Bertram to Helena by her willingness to permit Helena to take her (Diana's) place in an assignation with Bertram.

Diana   The Roman goddess of hunting, associated with women and childbirth. In *Pericles*, she appears in a dream to Pericles and sends him to the Temple of Diana to find his wife, Thaisa.

Dick the Butcher   In *2 Henry VI*, a butcher of Ashford, follower of Jack Cade.

Diomedes   In *Antony and Cleopatra*, an attendant of Cleopatra.

Diomedes   In *Troilus and Cressida*, a Greek commander who is sent to Troy to conduct Cressida to the Greek camp. She accepts his advances and gives him the love token that Troilus had given her.

Dion   In *The Winter's Tale*, a Sicilian lord who is sent with Cleomenes to the oracle at Delphi.

Dionyza   In *Pericles*, the wife of Cleon. She attempts the murder of Mariana, and with her husband is finally punished by being burned to death.

Dogberry   In *Much Ado About Nothing*, a foolish but self-admiring constable. Dogberry catches Borachio and Conrade after Borachio has staged a pretended assignation with Hero, and forces the truth from him. But because of Dogberry's inability to speak plainly Leonato fails to understand what has happened, and the result is near tragedy for Hero.

Dolabella   In *Antony and Cleopatra*, a friend of Octavius who succumbs to Cleopatra's charms and informs her that she is to be taken to Rome in triumph.

Don Adriano de Armado   ➤Armado, Don Adriano de.

Donalbain   In *Macbeth*, a son of Duncan, King of Scotland. He goes to Ireland after Duncan's murder and does not appear after II.iii.

Dorcas   In *The Winter's Tale*, a shepherdess.

Doricles   In *The Winter's Tale*, the name assumed by Florizel when in disguise.

Dorset, Marquess of   In *Richard III*, the historical Thomas Grey, eldest son of Lady Grey (Elizabeth Woodville), who later became Edward's Queen. When Dorset's brother, Lord Grey, and his uncle, Rivers, are executed by Richard, he joins Richmond in Brittany.

Double Falsehood   ➤*Cardenio, the History of.*

Douglas, Archibald, (4th) **Earl of**   In *1 Henry IV*, the historical Archibald Douglas, 4th Earl of Douglas, an ally of Hotspur at Shrewsbury; he almost kills King Henry and is later captured when the rebels flee.

Drayton, Michael   (1563–1631) English poet. He was buried in Westminster Abbey and his epitaph is said to be by Ben ➤Jonson. He wrote historical and topographical poems, including *Morti meriados* (1596, later emended as *The Barons' Wars*, 1603), and *Polyolbion* (1612, 1622). From 1597 to 1602 he wrote for the theatre. He knew Shakespeare, and, along with Jonson, was present at the "merry meeting" that, according to the notebooks of John Ward, vicar of Stratford-upon-Avon (1662–81), brought on a fever of which Shakespeare died.

Dromio of Ephesus and **Dromio of Syracuse**   In *The Comedy of Errors*, twin brothers, servants respectively of the twins Antipholus of Ephesus and Antipholus of Syracuse. The Dromio of Ephesus is a stupid servant, the Dromio of Syracuse a witty one. In Plautus's *Menaechmi*, from which this play is derived, there is only one servant.

Dryden, John   (1631–1700) English poet, playwright and critic, who adapted a number of Shakespeare's plays for the Restoration stage, including *The Tempest* (1667, with ➤Davenant), *All for Love* (a version of *Antony and Cleopatra*, 1677), and *Troilus and Cressida* (1679). He was also one of the earliest critics of Shakespeare. He became Poet Laureate in 1668.

Duke Senior   In *As You Like It*, the father of Rosalind. As his name suggests, he was "the elder duke," and he has no more specific name in the play. He is driven into exile by his brother, Frederick, but is eventually restored when Frederick repents.

Dull   In *Love's Labour's Lost*, a dim-witted constable who (at Armado's suit) arrests Costard for breaking the King's decree and wooing Jaquenetta.

Dumain   In *Love's Labour's Lost*, one of the three French lords attending the King of Navarre at his rural academy. He falls in love with Katherine. His song to her "On a day—alack the day" (IV.iii) appears also in *The Passionate Pilgrim*.

Duncan   In *Macbeth*, King of Scotland. The historical Duncan succeeded to the throne *c.* 1034 on the death of his grandfather Malcolm II, and was assassinated near Elgin in 1039 or 1040. In *Macbeth*, he is a gracious old man, murdered by Macbeth, who looks in horror at the "silver skin laced with golden blood" of the corpse and likens the result of his monstrous deed to "a breach in nature" (II.iii).

Dunsinane   ➤Birnam Wood.

E

Earl of Nottingham's Company ➤Lord Admiral's Men.

Earl of Oxford ➤authorship theories.

Earl of Pembroke's Men [Also, Pembroke's Men] An acting company whose patron was Henry Herbert, 2nd Earl of Pembroke. It flourished in the early 1590s. Shakespeare, along with Richard ➤Burbage, was a member of this company before he joined the ➤Lord Chamberlain's Men (1594). The company seems to have disbanded *c.* 1593, but reformed 1595–96 for a brief period. It performed the seditious play *The Isle of Dogs* (1597), by ➤Jonson and others. ➤Herbert, William.

Ecclestone, William English actor. He joined the ➤King's Men in 1614, probably as a shareholder, and is listed in the first folio (1623) of Shakespeare's plays as a principal actor.

Edgar In *King Lear*, the legitimate son of the Earl of Gloucester. He is banished by Gloucester as the result of a plot contrived by the bastard son, Edmund, and wanders, disguised as a mad beggar, on the heath, where he meets Lear and eventually becomes a guide to the blinded Gloucester. In the "cliff" scene (IV.vi), Edgar leads the blind Gloucester to what Gloucester believes to be the edge of the cliff and allows the blind man to "fall" so that he may be "saved" from the "fiend" who has led him there, and thus brings Gloucester to an acceptance of his affliction. Edgar is finally left with Albany to restore the kingdom.

Edmund In *King Lear*, the bastard son of the Earl of Gloucester. He contrives to have his legitimate brother Edgar banished, so that he can inherit his father's land, and allies himself with Goneril, Regan, and Cornwall against Lear. He intrigues with both Goneril and Regan separately and is finally killed in a duel by Edgar.

Edmund Ironside An anonymous Tudor manuscript history play, probably written in the 1590s, claimed by some to be an early work of Shakespeare, though the attribution is not widely accepted. Set in the eleventh century, it concerns the conflict between the English Edmund, King of the Saxons, and Canute, Prince of Denmark.

Edmund of Langley, Duke of York ➤York, (1st) Duke of.

Edmund, Earl of Rutland ➤Rutland, Edmund, Earl of.

Edward III A chronicle history play, published anonymously in 1596, and attributed to Shakespeare by some critics from the eighteenth century onwards. It was written between 1590 and 1594, and concerns events in the relations between England and France in the reign of Edward III, father of the Black Prince. Many critics support the view that Shakespeare was the author of four scenes including those between Edward III and the Countess of Salisbury, and a case has recently been made for his sole authorship. Following exhaustive computer analysis of the text in the USA, the editors of the Arden Shakespeare, the standard scholarly edition of the plays, announced in 1998 that they would be adding *Edward III* to the series early in the new century.

Edward IV ➤Edward, Earl of March.

Edward V ➤Edward, Prince of Wales.

Edward, Earl of March In *2 Henry VI*, the eldest son of Richard Plantagenet, Duke of York. In *3 Henry VI*, he shows his father his sword, bloody from the wounds of the Duke of Buckingham (I.i). On the death of his father he becomes Duke of York. He defeats the Lancastrians, is proclaimed king, as Edward IV, and marries Lady Grey. In *Richard III*, ill, he learns that the order for Clarence's death was executed despite his reversal of it (II.i). In the following scene word comes of his death.

Edward, Prince of Wales In *3 Henry VI*, the only son of Henry VI. He is disinherited when the Yorkists persuade the King to leave the crown to the heir of York, and is captured at Tewkesbury and killed.

Edward, Prince of Wales In *3 Henry VI*, the son of Edward IV. In *Richard III*, he is due to become king, as Edward V, on the death of his father, but he and his brother are put in the Tower and murdered by Richard, Duke of Gloucester.

Egeus In *A Midsummer Night's Dream*, the father of Hermia whose opposition to her marriage with Lysander causes the lovers to run away to the woods.

Eglamour In *Two Gentlemen of Verona*, a courtly knight who helps Silvia escape from Milan and from Thurio, whom her father wishes her to marry. Eglamour deserts her when she is captured by a band of outlaws.

Elbow In *Measure for Measure*, a foolish constable.

Eleanor, Duchess of Gloucester ➤Gloucester, Eleanor, Duchess of.

Elector Palatine's Company ➤Lord Admiral's Men.

Elinor, Queen [Also, Eleanor] In *King John*, the mother of John, a vigorous and outspoken woman. She follows him to France and he learns she has died there (IV.ii). She is the historical Eleanor of Aquitaine, first married to Louis VII of France and then to Henry II of England.

Elizabeth I (1533–1603) Queen of England (1558–1603), the daughter of Henry VIII and Anne Boleyn, to marry whom Henry divorced Catherine of Aragon. Elizabeth was regarded as illegitimate by Catherine's adherents and by Pope Clement VII. Thus her right to the throne was in question throughout the reign. Elizabeth was educated by teachers who followed the new Humanism; she was expert in languages, modern as well as Greek and Latin, and was known as an eloquent speaker. Raised a Protestant, she followed a policy of tolerance after her accession. In foreign affairs, she pursued a policy of aggressive resistance to the spread of the power of Spain. Unofficial war was waged constantly by privateers, bringing great fortunes to the royal treasury. During nearly thirty years of her reign England was at peace, until Philip II of Spain resolved to put a stop to English privateer raids on his shipping and to English support of the Dutch rebels. He dispatched the Invincible Armada; but the fleet of the Armada was caught off Calais and destroyed (1588). When Mary, Queen of Scots, fled the wrath of the Scots and sought refuge in England, Elizabeth kept her in custody for nearly twenty years and then reluctantly approved her execution because of the many plots to rescue Mary and to revive her claims to the thrones of both England and Scotland. Under Elizabeth, English coinage was standardized on a silver basis; a Statute of Artificers, a labour law, was enacted in 1563; and the Poor Laws of 1597 made parishes responsible for their own poor and set heavy penalties for vagabondage. The Acts of uniformity and of supremacy establishing the Church of England were passed by Parliament; the Archbishop of Canterbury drew up the Thirty-Nine Articles of convocation and edited a new edition of the Bible known as the "Bishop's Bible." Elizabeth's spinsterhood and the question of the succession were continuing problems. Several diplomatic marriages were suggested, in particular with the Duke of Anjou and subsequently the Duke of Alençon, but none came close to materializing and the Queen made much political capital out of her status as a royal virgin. When she died, in 1603, she was the only English ruler of adult years since the Norman Conquest in 1066 who had not married. She recognized clearly the problem that would face the kingdom at her death and part of her reluctance to order the execution of Mary, Queen of Scots, is traceable to the fact that Mary's son, James VI of Scotland, was the logical successor to the English throne. On Elizabeth's death, he became James I of England.

The four and a half decades of Elizabeth's reign mark a brilliant period in English history. The long period of official peace with other nations built up about Elizabeth a vibrant and active court whose energies were turned to other matters than war. England became in Elizabeth's time a world power, not yet as strong as Spain but soon to surpass her; the English navy grew to be second to none; commerce expanded and colonies were established where such explorers as Frobisher and Drake had gone. The print trade flourished in this period, which is well-known for such literary figures as the poets Spenser and Sidney, the playwrights ►Kyd, ►Marlowe, ►Greene, ►Lyly, and Shakespeare, and a range of other writers such as ►Raleigh and ►Bacon. Elizabeth was a patron of literature and of the theatre, and theatrical companies performed at court at various times throughout her reign. In 1583 she became patron of her own company, ➤Queen Elizabeth's Men. Tradition has it that Shakespeare's plays were much appreciated by Elizabeth, and that he wrote *The Merry Wives of Windsor* at her request, because she had been especially pleased by the character Falstaff, in *1* and *2 Henry IV*, and wished for a play showing him in love. There are few references to Elizabeth in Shakespeare's plays and sonnets, and most of these follow the conventions of flattery to the reigning monarch. The infant Elizabeth appears in *Henry VIII*, where her christening forms a climax, as a sign that a better time is in the offing for the English nation:

> This royal infant ...
> Though in her cradle, yet now promises
> Upon this land a thousand thousand blessings,
> Which time shall bring to ripeness.
>
> (V.v)

Elizabeth, Queen   ➤Grey, Lady.

Ely, Bishop of   In *Henry V*, a counsellor who supports the Archbishop of Canterbury in arguing for the legality of the King's proposed war with France.

Ely, Bishop of   ➤Morton, John.

Emilia   In *Othello*, the wife of Iago. She unwittingly assists her husband's plotting by giving him Desdemona's handkerchief. He murders her at the end of the play when she reveals this fact.

Emilia   In *The Winter's Tale*, a lady attendant on Hermione.

English Shakespeare Company   British theatrical company founded in 1986 by Michael ➤Bogdanov and Michael ➤Pennington to mount touring productions of Shakespeare. The opening production was of *The Wars of the Roses* (1987–88), a double cycle of eight history plays, which mixed the medieval and the modern in settings and costumes. Subsequent productions have included *Coriolanus* and *The Merchant of Venice* (1990), *Twelfth Night* (1991), *Macbeth* and *The Tempest* (1992), and *Romeo and Juliet* (1993).

Enobarbus   In *Antony and Cleopatra*, a friend of Antony. He gives the famous description of Cleopatra in her barge coming down the Cydnus (II.ii). Enobarbus deserts Antony, but dies of a heart broken by remorse at his betrayal of his friend when Antony sends his treasure after him.

Ephesus, Duke of   ➤Solinus.

Eros   In *Antony and Cleopatra*, the freed slave of Antony. He is devoted to Antony, and kills himself with his own sword when ordered by Antony to slay him.

Erpingham, Sir Thomas   In *Henry V*, one of Henry's officers.

Escalus In *Measure for Measure*, an old lord; he is deputy to Angelo, whom he urges to deal more leniently with offenders.

Escalus In *Romeo and Juliet*, the Prince of Verona. The real Romeo and Juliet supposedly lived during the reign (1301–04) of Bartolomeo della Scala. "Escalus" is a corruption of della Scala.

Escanes In *Pericles*, a lord of Tyre who appears with Helicanus, another lord.

Essex, Earl of In *King John*, a lord in attendance on the King.

Essex, (2nd) **Earl of** [Title of Robert Devereux] Son of Walter Devereux, 1st Earl of Essex of the Devereux line; a favourite of Queen Elizabeth. His secret marriage (1590) to the widow of Sir Philip ➤Sidney, Frances Walsingham, daughter of Elizabeth's secretary of state angered the Queen, but they were reconciled, and he became a member of the Privy Council in 1593. He led various military campaigns abroad, often without great success. In 1599 he was appointed Lord Lieutenant of Ireland, in which post he aroused the Queen's anger by the failure of his operations against the Irish rebels, and by his inability to follow orders from the Queen. He made a truce with Hugh O'Neill, the Earl of Tyrone, leader of the Ulster rebels, and leaving his post without authorization, returned (September 1599) to England to lay his defence before the Queen in person. He failed to regain his standing at court, was tried and stripped of his offices. He then formed a conspiracy with Charles Blount, Baron Mountjoy, and Henry Wriothesley, 3rd Earl of ➤Southampton, to compel Elizabeth by force of arms to dismiss his enemies in the council, the Cecil faction. On 8 February 1601, he led a group of his retainers through the streets of London, trying to arouse the citizenry to join him; but this half-formed uprising was met with apathy and he returned to his palace, Essex House, where he was captured. The day before, a group of Essex's followers had persuaded members of the ➤Lord Chamberlain's Men to perform a play about the deposition of Richard II, quite probably Shakespeare's. Essex was tried for treason; Francis ➤Bacon, who had consistently attempted to mediate between Essex and Elizabeth, prosecuted the charge. Essex was found guilty and executed for treason.

Euphronius In *Antony and Cleopatra*, an ambassador for Antony to Octavius.

Evans, Dame Edith (1888–1976) British actress specializing in comedy who played in Shakespeare for over forty years. Her first Shakespearean role was Cressida in *Troilus and Cressida*, directed by William Poel for the Elizabethan Stage Society in 1912. Among other roles she played Gertrude (1914), Mistress Ford (1917), Helena (1924), Portia (1925–26), Queen Margaret (1925–26), Katherina (1925–26), Cleopatra (1925–26), Rosalind (1925–26), Viola (1932), Queen Katherine (1958), and Volumnia (1959).

Evans, Henry   English theatre manager, an early leaseholder in the ➤Blackfriars theatre. In 1608 the lease was taken over by the ➤King's Men but it is probable that Henry Evans retained a share.

Evans, Sir Hugh   In *The Merry Wives of Windsor*, a comic Welsh parson. On the evening when Falstaff is being baited, Evans leads the children's revels as Fairy Queen.

Exeter, Duke of   In *Henry V*, the historical Sir Thomas Beaufort, an uncle of the King. He arrests Cambridge, Scroop, and Grey for treason, acts as ambassador to France, and goes with Henry on the French campaign, where he reports the deaths of Suffolk and York after the battle. In *1 Henry VI*, he mourns the death of Henry V, but looks forward to defeating the French under the young King, whose special governor he is (I.i). He plays the part of a peacemaker, but foresees the Wars of the Roses.

Exeter, Duke of   In *3 Henry VI*, the historical Henry Holland, a supporter of King Henry during the Wars of the Roses.

Exton, Sir Pierce of   In *Richard II*, the nobleman who overhears Henry IV's wish for Richard's death and murders Richard in Pomfret Castle. Holinshed reports this, possibly confusing him with Sir Nicholas Exton, who violently opposed Richard in Parliament.

Eyre, Sir Richard   (1943–   ) British theatre director who worked at the (Royal) National Theatre from 1981, serving as artistic director from 1988 to 1997. He has directed numerous Shakespeare productions, including *Hamlet* (1979) at the Royal Court Theatre, *Hamlet* (1989), *Richard III* (1990), *Macbeth* (1993), and *King Lear* (1997), all at the National. He has also promoted experimental Shakespeare productions during his administration at the ➤Royal National Theatre, including *Richard II* directed by Deborah Warner with Fiona Shaw in the title role.

F

Fabian   In *Twelfth Night*, a servant of Olivia. He joins Maria's plot against Malvolio because the latter has brought him into disfavour with Olivia.

Falstaff, Sir John   A celebrated character in *1* and *2 Henry IV* and *The Merry Wives of Windsor*. He was originally called Oldcastle, after his historical counterpart, the Protestant martyr Sir John Oldcastle, but objections from Oldcastle's descendants, the influential Cobham family, obliged Shakespeare to change the name. He is a fat witty knight, a version of the traditional comic character of the braggart soldier but with elements in him of the medieval Vice and the world of Carnival. The part may have been played by the famous clown, Will ►Kemp. Morgann in his essay on the *Dramatic Character of Sir John Falstaff* (1777) argued that Falstaff was not a coward, and proponents of this view have sought to see the "wholeness" of his character, looking upon his flight from Prince Henry and Poins at Gadshill as merely carrying a joke along. He characteristically gets out of this scrape by his quick wit: "Was it for me to kill the heir apparent? But beware instinct, the lion will not touch the true prince. I was a coward upon instinct." He provides a contrast to Hotspur, whom Prince Hal parodies (*1 Henry IV*, II.iii), and pretends to have killed Hotspur at Shrewsbury, although actually he played dead until Hal defeated Hotspur. In *2 Henry IV* he insults the Lord Chief Justice, defrauds Mistress Quickly, who is nearly bankrupt with debt, captures Colevile only because Colevile gives himself up, then assumes the airs of a hero and comments satirically on Justice Shallow's administration of justice and his feeble reminiscences of younger days. He is rejected by Hal, his former drinking companion, when the latter becomes King Henry V. In *Henry V*, his death is described by Mistress Quickly, and Pistol comments that "his heart is fracted and corroborate" (II.i). He appears again, according to legend at the request of Queen Elizabeth herself, in *The Merry Wives of Windsor* in amorous, but unsuccessful, pursuit of the two wives.

Fang   In *2 Henry IV*, a sheriff's officer who with Snare tries to arrest Falstaff.

Fastolf, Sir John   In *1 Henry VI*, a cowardly knight who flees from the Battle of Rouen. The historical Fastolf was an English soldier and benefactor of Magdalen College, Oxford, and was connected with Lollardry.

Faulconbridge, Lady   In *King John*, the widow of Sir Robert Faulconbridge and mother of Robert and Philip Faulconbridge. She confesses (I.i) to Philip that his father was the late King Richard I (the Lion-Hearted).

Faulconbridge, Philip [Also, Philip the Bastard] In *King John*, the illegitimate son of Richard I (the Lion-Hearted), and the half-brother of Robert Faulconbridge. He follows John in his French wars and is recognized by Queen Elinor as her grandson. He comments upon the politics involved in making peace with France, preferring instead a good open fight (which eventually occurs).

Faulconbridge, Robert In *King John*, the legitimate younger son of Lady Faulconbridge.

Feeble, Francis In *2 Henry IV*, one of Falstaff's recruits, characterized by Falstaff as "most forcible Feeble" (III.ii).

Fenton In *The Merry Wives of Windsor*, a penurious gentleman in love with Anne Page.

Ferdinand In *The Tempest*, the son of the King of Naples, who weds Miranda in a dynastic marriage.

Ferdinand, King of Navarre In *Love's Labour's Lost*, the King of Navarre who wishes to make his court a "little Academe." He, as well as each of his lords, soon breaks his vow to avoid women for three years (he falls in love with the Princess of France shortly after she appears in the play).

Feste In *Twelfth Night*, Olivia's jester, and a type of the wise fool, with resemblances to the Fool in *King Lear*. He takes part in the baiting of Malvolio, pretending to be Sir Topas, who treats Malvolio as a lunatic. He sings the well-known songs "O mistress mine" (II.ii), "Come away, come away, death" (II.iv), and "When that I was a little tiny boy" (V.i).

Fidele In *Cymbeline*, the name assumed by Imogen, when disguised as a boy.

Field, Nathaniel [Also, Nathan] (1587–1619) English actor, after 1610 a rival in fame to Richard ►Burbage, and occasional playwright. He is chiefly remembered as the author of *A Woman is a Weathercock* (acted *c.* 1609 and printed 1612) and *Amends for Ladies* (acted *c.* 1615 and printed in 1618). Initially a boy actor, he joined the ►King's Men in 1615, appearing in *The Loyal Subject* (by ►Fletcher) and *Bussy D'Ambois* (by ►Chapman), as well as various other popular plays.

Finsbury An open field area to the north of the City of London and adjacent to Shoreditch (the borough in which the Theatre and the Curtain were located). A shooting field in the early sixteenth century, Finsbury became a resort of the common people and was avoided by people of fashion. It was referred to by both Jonson and Shakespeare (*1 Henry IV*, III.i) in their writings.

Fitzwater, Lord In *Richard II*, a nobleman who accuses Aumerle of causing the Duke of Gloucester's death and challenges him to a duel.

Flaminius In *Timon of Athens*, a servant to Timon.

Flavius In *Julius Caesar*, a tribune of the people. With Marullus, his fellow tribune, he is opposed to the growth of Caesar's power.

Flavius In *Timon of Athens*, Timon's steward. Timon ignores his warning of the dangers of reckless spending, and after Timon's ruin, he visits him in his cave. Here Timon first curses him, then calls him "thou singly honest man" (IV.iii) and offers him gold if he will promise to "show charity to none" (IV.iii).

Fleance In *Macbeth*, the son of Banquo. He escapes when his father is murdered. Like his father, he has no basis in history (although he has been mentioned in Scottish tradition as an ancestor of the Stuart kings).

Fletcher, John (1579–1625) English playwright, who collaborated with ►Beaumont, Massinger, and Shakespeare. His earliest work in the theatre was on collaborative plays with Beaumont, including *Love's Cure* (c. 1605), and *Cupid's Revenge* (1607–08). His first solo play, *The Faithful Shepherdess* (1608–09) was not theatrically successful, and the best-known of his work, at least until recently, has been his collaborations with Beaumont, *Philaster* (1609) and *The Maid's Tragedy* (1610–11). It is now generally accepted that he collaborated with Shakespeare on *The* ►*Two Noble Kinsmen*, *Henry VIII*, and probably the lost play ►*Cardenio*. After Shakespeare's retirement from the stage, he became the chief dramatist for the ►King's Men, and he continued to write plays, alone or with collaborators, especially Massinger, until his death, probably of plague.

Fletcher, Lawrence (d. 1608) English actor, a member of the ►King's Men (1603), perhaps as a Groom of the Chamber.

Florence, Duke of In *All's Well That Ends Well*, a minor character. He accepts Bertram into his army.

Florio, John (1553–1625) English translator and promoter of the Italian language, London-born though of Italian descent. His phrase-book, *Florio his First Fruits* (1578), may have supplied Shakespeare with the title for *Love's Labour's Lost*: "We need not speak so much of love, all books are full of love, with so many authors, that it were labour lost to speak of love". His translation of Montaigne's *Essais* (1603) influenced Shakespeare (especially in *King Lear*), as well as other playwrights. He may have been personally known to Shakespeare. Other works include *A World of Words* (1598), an Italian-English dictionary, enlarged in 1611.

Florizel In *The Winter's Tale*, the Prince of Bohemia, in love with Perdita. He is temporarily estranged from his father Polixenes but is reunited with him when they meet at Leontes's court in Sicilia.

Fluellen In *Henry V*, a pedantic but courageous Welsh captain. Shakespeare uses the incident of Fluellen and the leek (symbol of Wales) to show the tolerance which must be practised as the price of unity among the British allies.

Flute, Francis   In *A Midsummer Night's Dream*, a bellows-mender. He plays the part of Thisby (Thisbe) in the interpolated play.

Fool   In *King Lear*, a household retainer and professional jester, companion of Lear in his wanderings on the heath. He often acts as the conscience of the King, reminding him continually of his folly in giving away his kingdom, and sits as a judge with Edgar (disguised as Tom o'Bedlam) in the mock trial of Lear's daughters (III.vi). He disappears from the play altogether in the course of this scene.

Fool   In *Timon of Athens*, a servant who arrives with Apemantus and jests with the servants of Timon's creditors (II.ii).

Forbes-Robertson, Sir Johnston   (1853–1937) British actor-manager, who appeared in many Shakespearean roles, including Romeo (1895), Othello (1897), Hamlet (1897), and Shylock (1906). He starred in a silent film of *Hamlet* (1913) after he had retired from the stage.

Ford, Master   In *The Merry Wives of Windsor*, a well-to-do gentleman and jealous husband. He assumes the name of Master Brook and induces Falstaff to confide to him his passion for Mistress Ford and his success in duping Ford, her husband.

Ford, Mistress   In *The Merry Wives of Windsor*, the wife of Ford. Falstaff writes identical love notes to her and Mistress Page, the "merry wives," and they contrive to expose him to public ridicule.

Forman, Simon   (1552–1611) English doctor, astrologer, and diarist, who kept a "Book of Plays" in which he made notes of visits to the theatre, including performances at the ➤Globe of *Macbeth* (20 April 1611), *Cymbeline* (undated), *Richard II* (20 April 1611, probably not Shakespeare's play), and *The Winter's Tale* (15 May 1611).

Forrest   In *Richard III*, a murderer (mentioned in IV.iii) hired by Tyrrel to kill the Princes imprisoned in the Tower.

Fortinbras   In *Hamlet*, the Prince of Norway. He aspires to recover the lands and power lost by his father. On the way to attack Poland, he marches through Denmark, where Hamlet encounters him, Hamlet's reaction being the soliloquy "How all occasions do inform against me" (IV.iv). He becomes the next king of Denmark at the end of the play.

Fortune, the   A public playhouse built off Golding Lane, outside the northern boundary of the City of London, in 1600 by ➤Henslowe. He was owner-manager with his son-in-law, ➤Alleyn, and intended it to rival the ➤Globe. The builder's contract for the theatre has survived, and provides much detail about costs, dimensions, construction, etc. In 1621 it was burned down but another round building, this time of brick, was put up in 1623. This was dismantled in 1649.

Francis In *1 Henry IV*, a drawer in a tavern, made fun of by Poins and Prince Hal.

Francis, Friar In *Much Ado About Nothing*, a friar who suggests to Leonato that he pretend Hero has died of grief, in order to revive Claudio's lost love.

Francisca In *Measure for Measure*, a nun.

Francisco In *Hamlet*, a soldier who, at the beginning of the play, is relieved from watch by Barnardo.

Francisco In *The Tempest*, a lord shipwrecked with Alonso.

Frederick, Duke In *As You Like It*, the usurping brother of the exiled duke.

Froth In *Measure for Measure*, a tapster and "foolish Gentleman" who is arrested by Elbow (II.i).

G

Gadshill   In *1 Henry IV*, a rascally companion of Falstaff. With Falstaff and others he robs travellers and is in turn robbed by Prince Hal and Poins. He supports Falstaff's lies when Prince Hal questions him about the episode.

Gallus   In *Antony and Cleopatra*, a friend of Octavius.

Ganymede   In *As You Like It*, the name assumed by Rosalind when disguised as a boy. In the period it had homoerotic associations.

Gardiner   In *Henry VIII*, the historical Stephen Gardiner (*c.* 1490–1555). He is secretary to the King, and later becomes Bishop of Winchester and leader of the attack on Cranmer as a heretic.

Gargrave, Sir Thomas   In *1 Henry VI*, an English officer.

Garrick, David   (1717–79) British actor, theatre manager, and adapter of Shakespeare, who did much to create the cult of Shakespeare in the mid-eighteenth century. He made his debut as Richard III in ►Cibber's adaptation, and was especially celebrated as Hamlet, Benedick, Romeo, King Lear, and Macbeth. He was manager of Drury Lane theatre from 1747 to 1776, and used the theatre as a showcase for his Shakespearean productions. He organized a Shakespeare Jubilee at Stratford-upon-Avon in 1769, which helped to establish the town as a site for Shakespearean pilgrimage.

Gaunt, John of   ►John of Gaunt.

George, Duke of Clarence   ►Clarence, George, Duke of.

Gerrold   In *The Two Noble Kinsmen*, a schoolmaster.

Gertrude   In *Hamlet*, the mother of Hamlet, and Queen of Denmark. Her rapid remarriage, to her dead husband's brother, occasions Hamlet's disgust. She is unaware of the true circumstances of her husband's death. She tries to protect Hamlet from Claudius's plotting. In the last scene she dies from the poison that Claudius has prepared for Hamlet.

Ghost   In *Hamlet*, the ghost of Hamlet's father, who appears to tell how Claudius poisoned him in his sleep and later to warn Hamlet against killing his mother. Ghosts also appear in *Richard III*, *Julius Caesar*, and *Macbeth* and are found in many other Elizabethan plays, often to reveal secret crimes or to awaken the consciences of various characters. According to tradition, ghosts could, if they chose, appear only to a single individual, they must return to the grave at daybreak, and (if they were messengers of the devil) they could not abide light, holy objects, or seasons (like Christmas) that were sacred in character. In *Hamlet* the ghost is an ambivalent figure; he speaks in I.v. as if returning from Purgatory, but Protestants did not believe in this concept, and argued that ghosts were devils sent to lure human beings to evil actions.

Gielgud, Sir John (1904–   ) British actor who has played all the main Shakespearean roles in a career that began in 1921 with an appearance as the Herald in *Henry V*. His most famous roles have been Romeo (1929, 1935), Hamlet (1929, 1930, 1934, 1936, etc.), King Lear (1940, 1950, etc.), and Prospero (1940, 1957, 1974), which he also played in the film *Prospero's Books* (1991). He has played Shakespearean roles in film, and on radio and television, and has directed a number of Shakespeare productions, including *Hamlet* (1934, 1964, etc.), *Romeo and Juliet* (1935), *Macbeth* (1953), and many others.

Gilburne, Samuel English actor, listed as one of the principal actors, in the first folio (1623) of Shakespeare's plays. He was probably a member of the King's Men (1605).

Glamis, Thane of In *Macbeth*, the title that Macbeth holds at the beginning of the play. The Witches show their recognition of him by hailing him "Thane of Glamis." There is in southern Scotland an actual village of Glamis (or Glammis) and a castle associated by tradition with Macbeth.

Glansdale, Sir William In *1 Henry VI*, an English officer.

Glendower, Owen In *1 Henry IV*, a Welsh ally of the Percys. His claim to supernatural powers and his boastfulness antagonize Hotspur and the two men exchange heated words (III.i). Glendower is not present at the battle of Shrewsbury.

Globe, the The London theatre, built by Richard and Cuthbert ►Burbage in 1599, most celebrated for its connections with Shakespeare. When the ►Theatre in Shoreditch was taken down, the timbers were carried to Bankside and used in the erection of the Globe. Among the first plays to be performed there were probably *Henry V* and *Julius Caesar*, and subsequently *Hamlet, Othello, King Lear*, and *Macbeth*. The Globe was polygonal in shape and open to the sky in the middle; the galleries and probably the stage were covered by a thatched roof. This caught fire as the result of a misfiring of a small cannon during the pageantry at a performance of *Henry VIII* in 1613, when the whole theatre burnt down. It was rebuilt in 1614, at a cost of £1400, this time with a tiled roof, but was pulled down during the Puritan regime in 1644. Shakespeare was a sharer in the ►Lord Chamberlain's Men (later the King's Men) who played at this theatre, and it was here that many of his plays were first performed. Excavations in 1989 uncovered a small part of the foundations of the Globe, now largely buried under a Georgian building. This discovery of the remains of a stair-turret confirms the view that admission to the Globe was on a different basis from the other theatres. The excavations fixed the location of the theatre, and demonstrated that its stage was to the south-west. They also testified to the accuracy of Wenceslas Hollar's depiction of the second Globe in his panorama of the 1630s. ➤International Shakespeare Globe Centre.

Gloucester, Duchess of In *Richard I*, the historical Eleanor de Bohun, widow of Thomas of Woodstock, Duke of Gloucester, whose murder (by Mowbray at the command of Richard II) she recalls to Gaunt with a demand for vengeance.

Gloucester, Earl of [Also, Gloster] In *King Lear*, the father of Edgar and Edmund. His story is taken from that of the Prince of Paphlagonia in Sidney's *Arcadia*. He is tricked by his bastard son, Edmund, into believing that his legitimate son, Edgar, is plotting against him. Seeking to help Lear, he is taken prisoner by Lear's daughter Regan and her husband Cornwall, and blinded. In IV.i. he speaks the lines "As flies to wanton boys are we to the gods;/ They kill us for that sport." Eventually he joins up with the disguised Edgar, and dies soon after Edgar has revealed his identity.

Gloucester, Eleanor, Duchess of In *2 Henry VI*, the historical Eleanor Cobham, wife of Humphrey of Gloucester. She desires to be Queen, engaging in sorcery for this purpose, and is betrayed by Richard, Duke of York. She is banished, after doing penance by walking three days about the street with a taper in her hand. Meeting Gloucester in the street, she chides him for permitting her shame and warns him against Suffolk, York, and Cardinal Beaufort.

Gloucester, Humphrey of In *2 Henry IV* and *Henry V*, the youngest son of Henry IV, who plays a minor part as Prince Humphrey of Gloucester and the Duke of Gloucester. In *1 Henry VI*, he is the King's uncle and quarrels with Henry Beaufort, Bishop of Winchester, because he suspects the Beaufort family of seeking to rule England. In *2 Henry VI*, he is the Protector of the King, until deprived of the protectorship by the influence of various enemies banded together. Later he is arrested on the false charge of torturing prisoners and purloining army payrolls and is executed.

Gloucester, Richard, Duke of In *2* and *3 Henry VI* and *Richard III*, the fourth son of Richard Plantagenet, Duke of York, and later Richard III. In *3 Henry VI*, Margaret refers to him as "that valiant crookback prodigy … that with his grumbling voice / Was wont to cheer his dad in mutinies" (I.iv), and he schemes in III.ii to achieve the crown by violence. After the battle of Tewkesbury he kills the Prince of Wales, murders Henry VI in the Tower, and goes on in *Richard III* to execute all those who stand between him and the throne, experiencing no setbacks until Buckingham's refusal to kill the Princes in the Tower. This murder, eventually perpetrated by Tyrrel, represents the height of Richard's successful villainy, and after it his fortunes decline. On the eve of the battle with the Earl of Richmond he is visited by the ghosts of his victims. He dies in the battle. The character is partly conceived of in terms of a "Machiavel", but is also related to the medieval Vice in his wit and self-display.

Gobbo, Launcelot   In *The Merchant of Venice*, a comic servant. In a casuistical soliloquy (II.ii) he persuades himself that to stay with Shylock, as his conscience bids him, would be to serve the devil; and to run away, as the fiend, who is the devil, bids him, is to obey more friendly counsel. He leaves Shylock and helps Lorenzo escape with Jessica.

Gobbo, Old   In *The Merchant of Venice*, the half-blind father of Launcelot Gobbo. Appearing in II.ii with a present for Shylock, he is persuaded by Launcelot to give it to Bassanio, thus aiding Launcelot to enter Bassanio's service.

Goffe, Matthew   In *2 Henry VI*, a follower of Jack Cade.

Goneril   In *King Lear*, the eldest daughter of Lear. She despises her husband Albany for his kindness towards Lear, whom she has driven from her house. Planning to put Edmund, whom she loves, in Albany's place by killing the latter, she jealously poisons her sister Regan when she discovers that Regan too loves Edmund. Goneril finally commits suicide.

Gonzago   In *Hamlet*, the king who is murdered in the interpolated play. The name of the character is not mentioned in the Dramatis Personae for *Hamlet*.

Gonzalo   In *The Tempest*, an "honest old counsellor" who gave supplies and books to Prospero and Miranda when they were set adrift. He is shipwrecked with Alonso on Prospero's magic isle.

Gough, Robert   (d. 1624). English actor included in the list of principal actors in the first folio (1623) of Shakespeare's plays; he was a member of the ►Lord Chamberlain's Men and subsequently of the King's Men, becoming a shareholder in 1611.

Governor of Harfleur   In *Henry V*, the governor who surrenders his town to Henry (IV.iv).

Gower   In *2 Henry IV*, an officer in the royal army. In *Henry V*, he tells Fluellen that the King has ordered all the prisoners killed (IV.vii).

Gower   In *Pericles*, a character who appears as chorus and presenter of the action. He represents the medieval poet John Gower, author of the play's principal source, and speaks in a deliberately archaic idiom using octosyllabic couplets or sometimes decasyllabics, in couplets or alternating quatrains. His part may have been written by George ►Wilkins, probably Shakespeare's collaborator on the play.

Grandpré   In *Henry V*, a French lord who vividly describes the worn and desperate appearance of the English army on the morning of Agincourt (IV.ii).

Gratiano In *The Merchant of Venice*, one of Bassanio's companions. He is a garrulous character and one of Shylock's chief persecutors. He marries Nerissa.

Gratiano In *Othello*, the brother of Brabantio. As the uncle of Desdemona, he succeeds to Othello's fortunes after Othello has killed both Desdemona and himself.

Green In *Richard II*, a servant of the King.

Greene, Robert (1558–92) English dramatist, novelist, and poet. His comedies, such as *The Honourable History of Friar Bacon and Friar Bungay* (*c.* 1591), and *The Scottish History of James IV* (*c.* 1591) may have influenced Shakespeare. His narrative romance, *Pandosto, the Triumph of Time* (1588), was the main source for *The Winter's Tale*. In his pamphlet *Greene's Groatsworth of Wit* (1592) appears the earliest printed allusion to Shakespeare (not by name), whom Greene attacks as the countryman trying to write plays, the actor attempting to enter the circle of university men, the "upstart Crow … an absolute *Iohannes fac totum* .. the onely Shake-scene in a countre." (►*Groatsworth of Wit*).

Gregory In *Romeo and Juliet*, a servant to Capulet. He and Sampson fight with the servants of Montague in the first scene.

Gremio In *The Taming of the Shrew*, a rich but old suitor of Bianca, a type of the Pantaloon. He describes the marriage of Petruchio and Katherina (III.ii).

Grey, Lady In *3 Henry VI*, the historical Elizabeth Woodville. In the play she is the widow of Sir John Grey, and pleads for her husband's confiscated property, getting instead a proposal of marriage from Edward IV. This causes Warwick to desert him. In *Richard III*, as Queen Elizabeth, she attempts to make peace between Richard and her relations. When Edward dies, she takes the Prince off to sanctuary, from which Richard fetches them. With the Duchess of York and Margaret she learns to curse Richard, who despoils her of her brothers and children, much as Margaret has been despoiled of hers. Richard attempts to persuade her to allow him to marry her daughter Elizabeth, but she has privately arranged for Elizabeth to marry Richmond.

Grey, Lord In *Richard III*, a son of Queen Elizabeth (Lady Grey) by her former husband. Grey and Rivers are executed by order of Richard at Pomfret.

Grey, Sir Thomas In *Henry V*, a conspirator with Scroop and Cambridge against the King. When he is discovered, he claims joy that he is "prevented from a damned enterprise" (II.ii).

Griffith In *Henry VIII*, a gentleman usher to Queen Katherine.

Groatsworth of Wit [Full title, *Greene's Groatsworth of Wit Bought with a Million of Repentance*] A tract by Robert ►Greene, posthumously published in 1592. It was prepared for the press by Henry ►Chettle, sometimes thought to have been its true author. Roberto, the young man whose conversion and adventures are related, corresponds in some, though not in all, respects to Robert Greene himself. ►Marlowe, Peele, and probably ►Nashe are warned to repent of their wild ways. The exhortation to Peele contains a passage attacking Shakespeare.

Grumio   In *The Taming of the Shrew*, a servant of Petruchio.

Guildenstern   In *Hamlet*, a former school friend of the Prince. With Rosencrantz, he spies on Hamlet, under Claudius's orders, and is killed when Hamlet substitutes Rosencrantz's and Guildenstern's names for his own in instructions sent by Claudius.

Guiderius   In *Cymbeline*, the son of Cymbeline. He is disguised under the name of Polydore and brought up as the son of Morgan.

Guildford, Sir Henry   In *Henry VIII*, a gentleman of the court.

Gurney, James   In *King John*, a servant of Lady Faulconbridge.

H

Hal, Prince In *1* and *2 Henry IV*, the historical Henry, Prince of Wales, one of Falstaff's boon companions. ➤Henry V.

Hall, Sir Peter (1930–   ) British theatre director known for his long association with Shakespeare, whose plays he has directed since 1956, when he began with *Love's Labour's Lost* at the ➤Shakespeare Memorial Theatre, Stratford-upon-Avon. He has been director at the ➤RoyalShakespeare Company (1960–68), the National Theatre (1973–88), and the OldVic (1996–97). At the National Theatre he directed among other work *Hamlet* (1975), *Othello* (1980), and *The Tempest* (1988).

Hamlet In *Hamlet*, the central character, Prince of Denmark. In his first scene (I.ii) he spurns the overtures of Claudius ("A little more than kin, and less than kind"), expresses disgust at his mother's hasty remarriage, and longs to die. The revelation by his father's ghost that his death was not a natural one fills him with anguish, and he plans to devote his whole being to avenging his father's murder. In order to do this, he pretends to be mad, but he does not convince Claudius. To test the Ghost's authenticity, he arranges for the performance of a play depicting a murder, at which Claudius betrays his guilt. In Gertrude's room, he stabs Polonius in mistake for Claudius. He is sent away to England but contrives to return, and finally kills Claudius in a confrontation that brings about his mother's death and also his own. The Romantic critics, led by S. T. Coleridge, tended to see Hamlet in psychological terms, as an individual torn by doubt and seeking to form a course of action. Goethe, in an interpretation influential in the nineteenth century, saw Hamlet as too sensitive a being to deal with a situation not of his own making. Following Freud, and his disciple Ernest Jones, many critics have interpreted Hamlet as a man whose psychological problems result from his subconscious Oedipus complex. More recently, Hamlet's characterization has been seen as innovatory in the creation of a literary subjectivity or sense of inwardness. He remains Shakespeare's best known character and continues to be redolent of mystery and enigma.

Hamlet [Full title, *The Tragedy of Hamlet, Prince of Denmark*] A tragedy by Shakespeare, now regarded as one of the major canonical works in English literature. The story of Hamlet is a very old one, and the name in the form Amlotha appears *c.* 1230 in a fragment of verse in the *Prose Edda* of the Icelandic poet Snorri Sturluson. The earliest writer to put the story into an extant literary form was the Dane Saxo Grammaticus who included it in his Latin *Historia Danica* at the end of the twelfth century. François de Belleforest expanded Saxo's version in his

Histoires Tragiques (1582), a collection that Shakespeare had already used, and it is generally thought that Belleforest's tale was the true source of *Hamlet*, although it has been claimed that Shakespeare also knew Saxo's version. In fact, the two versions are substantially similar and contain all the major elements of the play, including fratricide and incest, committed by the wicked King Feng (Claudius), Amleth's uncle, Amleth's desire to avenge his murdered father, his feigned madness, the use of a woman as a decoy to trap Amleth and betray his disguise, the machinations of a spying friend of King Feng's who hides like Polonius in the Queen's bedchamber when Amleth comes to confront her, the murder of this character, and a scene in which Amleth upbraids his mother for her conduct. As in *Hamlet*, the King dispatches Amleth to England with a letter secretly commanding his death, but Amleth discovers this, changes the letter, returns to his home, in this case Jutland, and finally avenges himself by burning Feng's palace and all his followers, and killing Feng after exchanging swords with him. Belleforest made certain alterations to Saxo's tale that Shakespeare did not use, such as making Feng's murder of his brother take place in public at a banquet, but he did add two important details: he referred to Amleth's "over-great melancholy," and he made it clear that Feng and the Queen had committed adultery before the murder. Neither Saxo nor Belleforest includes a ghost, a play equivalent to *The Mousetrap*, Laertes, Fortinbras, the madness and drowning of the Ophelia character, or a graveyard scene.

The relationship between Shakespeare's play and Saxo and Belleforest is complicated by the fact that there clearly existed an earlier play of *Hamlet* that seems to have been known by 1589, since there is a reference to it in Thomas ►Nashe's preface to Robert ►Greene's romance *Menaphon*, published in that year. The passage in question seems to refer also to Thomas ►Kyd, author of *The Spanish Tragedy*, who is thought by many to have been the author of this first *Hamlet* (usually known as the ►*Ur-Hamlet*, "Ur" meaning "source"). It is possible that he wrote the *Ur-Hamlet* just after the highly successful *Spanish Tragedy*, which has many features in common with Shakespeare's *Hamlet*, in an effort to capitalize on *The Spanish Tragedy's* popularity. Philip ►Henslowe refers to a production of *Hamlet* at the Newington Butts playhouse in 1594, and Thomas ►Lodge in his pamphlet *Wit's Miserie* (1596) speaks of a ghost crying "like an oister wife, Hamlet, revenge," but the ghost in Shakespeare's play has neither these words nor this manner. ►Dekker in *Satiromastix* (1601) has a character say "My name's Hamlet revenge," and refer to Paris Garden, where the ►Lord Chamberlain's Men probably acted the *Ur-Hamlet* in 1596. It is therefore very likely that Shakespeare's *Hamlet* was influenced by the *Ur-Hamlet*, and perhaps that he found in it some of the features of his play that were not in Saxo or Belleforest, such as the ghost, *The Mousetrap* play, and the madness and death of Ophelia, all of which would have been likely ingredients of a Senecan revenge play by Thomas Kyd.

A number of other sources are also thought to have contributed to Shakespeare's *Hamlet*. The presentation of the Ghost, if it did not come from the *Ur-Hamlet*, was likely to have been influenced by ►Seneca's ghosts, in the *Agamemnon* or the

Troades, both of which were available in translation, and also by contemporary ghost-lore such as that in Reginald Scot's *The Discoverie of Witchcraft* (1584) or Lavater's *Of Ghosts and Spirites*. The murder of Gonzago perhaps came from contemporary accounts of the death, said to be by poison, of Francesco Maria I, Duke of Urbino, in 1538, although the use of the play "The Murder of Gonzago" (*The Mousetrap*) to discover Claudius's guilt may have been suggested by the anonymous play, *A Warning for Faire Women* (1599), in which there is a discussion of murders miraculously revealed. Aeneas's tale of Dido probably came from ►Marlowe's *The Tragedie of Dido Queene of Carthage* (1594) and perhaps from Virgil also. The similarities between *Hamlet* and the *Oresteia* of Aeschylus are fascinating, particularly in the matters of the hero's madness, the part played by the faithful friend, and the question of revenge taken against the Queen, but Shakespeare did not know Aeschylus's trilogy in Greek and no translation was available.

Hamlet was played in 1600 or 1601 and printed first in 1603. The textual situation is complex and remains in contention. Three early versions exist. The play was entered on the Stationers' Register on 26 July 1602, as "A booke called the Revenge of Hamlett Prince Denmarke as yt was latelie Acted by the Lord Chamberleyne his Servantes." This was a very imperfect text, known as the first (or "bad") quarto, possibly based on the *Ur-Hamlet*, and less than half the length of the second quarto. The second quarto, published in 1604, was a good text, thought by many to have been set from Shakespeare's own manuscript. The third quarto was a reprint of the second, and the fourth appeared in 1611. There is a fifth quarto, undated. No others appeared during Shakespeare's lifetime. The text in the first folio (1623) has several important differences from the 1604 quarto; it may have been set from a promptbook put together from the second quarto for use in the playhouse. The German play *Der Bestrafte Brudermord, oder Prinz Hamlet aus Doennemark* (Fratricide Punished, or Prince Hamlet of Denmark) is now thought to be a corrupt version of the *Hamlet* produced at Dresden in 1626, with resemblances to the "bad" first quarto. Richard ►Burbage may have been the first actor to play the part of Hamlet. The play was revived in the Restoration, one of only a few of Shakespeare's works to be presented with little adaptation.

Dramatis Personae

Claudius, King of Denmark	Guildenstern, *courtier*
Hamlet, *son to the late, and nephew to the present King*	Osric, *courtier*
	A Gentleman
Fortinbras, Prince of Norway	A Priest
Horatio, *friend to Hamlet*	Marcellus, *an officer*
Polonius, *Lord Chamberlain*	Barnardo, *an officer*
Laertes, *his son*	Francisco, *a soldier*
Voltemand, *courtier*	Reynaldo, *Polonius's servant*
Cornelius, *courtier*	A Captain
Rosencrantz, *courtier*	English Ambassadors

Players
Two Clowns, Grave-diggers
Gertrude, Queen of Denmark, *and*
    mother to Hamlet

Ophelia, *daughter to Polonius*
Lords, Ladies, *Officers, Soldiers, Sailors,*
    Messengers, and Attendants
Ghost of Hamlet's Father

The Story. Hamlet, Prince of Denmark, returns from university in Wittenberg to the royal castle of Elsinore to find that his father has recently died and his mother, Gertrude, has married his father's brother Claudius, now ruling as King. Hamlet's initial dismay at the unseemly haste of the marriage turns to horror when he learns from his father's Ghost that his father was murdered by Claudius, and he determines to avenge his father by killing the murderer. To conceal his designs from Claudius, Hamlet feigns madness and spurns Ophelia, the daughter of the Lord Chamberlain Polonius, whom he had previously courted. To test the truth of the Ghost's information he stages a play before the King that re-enacts the circumstances of the murder. Utterly convinced of the King's guilt by his reaction to this, Hamlet nevertheless hesitates to kill Claudius when he comes upon him at prayer, and instead goes to his mother's room and violently reproaches her for her "incestuous" marriage. Hearing a noise behind the arras and thinking it is Claudius, he kills the eavesdropping Polonius. Claudius, now keenly aware of Hamlet's purpose, sends Hamlet to England with instructions that he be killed. En route, Hamlet encounters the army of Fortinbras, a Norwegian prince, marching to recapture a piece of land from Poland. The ship in which he is sailing to England is intercepted by pirates and he returns to Denmark to discover that in his absence Ophelia has gone mad and drowned herself. Laertes, son of Polonius and a former friend of Hamlet, has meanwhile returned to avenge his father's death and is persuaded by Claudius that he should participate in a scheme to kill Hamlet. A fencing match is arranged between the two young men, for which Laertes's foil is to be poisoned. Laertes wounds Hamlet and thus ensures his death, but Hamlet seizes the poisoned foil and kills Laertes, who, dying, reveals the treachery. Gertrude also dies, having drunk unwittingly from a poisoned chalice prepared by Claudius for Hamlet; and Hamlet then stabs the King with the poisoned sword and compels him to drain the chalice left unfinished by Gertrude. Fortinbras enters, to succeed to the throne of Denmark.

Hands, Terry   (1941–   ) British theatre director who has worked mainly with the ►Royal Shakespeare Company, becoming artistic director from 1986 to 1991. Recently he has directed *The Merry Wives of Windsor* at the Royal National Theatre (1995).

Harcourt   In *2 Henry IV*, a member of the King's party who announces to Henry the victory of the sheriff of Yorkshire (IV.iv).

Hastings, Lord   In *2 Henry IV*, a rebel who is arrested after making peace with Prince John.

Hastings, Lord   In *3 Henry VI*, and *Richard III*, a loyal supporter of Edward IV, whom he helps to escape from prison. Although Edward's Queen is his enemy, he refuses to help Richard to the throne after Edward's death, is accused by Richard of treachery, and is executed.

Hathaway, Anne   (1555/6–1623) The maiden name of the wife of William Shakespeare. According to the records of the diocese of Worcester, a licence was issued on 27 November 1582 for the marriage of William Shakespeare and Anne Whateley of Temple Grafton. On 28 November, certain friends of the deceased father of Anne Hathway or Hathaway of Stratford posted a bond as security in the matter of the marriage of this Anne to William Shakespeare. It is generally supposed that the name Whateley in the first entry was a clerical error. The licence in question was a special one permitting the marriage after only one publication of the banns; the normal triple publication would have made it impossible, for various reasons, to proceed with the ceremony in less than two months. Anne was in fact already pregnant. Her first child, Susanna, presumably Shakespeare's child, was christened on 26 May 1583. Subsequently, she bore twins, who were christened Hamnet and Judith on 2 February 1585, and these three, so far as the records show, were her only children. Anne lived to the year 1623, and the inscription on her tombstone says she was sixty-seven years of age at her death, which indicates that she was eight years older than her husband. In his will, Shakespeare had left her only his second-best bed, possibly because by local custom she would anyway have had a life interest in one-third of his estate and the right to live at New Place during her lifetime. The house now known as Anne Hathaway's cottage was Hewland, a farmhouse in the village of Shottery, bought by her brother in 1610.

Hecate   In *Macbeth*, a superior of the Witches, borrowed from lore already old in Shakespeare's day; she is also referred to in *A Midsummer Night's Dream* (V.ii). In Greek mythology she was the goddess of the moon and the night, and had power in three realms: the heavens, the earth, the lower world. In *Macbeth* (III.v), she scolds the Witches for acting without her advice. Her speeches are now often attributed to Thomas ►Middleton, who later (about 1612) wrote a play called *The Witch*.

Hector   In *Troilus and Cressida*, a son of Priam, King of Troy and husband of Andromache. He challenges the Greeks to single combat, fights with Ajax, and is later murdered by the jealous Achilles.

Helen   In *Troilus and Cressida*, the beautiful wife of Menelaus. Her elopement with Paris caused the Trojan War.

Helena   In *All's Well That Ends Well*, the heroine, who cures the king of a mysterious ailment and thereby wins the right to choose herself a husband. She names Bertram, Count of Rousillion, who is unwilling to live with her, but she pursues him until she fulfils the conditions he has set for acknowledging her as his wife.

Helena In *A Midsummer Night's Dream*, an Athenian maiden in love with Demetrius, who had loved her until he switched his affections to Hermia. Puck accidentally contrives that both Demetrius and Lysander should fall in love with her, but at Oberon's instruction restores both lovers to their senses, and in the end Helena obtains Demetrius.

Helenus In *Troilus and Cressida*, a Trojan prophet, son of Priam. He favours giving Helen back to the Greeks.

Helicanus In *Pericles*, the faithful minister of Pericles.

Heminges, John [Also, Hemminge] (*c.* 1556–1630) English actor. In 1593 he belonged to ►Strange's Men, a company of Elizabethan actors, and toured with Edward ►Alleyn. He probably joined the ►Lord Chamberlain's Men in 1594, about the time the company was formed, and became a sharer in 1599. He seems to have been treasurer of the King's Men, later formed from the Lord Chamberlain's company. He played in *1 Henry IV*, and in ►Jonson's *Volpone, The Alchemist*, and several other of his plays. With Henry ►Condell he edited the first folio edition of Shakespeare's plays, published in 1623. He was closely associated with Shakespeare, who left him 26s. 8d. in his will to buy a mourning ring.

Henry IV ►Bolingbroke, Henry.

1 Henry IV [Full title, *The First Part of King Henry the Fourth*] A historical play by Shakespeare, first acted *c.* 1597 and printed in 1598. The existence of five other quarto texts before the publication of the first folio (1623) testifies to the play's contemporary popularity. Shakespeare's main source was ►Holinshed's *Chronicles* (second edition, 1587). The action of the play takes place over a year, from June 1402 to July 1403. Although this was a shorter space of time to be dramatized than in many of Shakespeare's histories, nonetheless a number of events recorded in Holinshed had to be omitted and others compressed or rearranged. Henry IV's references to a crusade are taken from Holinshed's account of the last year of his reign, and he is depicted as an old man, although at the time of the battle of Shrewsbury he was only thirty-seven. The defeat of Mortimer at the hands of Glendower and the victory of Sir Walter Blunt's forces at Holmedon over the Earl of Douglas did not take place on the same day, as recorded in I.i, Prince Henry did not slay Hotspur at Shrewsbury, nor were they in fact the two young rivals that Shakespeare depicts; Prince Henry was fifteen and Hotspur thirty-nine. The character of Hotspur's wife, whom Shakespeare called Kate and Holinshed Elinor, was virtually Shakespeare's invention. Shakespeare probably supplemented Holinshed's account with *A Mirrour for Magistrates* (1559), which contained accounts of Glendower and Northumberland, although he does not take over the *Mirrour's* characterization of Glendower as a man of evil life who deserved his wretched death. Some details in the play come from Samuel ►Daniel's *The First Fowre Bookes of the Civile Wars* (1595), in which Hotspur was presented as a rash young man and Hal saves his father on the battlefield from death at the hands of the Earl of Douglas. Daniel's view of Henry IV's reign as overshadowed by an avenging nemesis on account of his usurpation of the throne may also have influenced Shakespeare. An anonymous play called *The Famous Victories of Henry the Fifth*, published in 1598, though possibly written ten years earlier, supplied elements and characters for the comic plot of *1 Henry IV*, including the robbery at Gadshill, Prince Henry's tavern life, the parodying of authority, and the characters of Ned Poins, Gadshill, and "Jockey Old Castle," whom Shakespeare took over, transformed, and renamed Falstaff. The relationship between *1 Henry IV* and *2 Henry IV* remains unclear, although it has been convincingly argued that Shakespeare only decided on a two-part play when already embarked on Part One. The sequel to both parts is *Henry V* and together with *Richard II* these plays comprise a historical sequence that is often known as Shakespeare's second tetralogy (the first tetralogy consisting of the *Henry VI* plays and *Richard III*).

Dramatis Personae

King Henry IV
Henry, Prince of Wales (Prince Hal)
Prince John of Lancaster
Earl of Westmoreland
Sir Walter Blunt
Thomas Percy, Earl of Worcester
Henry Percy, Earl of
  Northumberland
Henry Percy (Hotspur)
Edmund Mortimer
Richard Scroop, Archbishop of York
Archibald, Earl of Douglas
Owen Glendower
Sir Richard Vernon

Sir John Falstaff
Sir Michael
Poins
Gadshill
Peto
Bardolph
Lady Mortimer, *daughter to*
  Glendower, and wife to Mortimer
Lady Percy, *wife of Hotspur*
Mistress Quickly
Lords, Officers, Sheriff, Vintner,
  Chamberlain, Drawers, Carriers,
  Travellers, and Attendants

The Story. When Henry IV refuses to ransom Lady Percy's brother, Edmund Mortimer, rightful claimant to the throne, from his captor Owen Glendower, the Percys refuse to give their Scottish prisoners to Henry. Moreover, Henry Percy (nicknamed Hotspur), with his father, Northumberland, and his uncle, Worcester, determine to raise a rebellion against Henry with Glendower, Mortimer, Scroop, Archbishop of York, and Douglas. Meanwhile Prince Hal, the young Prince of Wales, is amusing himself with the companionship of Sir John Falstaff and his carousing friends in the tavern in Eastcheap; when the play opens they are laying their plans to rob a group of travellers. But Prince Hal and Poins arrange not to be present at the robbery so that they may be able to attack and put to flight Falstaff and his companions, which they are able to do easily and without being recognized. The prank is revealed at the Boar's Head tavern after Falstaff has given his exaggerated version of the adventure (from which Sir John emerges, by his own account, as a courageous fighter), and much merriment ensues. Hal and Falstaff then create an impromptu play, staging the confrontation between Hal and his father the King, which is due to take place. Soon after, Hal meets his father and is strongly rebuked for his irresponsibility. He is given part of the royal forces to lead against the rebels, who have, meanwhile, been arguing about how to divide the kingdom when they have captured it. At Shrewsbury, Hotspur and Douglas learn that they have been deserted by Northumberland and Glendower, but prepare nevertheless to meet the advancing royal army. Worcester does not deliver to his rebel allies the King's offer of peace terms, and in the following battle the rebels are severely defeated. Hal slays Hotspur, and then colludes with Falstaff when he claims to have done so. The play ends with the King preparing to suppress the rebellion for good.

2 Henry IV [Full title, *The Second Part of King Henry the Fourth*]   A historical play by Shakespeare, first acted *c.* 1598 and printed in 1600. As in *1 Henry IV* Shakespeare's main source for the historical part of his play was ➤Holinshed's *Chronicles* (second edition, 1587), on which he depended more than for the first play, since Samuel ➤Daniel's *The Civil Warres between the Two Houses of Lancaster and York* (1595) was of less use to him. He had a wider span of time to compress, the period from 1403 to Henry V's accession in 1413, and in various ways he adjusted and modified Holinshed to make his long account more tractable. The rebellions against Henry IV by Northumberland's faction and the Archbishop of York are condensed from a number of separate uprisings. Northumberland's crafty escape to Scotland so as to avoid confrontation with the royal forces at Gaultree is Shakespeare's invention; in Holinshed, the Archbishop moved too quickly for Northumberland to keep up with him, although Northumberland finally died bravely in battle. Henry IV's illness is predated so as to add force to the presentation of chaos in the realm from the start; this may be due to the influence of Daniel, where the King's bad conscience is related to his sickness, for in Holinshed his illness is not mentioned before 1411. In Shakespeare the King hears the news of Northumberland's death shortly before his own death, although the events actually took place five years apart. Daniel's poem influenced Shakespeare's presentation of Henry IV, especially of the burden of guilt that the King expresses in IV.v. John ➤Stowe's *Chronicles of England* (1580) and *Annales of England* (1592) may also have been used for this scene, particularly Stowe's emphasis on the advice given by the dying King to his son; the solemn vows of Henry V in V.ii, to rule his realm justly may also have been influenced by Stowe. The anonymous play, *The Famous Victories of Henry the Fifth*, published in 1598 though written earlier, is an important source; Shakespeare takes up its theme of the Prince's ambiguous attitude towards his father but makes it very clear that Hal's apparent indifference and cynicism are only a pose. He makes use of the scene in which the Prince repents at his father's bedside for IV.v, in particular in the details of the music that the King calls for, the King's dozing and then awakening to find the crown gone, and the Prince's weeping. In *The Famous Vic-*

tories the Prince is shown boxing the ears of the Lord Chief Justice, whereas in *2 Henry IV* this incident is mentioned but not presented. At Henry V's coronation, Shakespeare uses the scene from the older play where the new King's former companions await his arrival, expecting to be taken into royal favour but instead finding themselves banished, though it is Ned (Poins) in *The Famous Victories* who steps forward to present himself to the King, not Falstaff. But *The Famous Victories* does not account for much of the comic plot. Mistress Quickly, Doll Tearsheet, Pistol, and the characters of the Gloucestershire countryside are Shakespeare's invention. The title page of the 1600 quarto text describes the play as *The Second Part of Henry the Fourth, Continuing to His Death, and Coronation of Henry the Fifth. With the Humours of Sir John Falstaff, and Swaggering Pistol.* The proportion of the play given over to "low" comic material has expanded from Part One, and this was clearly thought to be one of the play's attractions. But in this play, Prince Hal is less involved with Falstaff and his companions than before, and the transition to his role as king is well under way.

Dramatis Personae

Rumour, *the presenter*
Epilogue
King Henry IV
Henry, Prince of Wales, *afterwards*
    King Henry V
Thomas, Duke of Clarence
Prince John of Lancaster, *son of King*
    Henry the Fourth
Humphrey, Duke of Gloucester, *son*
    of King Henry the Fourth
Earl of Warwick
Earl of Westmoreland
Earl of Surrey
Gower
Harcourt
Blunt
Lord Chief Justice
A Servant of the Chief Justice
Earl of Northumberland
Scroop, Archbishop of York
Lord Mowbray
Lord Hastings

Lord Bardolph
Sir John Coleville
Travers
Morton
Sir John Falstaff
Bardolph
Pistol
A Page
Poins
Peto
Shallow *and* Silence, *country justices*
Davy, *Shallow's servant*
Mouldy, Shadow, Wart, Feeble, *and*
    Bullcalf, *recruits*
Fang *and* Snare, *sheriff's officers*
Lady Northumberland
Lady Percy
Mistress Quickly
Doll Tearsheet
Lords and Attendants, Officers, Soldiers,
    Messenger, Porter, Drawers, Beadles,
    Grooms, etc.

The Story. As the play opens, Westmoreland and Lancaster are preparing to lead an army against the remaining rebels. In London the King has commissioned Falstaff to go on the expedition to enlist soldiers en route. Prince Hal and Falstaff finally leave their friends at the Boar's Head tavern and set out for the north, Fal-staff bidding Mistress Quickly and Doll Tearsheet an emotional farewell. In Glouces-ter, at the home of Justice Shallow, Falstaff allows recruits to buy themselves off and enlists only a few poor and ragged men. Northumberland again deserts the rebels, and York, Mowbray, Hastings, and the others face the royal forces with a low morale. Lancaster tricks them into disbanding by promising to redress their wrongs, and then has them executed. The King is too sick and weary of his duties to re-joice over the defeat of the rebels; after doubting Hal's loyalty, he is reconciled with his son, and dies soon after. Hearing that Hal is now Henry V, Falstaff hurries to London, but is there rejected by the new King.

Henry V In *Henry V*, the King of England. Historically, he came to responsibil-ity early and when not yet sixteen was commander of the royal forces at Shrews-bury against the Percys; an unfounded legend says that he personally killed Harry Percy (Hotspur) at that battle. He succeeded to the throne on 20 March 1413 and immediately set about arranging matters to secure domestic peace, among other things restoring to their former positions those who had lost their titles or lands. In 1415, a plot by Richard, Earl of Cambridge, to make the Earl of March king was discovered. Cambridge was executed. Against the rebellious Lollards Henry V firmly enforced the anti-Lollard statute *De Heretico Comburendo* of 1401, Sir John Oldcastle being one of those burned (1417) for his part in the revolt of 20,000 Lol-lards in 1414. Henry decided to embark on a career of reconquest in France, prin-cipally because of French support of the Welsh during Glendower's rebellion in his father's reign, but also, according to some historians, to divert attention from do-mestic complaints. He crossed to France in 1415, besieged and took Harfleur, and marched on Calais. At Agincourt, his army of 13,000, thinned by disease, was faced by 50,000 French; on 25 October 1415, St Crispin's Day, the battle was fought; the French were routed with great loss, and Henry continued on to Calais. He returned almost at once to England. In 1417, having completed preparations, Henry again crossed the Channel. He took Caen and besieged Rouen; most of Normandy fell into his hands, and after the fall of Rouen in 1419 his army approached Paris. By the Treaty of Troyes (21 May 1420), he attained his principal aims. He was to marry Catherine of Valois, daughter of Charles VI of France; he would serve as regent for the insane King; and he was to be the King's heir, the Dauphin being specifically excluded. On 2 June he married Catherine; in December he made a triumphal entry into Paris. He returned with his queen to England to have her crowned and to have the treaty ratified, but in his absence a revolt occurred in Normandy. Henry returned to France and, while besieging Meaux (1421–22), weakened his health and died the following summer. He was succeeded by his nine-month-old son Henry VI. Henry is often considered the ideal knightly king, and he modelled him-self deliberately in the image of King Arthur and Godfrey of Bouillon. He is said on doubtful authority to have been wild and dissolute in his youth (probably a story spread by prejudiced religious controversialists who disliked his friendship with the

Lollard Oldcastle), and is so represented by Shakespeare; Shakespeare also allows him to be seen in maturity as "the mirror of all Christian kings" (Chorus 2) and "this star of England" (Final Chorus).

Henry V [Full title, *The Life of King Henry the Fifth*]   A historical play by Shakespeare, first acted before 1600 (it may have been the first play in the new ►Globe theatre), printed in 1600 in what is often regarded as a "bad" quarto, which was reissued in 1602 and 1619, and again in a more authoritative version in the first folio (1623). The main historical source was Book III of ►Holinshed's *Chronicles* (second edition, 1587), but Shakespeare also went independently to Holinshed's source, Hall's *The Union of the Two Noble and Illustre Famelies of Lancastre and Yorke* (1548) for some details. The main outline of the historical events is common to both, but some passages in the play can be separately derived from one or the other. For instance, Fluellen's reference to the effects of countermining (III.ii) comes from Holinshed, as does Westmoreland's wish for more men (IV.iii) and Henry's threat to the French horsemen (IV.vii). The Archbishop of Canterbury's speech on the Salic Law (I.ii) follows Holinshed very closely. From Hall come Henry's conversation with his nobles on England's relations with Scotland (I.ii), the placing of the tennis balls incident after the proroguing of Parliament, and the stress on the theme of the unity of England and France. Shakespeare may also have used other chronicles including the *Vita et Gesta Henrici Quinti* by "Titus Livius," translated into English in 1513. Earlier plays on the life of Henry V were in existence, including the anonymous *The Famous Victories of Henry the Fifth*, which Shakespeare had already used for his Henry IV plays, and a lost play, referred to by Nashe in 1599, that may have been a source both for Shakespeare's three plays dealing with Henry V and also for *The Famous Victories*. *The Famous Victories* included the tennis balls scene, scenes showing the attitude of the common people to the war, the encounter of an English clown with a French soldier, and a scene with Henry as a blunt and matter-of-fact suitor, all of which Shakespeare may have used. He rearranged the material of the sources so as to concentrate on the heroic struggle between England and France, and in particular on the battle of Agincourt, and to show Henry as an ideal king, brave, active, and fully aware of his responsibilities and duties. The play was formerly regarded as unambiguously patriotic, but modern critics have found elements of the ironic and equivocal in its handling of war and kingship, particularly if it is seen in conjunction with the other component plays of Shakespeare's second tetralogy, *Richard II* and *1* and *2 Henry IV*. The play is one of the few that can be dated exactly as to its composition, this being between March and September 1599, from a reference to the Earl of Essex's expedition to Ireland in the Chorus to Act V.

Dramatis Personae

King Henry V	Duke of Bedford
Humphrey, Duke of Gloucester	Duke of Exeter

Duke of York

Earls of Salisbury, Westmoreland, *and* Warwick

Archbishop of Canterbury

Bishop of Ely

Earl of Cambridge

Lord Scroop

Sir Thomas Grey

Sir Thomas Erpingham

Gower, *an Englishman*

Fluellen, *a Welshman*

Macmorris, *an Irishman*

Jamy, *a Scot*

Bates

Court

Williams

Pistol

Nym

Bardolph

Boy

A Herald

Charles the Sixth, King of France

Lewis, the Dauphin

Dukes of Burgundy, Orleans, and Bourbon

The Constable of France

Rambures

Grandpré

Montjoy

Governor of Harfleur

Ambassadors to the King of England

Isabel, Queen of France

Katherine, *daughter to Charles and Isabel*

Alice

Hostess of a tavern in Eastcheap, formerly Mistress Quickly, *and now married to Pistol*

Lords, Ladies, Officers, French and English Soldiers, Citizens, Messengers, and Attendants

Chorus

The Story. Henry V, supported in his claim to the throne of France by the arguments of the Archbishop of Canterbury, and angered by the insulting gift of tennis balls from the French Dauphin (a gift meant to underline the fact of Henry's youthful follies), sets forth to invade France. Before he leaves he discovers the conspiracy of Grey, Scroop, and Cambridge and orders their execution. At the Boar's Head tavern, Mistress Quickly describes the death of Falstaff, and his old cronies (Pistol, Nym, and Bardolph) thereupon enlist in the army. In France, before Harfleur, Henry urges on his men, "Once more into the breach, dear friends, once more; / Or close the wall up with our English dead" (III.i). He captures Harfleur and proceeds to face a much larger French army at Agincourt. The evening before the battle, the King, disguised as a common soldier, mingles in the ranks to test their confidence in him. Later in the evening he rejoices with his nobles that the English are outnumbered five to one. He would not wish for one man more who would lessen the honour that "We few, we happy few, we band of brothers" (IV.iii) will have in facing such a superior force. The English are victorious on the following day, and in the Treaty of Troyes, Henry obtains the hand of the Princess Katherine and the promise of the French throne upon the death of the French King then reigning.

Henry VI In *1, 2,* and *3 Henry VI*, the King of England. Historically, he succeeded to the English throne at the age of not quite nine months, under the protectorship of his uncle John, Duke of Bedford, the protectorship being exercised in England by Bedford's brother Humphrey, Duke of Gloucester, during Bedford's absence as regent in France. He married Margaret of Anjou in 1445; their only son Edward was born in 1453. Henry was a weak king, and the rule was always in the hands of others. Then York claimed the throne for himself and the nobles divided into factions and took arms; the Wars of the Roses began. Henry was restored as King in 1470, but in 1471 Queen Margaret's army was defeated at Tewkesbury, where Prince Edward was killed. Henry died in the Tower soon afterwards, probably murdered. In the play Richard of Gloucester is the murderer.

1 Henry VI [Full title, *The First Part of King Henry the Sixth*]   A historical play now thought to have been written by Shakespeare in collaboration with other writers, one of whom is likely to have been ➤Nashe. It may well have been first acted on 3 March 1592 (if ➤Henslowe's reference in his diary entry of that date to a performance of "Harry the VI" can be taken to apply to this play). Some scholars believe it to have been written later than *2* and *3 Henry VI*. It was first printed in the first folio (1623). It seems to be alluded to by Nashe in *Piers Penniless* (1592), where the popularity of Talbot's role is mentioned. Shakespeare's main sources were chronicles of English history, first Edward Hall's *The Union of the Two Noble and Illustre Famelies of Lancastre and Yorke* (1548), perhaps Richard Grafton's *A Chronicle at Large* (1569), which plagiarized from Hall, and also ➤Holinshed's *Chronicles* (second edition, 1587) and Robert Fabyan's *The New Chronicles of England and France* (1516). He did not follow the sequence of events given in these chronicles, and he departed much more violently from historical fact than in his later histories. For instance, the first scene of the play shows Henry V's funeral, which took place in 1422, interrupted by news from France combining events from 1436 (the loss of Paris) and 1429 (the crowning of the Dauphin), and concludes with Bedford's departure to fight at Orleans (1428–29) and Winchester's confession that he intends to steal away the baby King Henry VI (1425?). In order to write a patriotic play, probably one intended to be topical at a time when English forces were fighting in France, Shakespeare had to distort history completely by turning the two-year truce that preceded Henry VI's marriage with Margaret of Anjou (V.v) into a triumphant peace with Charles the Dauphin swearing allegiance to Henry VI. Shakespeare used Holinshed most in Act I, but not very much afterwards, except for the Joan of Arc material. The presentation of Joan in the play is much more complex and ambiguous than in Holinshed or any other chronicle; she is Amazon, shrew, whore, and finally witch. Hall's chronicle supplied the main material for Acts II to V, supplemented by Fabyan, Geoffrey of Monmouth's *Historia Regum Britanniae* and Hardyng's *Chronicle* for the account of Bedford carried to battle in a litter (III.ii), and a journal of the *Siege of Rouen* (1591) probably by Sir Thomas Coningsby. Some scenes, for instance the Temple Garden scene (II.iv), those concerning Talbot and his son (IV.vi–vii), and the wooing of Margaret by Suffolk (V.iii), have no basis in the chronicles.

Dramatis Personae

King Henry VI	*A Lawyer*
Humphrey, Duke of Gloucester	Charles, Dauphin, *afterwards* King of
Duke of Bedford	France
Thomas Beaufort, Duke of Exeter	Reignier, Duke of Anjou
Henry Beaufort, Bishop of	Duke of Burgundy
Winchester	Duke of Alençon
John Beaufort, Earl of Somerset	Bastard of Orleans
Richard Plantagenet, Duke of York	*Governor of Paris*
Earl of Warwick	*Master-Gunner of Orleans and his Son*
Earl of Salisbury	*General of the French forces in*
Earl of Suffolk	*Bordeaux*
Lord Talbot	*A French Sergeant*
John Talbot, *his son*	*A Porter*
Edmund Mortimer	*An old Shepherd, father to Joan la*
Sir John Fastolf	*Pucelle*
Sir William Lucy	Margaret
Sir William Glansdale	Countess of Auvergne
Sir Thomas Gargrave	Joan la Pucelle (Joan of Arc)
Mayor of London	*Lords, Warders of the Tower, Heralds,*
Woodvile	*Officers, Soldiers, Messengers, and*
Vernon	*Attendants, Fiends appearing to Joan*
Basset	*la Pucelle*
Mortimer's Keepers	

The Story. The play begins with the death of Henry V and the accession of the boy King Henry VI to the throne. With the strong hand of Henry V no longer controlling the realm, dissension immediately breaks out between the great nobles, particularly between Gloucester and Winchester, and between the factions of York and Lancaster (thus portending the Wars of the Roses). The English domain in France fares worst of all: Orleans is relieved and the English are driven steadily back towards the coast by the French under Joan of Arc. Talbot, who meets his death during the course of the play, is the only really powerful figure on the English side, and the play comes to an end as Henry prepares to enter upon marriage with Margaret of Anjou in an effort to bolster the crumbling fortunes of his realm.

2 Henry VI [Full title, *The Second Part of King Henry the Sixth*] A historical play attributed to Shakespeare, written between 1589 and 1591 and published in 1594 in a "bad" quarto that is thought by some to be a memorial reconstruction made from the piece as performed but by others to be an early version by Shakespeare of the text that subsequently appeared in the first folio (1623). Its original title was *The First Part of the Contention betwixt the two Famous Houses of York and Lancaster* ... The main source was either Hall's chronicle, *The Union of the Two Noble and Il-*

lustre Famelies of Lancastre and Yorke (1548) or Grafton's plagiarized version of it, *A Chronicle at Large* (1569). Shakespeare supplemented this with some elements from ►Holinshed's *Chronicles* (second edition, 1587), and perhaps John Foxe's *Acts and Monuments of Martyrs* (1583 edition), for the false miracle of Simpcox (II.i), and an anonymous play, *The Life and Death of Jack Staw* (published 1593/4) for the Jack Cade scenes. Shakespeare departed from history much less than for *1 Henry VI*, although he did make some modifications to the outline of the events of eleven years from 1444 to 1455, as given in Hall and Grafton. The fall of Gloucester is accentuated when he is accused in the play (III.i) of crimes that were in fact ascribed to others and it was Shakespeare, not the chroniclers, who made Suffolk an accomplice in Gloucester's murder. Some details for Jack Cade's rebellion came from Holinshed's or Grafton's account of the Peasants' Revolt of 1381, and Shakespeare showed Cade's followers as much more unruly than in the chronicles. The character of York is both blackened and made more dynamic than historical fact would suggest, in order to give the play a developing centre of interest and to prepare for York's part in *3 Henry VI* as the father of Richard of Gloucester. York's sons Edward (the future Edward IV) and Richard (Richard III), already a "heap of wrath, foul indigested lump" (V.i), are introduced at the end of the play to look forward to the sequel, although in 1455 when the battle with which the play ends took place Richard was a child of three.

Dramatis Personae

King Henry VI
Humphrey, Duke of Gloucester
Cardinal Beaufort
Richard Plantagenet, Duke of York
Edward, Earl of March
Richard, Duke of Gloucester
Duke of Somerset
Duke of Suffolk
Duke of Buckingham
Lord Clifford
Young Clifford
Earl of Salisbury
Earl of Warwick
Lord Scales
Lord Say
Sir Humphrey Stafford
William Stafford, *his brother*
Sir John Stanley
Sir William Vaux
Matthew Goffe
Walter Whitmore

A Sea Captain, Master, and Master's-Mate
Two Gentlemen, prisoners with Suffolk
John Hume
John Southwell
Roger Bolingbroke, *a conjurer*
Thomas Horner
Peter
Clerk of Chatham
Mayor of St Albans
Simpcox
Jack Cade
George Bevis, John Holland, Dick the Butcher, Smith the Weaver, Michael, *etc.*
Alexander Iden
Two Murderers
Margaret, *Queen to King Henry*
Eleanor, Duchess of Gloucester
Margery Jourdain, *a witch*
Wife to Simpcox

Lords, Ladies, and Attendants, Herald,	Prentices, Falconers, Guards, Soldiers,
Petitioners, Aldermen, a Beadle,	Messengers, etc.
Sheriff and Officers, Citizens,	A Spirit

The Story. The marriage of Henry to Margaret of Anjou has worsened rather than helped Henry's position in England; it has added to Henry's other troubles Gloucester's resentment at the cession of Maine and Anjou as the price of the marriage and added no equivalent stabilizing factor to his rule. Margaret, supported by York and Suffolk, intrigues against Gloucester, contriving first to have the Duchess of Gloucester arrested as a sorceress and finally securing the murder of Gloucester himself. Various other historical events, including the uprising under Jack Cade and the banishment of Suffolk, Margaret's lover, are also brought into the action of the play. At the end, the York–Lancaster dissension culminates in the initial struggle of the Wars of the Roses; the play ends with the death of Somerset in 1455 and the Battle of St Albans.

3 Henry VI [Full title, *The Third Part of King Henry the Sixth*] A historical play by Shakespeare, written between 1589 and 1591 and published in 1595. It was first performed sometime before September 1592, and appears in the first folio (1623). As with *2 Henry VI*, the early text (in this case an octavo) differs from that printed in the folio. Many editors now believe the earlier version to be a memorial reconstruction of an abridged version of the folio text. Its original title was *The true Tragedie of Richard Duke of York, and the Death of Good King Henry the Sixt…* (it was reprinted, under this title, with *2 Henry VI* under its original title, in 1619 as the second half of a two-part work entitled *The Whole Contention betweene … Lancaster and Yorke …*). ➤Greene parodies a line from this play, "O tiger's heart wrapped in a woman's hide" (I.iv) in *Greene's* ➤*Groatsworth of Wit*, published in September 1592. As in *2 Henry VI* the main source was Hall's chronicle, *The Union of the Two Noble and Illustre Famelies of Lancastre and Yorke* (1548). Shakespeare also used ➤Holinshed's *Chronicles* (second edition, 1587), especially for the scene of York's death at the hands of Clifford and Queen Margaret (I.ii), and probably Fabyan's *The New Chronicles of England and France* (1516). He knew *A Mirrour for Magistrates* and may have taken from it the idea that Richard of Gloucester murdered Henry VI. As in *2 Henry VI* the events of several years (1460–71) are compressed and rearranged, though Shakespeare stays closer to historical fact than in *1 Henry VI*. Acts I and II deal with the battles of 1460–61 in which York and his young son Rutland are slain by Clifford, and Clifford slain and his body brutalized by York's other sons, Acts III and IV with Edward IV's marriage to Lady Grey (1464), its political repercussions, and the rival diplomacy of the different factions, and Act V with the campaigns of 1471. Shakespeare develops the character of Richard of Gloucester (b. 1452), who was historically only a youth during the events of this play, and contrasts him with the weak but saintly Henry VI; it seems that *Richard III* was already in the playwright's mind. In fact Richard and his brother George (Clarence) were in France for a period in 1461, and could not have been present at the battles in II.iii–vi, where Richard is called a "foul misshapen stigmatic" by Queen Margaret and drawn into combat with Clifford.

Dramatis Personae

King Henry VI
Edward, Prince of Wales, *his son*
Lewis the Eleventh, King of France
Duke of Somerset
Duke of Exeter
Earl of Oxford
Earl of Northumberland
Earl of Westmoreland
Lord Clifford
Richard Plantagenet, Duke of York
Edward, Earl of March, *afterwards* King Edward the Fourth
Edmund, Earl of Rutland, *son to the Duke of York*
George, Duke of Clarence, *son to the Duke of York*
Richard, Duke of Gloucester, *son to the Duke of York*
Duke of Norfolk
Marquess of Montague
Earl of Warwick
Earl of Pembroke
Lord Hastings
Lord Stafford

Sir John Mortimer, *uncle to the Duke of York*
Sir Hugh Mortimer, *his brother*
Henry, Earl of Richmond
Earl Rivers
Sir William Stanley
Sir John Montgomery
Sir John Somerville
Tutor to Rutland
Mayor of York
Lieutenant of the Tower
A Nobleman
Two Keepers
A Huntsman
A Son that has killed his Father
A Father that has killed his Son
Queen Margaret
Lady Grey, *afterwards Queen to Edward the Fourth*
Lady Bona, *sister-in-law to the King of France*
Soldiers, and other Attendants on King Henry and King Edward, Messengers, Watchmen

The Story. Henry yields to York the succession to the throne, whereupon Queen Margaret, furious that her son should be disinherited, seeks (with the help of Clifford) to resolve the matter on the field of battle. At Wakefield, she is victorious; York himself is captured and subsequently killed. But York's sons Edward (who is to rule England as Edward IV) and Richard (who is also to rule England, as Richard III) vanquish Margaret and the Lancastrians at Towton, capturing Henry himself (now only a figurehead in the affairs of the kingdom) and making possible the crowning of Edward as King. However, the matter is not yet settled; dissension within the Yorkist ranks makes further fighting inevitable, and the throne remains in dispute until the Lancastrian faction is finally defeated at Tewkesbury. Margaret's son is slain, and Richard ruthlessly murders Henry VI.

Henry VII ▸Richmond, Henry Tudor, Earl of.

Henry VIII In *Henry VIII*, the King of England. Historically, the second and only surviving son of Henry VII and Elizabeth of York, he reigned from 1509 to 1547. After the death of his older brother Arthur, he became (1503) Prince of Wales. He succeeded his father on 22 April 1509, and on 3 June married Catherine of Aragon, widow of his brother. Henry's marriage had required a papal dispensation, one about which both the Pope and the Archbishop of Canterbury had had doubts at the time. After several miscarriages, Catherine bore a daughter in 1516, the future Queen Mary I, and never again gave birth to a live child. In 1527 Henry began proceedings for a divorce from the forty-two-year-old Catherine, alleging the invalidity, despite the papal dispensation, of the marriage with a deceased brother's wife. He wished now to marry Anne Boleyn, younger sister of a previous mistress. Pope Clement VII appointed (1528) a commission to sit in England, composed of Wolsey, appointed papal legate for the purpose, and Lorenzo Campeggio, Bishop of Salisbury, the regular papal legate, to hear and decide on the case; but in 1529, Campeggio having delayed a decision on papal orders, the case was called to Rome for hearing. Wolsey was very shortly dismissed and Cranmer was put in charge of the negotiations. Cranmer held that the marriage was invalid and that the Pope had been incompetent to grant a dispensation. Anne Boleyn was carrying Henry's child, and the marriage had to be arranged quickly. Cranmer secretly performed the ceremony on 25 January 1533, and on 23 May, as Archbishop of Canterbury since March, declared the marriage with Catherine void and that with Anne Boleyn valid (28 May 1533). Elizabeth, the future queen, born on 7 September 1533, was thus legitimatized. Henry's marriage to Anne Boleyn ended on 19 May 1536, when she was executed for adultery. Henry subsequently married Jane Seymour (1536), Anne of Cleves (1540), Catherine Howard (1540), and Catherine Parr (1543), who survived him. By these six marriages, Henry had three children: Mary, daughter of Catherine of Aragon, who reigned as Mary I; Elizabeth, the daughter of Anne Boleyn; Edward VI, the son of Jane Seymour, who was Henry's immediate successor. Henry's principal advisors were Wolsey, More, Cranmer, and Cromwell. Wolsey, deprived of his magnificence, died in disgrace in 1530. More was beheaded for his adherence to the original succession in 1535 and Cromwell for treason in 1540. Cranmer alone of the king's principal aides outlived him, to die at the stake in 1556.

Henry VIII [Full title, *The Famous History of the Life of King Henry the Eighth*: originally known as *All is True*.] A historical play written by Shakespeare, probably in collaboration with John ►Fletcher, although there is no external evidence to support this. Fletcher is thought to have written part or all of I.iii–iv, III.i, V.ii–iv. It was first acted on 29 June 1613 (an exact date is possible because it is known that the cannon fired during the performance started the fire that burned the ►Globe theatre to the ground on that day), and published in the first folio (1623). The main source was ►Holinshed's *Chronicles* (second edition, 1587), but Shakespeare also relied heavily on an earlier play about Henry VIII, Samuel ►Rowley's *When You See*

Me You Know Me, published in 1605 and reprinted in 1613. Rowley also used Holinshed, so that certain similarities between his play and Shakespeare's were almost inevitable, but there is plenty of evidence to show that Shakespeare undoubtedly did use his play. In both plays King Henry is similarly presented, leaning on the shoulder of one of his intimates as he walks in his gallery, growing angry when interrupted in his privacy, influenced by the persuasive rhetoric of Wolsey; Wolsey's downfall is accounted for in similar terms; the announcement of Elizabeth's birth, the rewarding of the person who brings the news, and the allusion to the baby's resemblance to her father in Shakespeare's play resemble the same incidents in Rowley's. But Shakespeare omits Rowley's scenes with the King's fools and also the account of the King's night visit in disguise to the city when he becomes involved in a brawl and is put in prison. Rowley's play is not much concerned with Wolsey's fall, and he does not deal with the divorce from Katherine or the marriage to Anne Boleyn; Shakespeare goes to Holinshed for these. Shakespeare concentrates the events of twenty years into his play, often anticipating time, as when he places Henry's meeting with Anne before Buckingham's condemnation, when in fact Buckingham was executed in 1521 and Henry did not meet Anne until 1526 or 1527, and he makes Katherine die before Elizabeth was born whereas she actually died three years afterwards. He made a little use of Hall's *The Union of the Two Noble and Illustre Famelies of Lancastre and Yorke* (1548), for instance, for Suffolk's announcement that Cardinal Campeius has stolen away to Rome (III.ii), and also of John Speed's *History of Great Britain* (1611) for some of the images in Wolsey's speeches (III.ii), and Foxe's *Actes and Monuments of Martyrs* (1583 edition) for the intrigues of Gardiner against Cranmer (V.i). In mode and style *Henry VIII* combines national history with tragicomic romance. It has much in common with Shakespeare's later plays, such as *The Winter's Tale* and *The Tempest*, in particular the providential outcome whereby a virtuous daughter (in this case the baby Elizabeth I) redeems her father.

Dramatis Personae

King Henry VIII	Lord Abergavenny
Cardinal Wolsey	Lord Sandys
Cardinal Campeius	Sir Henry Guildford
Caputius	Sir Thomas Lovell
Cranmer	Sir Anthony Denny
Duke of Norfolk	Sir Nicholas Vaux
Duke of Suffolk	*Secretaries to Wolsey*
Duke of Buckingham	Cromwell
Earl of Surrey	Griffith
Lord Chamberlain	*Three Gentlemen*
Lord Chancellor	*Garter King-at-Arms*
Gardiner	Doctor Butts
Bishop of Lincoln	*Surveyor to the Duke of Buckingham*

Brandon	*An Old Lady*
Door-keeper of the council-chamber	Patience
Porter, and his Man	*Several Lords and Ladies in the Dumb-*
Page to Gardiner	*shows, Women attending upon the*
A Crier	*Queen, Scribes, Officers, Guards, and*
Queen Katherine	*other Attendants*
Anne Bullen	*Spirits*

The Story. Buckingham, about to expose the ambitious Cardinal Wolsey to the King, is arrested for high treason at the instigation of Wolsey. Queen Katherine (in history, Catherine of Aragon, mother of Queen Mary) pleads with Henry to remove certain oppressive taxes and to pardon Buckingham. The first request the King grants, but the trial and execution of Buckingham are carried out. Meanwhile, the King has met Anne Bullen (in history, Anne Boleyn, mother of Queen Elizabeth) at a party given by Wolsey and has fallen in love with her. He hopes to get a divorce from Katherine on the grounds that his marriage was not permissible for reasons of near relationship, Katherine being his brother's widow (in the eyes of the Elizabethans, this made the match almost incestuous). Wolsey halts proceedings on the divorce because he realizes that if they are completed Henry will marry Anne, and he opposes her on religious grounds. The King discovers the duplicity of Wolsey, and the Cardinal retires. Cranmer, Archbishop of Canterbury, annuls the marriage to Katherine, who shortly dies of a broken heart. Henry secretly marries Anne, but Cranmer, accused of heresy, is brought to trial; however, the King gives him a ring for protection, and later honours him by asking him to be the godfather of Elizabeth. The christening is the final scene of the play.

Henry, Prince   In *King John*, the son of John. After John's death the lords swear loyalty to him (as Henry III).

Henry, Prince of Wales   ➤Henry V.

Henry Bolingbroke   ➤Bolingbroke, Henry.

Henry Percy   ➤Hotspur.

Henslowe, Philip   (d. 1616) English theatre manager. He was a servant of the bailiff of Viscount Montague, whose town house was in Southwark. Henslowe took care of the property there, and gradually made money and bought property. In 1585 he bought land on the ➤Bankside, and in 1587 built the ➤Rose theatre there. In 1592 he began to keep the accounts of his theatrical ventures in his *Diary*. After 1594 he became manager of the ➤Lord Admiral's Men. In 1600 he built, with Edward ➤Alleyn, his son-in-law, the ➤Fortune theatre and in 1613–14 the ➤Hope, the builder's contract for which survives. The *Diary* and other papers were lost in a mass of printed material at Dulwich College until 1790, when Edmund Malone recovered them for his variorum edition of Shakespeare. The *Diary* contains among other things a list of companies performing at the Rose, names of plays, and Henslowe's receipts as theatre owner for performances; and accounts of his advances to the Lord Admiral's Men for plays, costumes, properties, and licensing fees, and to the actors themselves. The record covers the years 1592–1603.

Herbert, Sir Walter   In *Richard III*, a supporter of Richmond.

Herbert, William [Title, 3rd Earl of Pembroke] (1580–1630) Statesman and patron of poets. He was educated privately by Samuel ➤Daniel, author of the *Delia* sonnets, and later at New College, Oxford. Soon after he became (1601) Lord Herbert of Pembroke, he was disgraced, imprisoned, and exiled from court because of his affair with Mary Fitton, maid of honour to Elizabeth. He was the patron of ➤Jonson, Massinger, and Inigo ➤Jones the architect, among others. He was chancellor (1617–30) of Oxford University, Pembroke College (formerly Broadgates Hall) being renamed (1624) in his honour. To him and his brother Philip, ➤Heminges and ➤Condell dedicated the first folio (1623) of Shakespeare; he has sometimes been regarded as the "Mr. W.H." to whom the Sonnets of Shakespeare are dedicated.

Hereford, Duke of   ➤Bolingbroke, Henry.

Hermia   In *A Midsummer Night's Dream*, an Athenian lady, the daughter of Egeus, in love with Lysander.

Hermione   In *The Winter's Tale*, the Queen of Sicilia, wife of the jealous Leontes. She is the Bellaria of Greene's *Pandosto*, the story from which *The Winter's Tale* was taken. She appears to die at the news of Mamillius's death, but in fact survives, and is preserved secretly by Paulina for sixteen years, to be reunited with the repentant Leontes at the end of the play.

Hero   In *Much Ado About Nothing*, the daughter of Leonato, and friend and cousin of Beatrice. When denounced by Claudio at the church as unchaste, she faints, and on Friar Francis's advice it is announced she is dead. When Claudio repents his false accusation of her, she is brought to him veiled, and the two are reconciled.

Hippolyta   In *A Midsummer Night's Dream*, the Queen of the Amazons, betrothed to Theseus.

Hippolyta   In *The Two Noble Kinsmen*, the wife of Theseus and sister of the heroine, Emilia. She begs Theseus to spare Palamon and Arcite.

Holinshed's *Chronicles*   A prose historical work (published 1577, in two folio volumes, and a second edition in three volumes in 1587) by Raphael Holinshed (*c.* 1529–80), with the assistance of William Harrison, Richard Stanyhurst, and others. Both editions were subject to government censorship. Shakespeare drew much from the *Chronicles* (probably from the 1587 edition) for *Macbeth*, *King Lear*, *Cymbeline*, *Richard II*, *Richard III*, and all his *Henry* (*IV*, *V*, *VI*, *VIII*) plays.

Holland, John   In *2 Henry VI*, a follower of Jack Cade.

Holm, Ian   (1931–) British actor who has appeared in Shakespeare for the ➤Royal Shakespeare Company and at the Royal National Theatre, making his debut at the ➤Shakespeare Memorial Theatre, Stratford-upon-Avon in 1954. Recently he has played King Lear (Royal National Theatre, 1997) and Fluellen in Kenneth ➤Branagh's film of *Henry V*.

Holofernes   In *Love's Labour's Lost*, a pedantic schoolmaster who takes the part of Judas Maccabaeus in the masque of the Nine Worthies.

honorificabilitudinitatibus   The longest word in Shakespeare, in *Love's Labour's Lost* (V.i). It appears in other contemporary writing, and has been traced back to Dante's *De vulgari eloquentia* (*c.* 1300) and earlier.

Hope, the   A playhouse built for Philip ➤Henslowe on the ➤Bankside, Southwark, in 1613. Ben ➤Jonson's *Bartholomew Fair* was produced on the occasion of its opening in October 1614. It also doubled as a pit for the baiting of bears and bulls. It was a round building near the ➤Globe and was demolished in 1656.

Horatio   In *Hamlet*, a close friend and confidant of Hamlet, charged by Hamlet at the end of the play to "report me and my cause aright / To the unsatisfied" (V.ii).

Horner, Thomas   In *2 Henry VI*, an armourer accused of treasonable sayings by his apprentice. In a combat with the apprentice, Peter Thump, he is mortally wounded and confesses his treason.

Hortensio   In *The Taming of the Shrew*, a suitor of Bianca. He persuades Petruchio to marry Katherina, Bianca's older sister, so that he may marry Bianca; he woos her in disguise as Licio, a tutor, but she marries Lucentio, and he marries a widow instead.

Hortensius   In *Timon of Athens*, a servant.

Host   In *The Merry Wives of Windsor*, the keeper of the Garter Inn, who participates in the schemes of his guests. He urges Dr Caius to fight with Evans, and when the two realize that they have been fooled they steal his horses. He helps Fenton court Anne Page.

Host   In *The Two Gentlemen of Verona*, the hospitable character who takes Julia in search of Proteus (IV.ii).

Hotspur   In *Richard II* and *1 Henry IV*, Sir Henry (or Harry) Percy, son of Northumberland. He leads the northern rebellion against Henry IV and is killed at Shrewsbury. Shakespeare makes him the same age as Prince Hal (the historical Hotspur was twenty years Hal's senior) to sharpen the contrast between the man who thinks "it were an easy leap / To pluck bright honour from the pale-faced moon" (*1 Henry IV*, I.iii) and Prince Hal, regarded by his father as a wastrel. The historical Hotspur (1364–1403) fought alongside his father at Homildon Hill in 1402 and captured the Earl of Douglas. He attempted to arrange an exchange of prisoners with Henry IV, seeking to use Douglas as ransom for his (Percy's) brother-in-law Edmund Mortimer. Henry IV refused, and Percy, angered by this refusal, associated himself with Owen Glendower in his war against the King. It was during this war that Percy was killed at Shrewsbury.

Howard, Alan (1937–   ) British actor who played various Shakespearean roles during a lengthy period with the ►Royal Shakespeare Company (1966–80), notably Achilles in *Troilus and Cressida* (1968), Theseus and Oberon in Peter ►Brook's production of *A Midsummer Night's Dream* (1970), Hamlet (1970), and Coriolanus (1977). He has recently played Macbeth at the ►Royal National Theatre (1997) and King Lear at the Old Vic (1997).

Hubert de Burgh In *King John*, the King's chamberlain. Ordered to kill John's young nephew, Hubert is softened by Arthur's entreaties, lets him live unharmed, and reports to the King that Arthur is dead. When Arthur is discovered dead (he is accidentally killed while trying to escape), Hubert is suspected of responsibility.

Hume, John In *2 Henry VI*, a priest bribed to undertake witchcraft on behalf of the Duchess of Gloucester.

Hutt, William (1920–   ) Canadian actor and director, who has worked regularly with the Stratford (Ontario) Shakespeare festival since its inception in 1953. His parts have included Polonius (1957), Prospero (1962, 1976), Richard II (1964), and King Lear (1972, 1988, 1996).

Hymen The classical god of marriage. He appears as a character in *As You Like It* and in *The Two Noble Kinsmen*.

I

Iachimo In *Cymbeline*, an Italian courtier who deceives Posthumus in order to win a wager that the latter's wife, Imogen, is unchaste.

Iago In *Othello*, Othello's ensign, passed over for promotion to lieutenant in favour of Cassio. Iago successfully plots to get Cassio demoted, and to persuade Othello that Desdemona is having an affair with Cassio. His villainy is finally revealed by his wife, but only after Desdemona's death

Iden, Alexander In *2 Henry VI*, the slayer of Jack Cade.

Ides of March In *Julius Caesar*, 15 March, the day on which Caesar is murdered. According to the Roman calendar the Ides occurred on the fifteenth of March, May, July, and October, and on the thirteenth of the other months.

Illyria, Duke of ➤Orsino.

Imogen [Also, Innogen] In *Cymbeline*, the daughter of Cymbeline, and wife of Posthumus. She continues to love her husband despite his rejection of her when he believes her to have been unfaithful to him with Iachimo. She undergoes much suffering for Posthumus's sake, but they are finally reunited.

Inns of Court Legal societies at London that have the exclusive privilege of calling candidates to the bar, and their precincts or premises. They are the Inner Temple, Middle Temple, Lincoln's Inn, and Gray's Inn. The first two originally belonged to Knights Templar (whence the name Temple). These inns had their origin about the end of the thirteenth century. In Shakespeare's day, the students were all young men of the elite classes, and the Inns were regarded as the third university of England (after Oxford and Cambridge). Membership carried social privileges, including an entrée to the court.

International Shakespeare Globe Centre Institution on the South Bank of the Thames in London, close to the site of the original ➤Globe theatre, which consists of a reconstruction of the Globe and various associated buildings. This centre is the culmination of the project initiated by Sam ➤Wanamaker. The theatre opened in 1996 with Mark ➤Rylance as artistic director and offers an annual summer season of plays by Shakespeare and his contemporaries. Productions have included *The Two Gentlemen of Verona* (1996), *Henry V* and *The Winter's Tale* (1997), and *As You Like It* and *The Merchant of Venice* (1998).

Iras In *Antony and Cleopatra*, one of the two female attendants (the other being Charmian) who die with Cleopatra.

Ireland, William Henry (1775–1835) British lawyer's clerk who forged a number of documents supposedly by or relating to Shakespeare, including letters to the Earl of ►Southampton and Anne ►Hathaway, and a play called *Vortigern*. This last was performed at Drury Lane in 1796, just after the exposure of these forgeries by the scholar Edmund Malone.

Iris In *The Tempest*, a character in the masque celebrating the betrothal of Ferdinand and Miranda; the classical goddess of the rainbow.

Irving, Sir Henry (1838–1905) Celebrated British actor-manager, who was the first actor to be knighted (1895). His first success was as Hamlet (1874), and he subsequently played many roles, including Richard III, Shylock, Othello, and Macbeth, often with Ellen ►Terry as his leading lady.

Isabel In *Henry V*, the Queen of Charles VI of France. She is present at the meeting of the two Kings (V.ii).

Isabella In *Measure for Measure*, a novice nun, the sister of Claudio. Angelo offers to save her brother from execution, if she will sleep with him. At the Duke's contrivance, she is replaced in Angelo's bed by Mariana. At the end of the play, the Duke proposes marriage to her.

J

Jacobi, Sir Derek (1938–) British actor who has played Shakespearean parts for several companies, including Touchstone (Old Vic, 1967), Pericles and Hamlet (1977, Prospect Theatre Company), and Benedick and Prospero (1982, ►Royal Shakespeare Company). More recently he has directed *Hamlet* for the Renaissance Theatre (1988) and appeared in films of *Henry V* (Chorus, 1989), and *Hamlet* (Claudius, 1996).

Jailer In *The Two Noble Kinsmen*, the keeper of the jail where Palamon and Arcite are confined.

Jailer's Daughter In *The Two Noble Kinsmen*, the daughter of the Jailer. She goes mad with unrequited love for Palamon, who is a nobleman, but is cured when her suitor impersonates him. She has more soliloquies than any other female character in a Shakespeare play.

James I [Also, James VI (of Scotland)] (1566–1625) King of England, Scotland, and Ireland (1603–25); son of Lord Darnley and Mary, Queen of Scots. He became King of Scotland as James VI on 24 July 1567, on the abdication of his mother; and by virtue of his descent, through both his father and his mother, from Margaret Tudor, daughter of Henry VII, succeeded to the English throne when Elizabeth died without issue on 24 March 1603. He was crowned King of England (and Ireland) on 25 July 1603. He was the author of a number of political works, as well as a treatise on witchcraft, and an attack on tobacco. The Duc de Sully characterized him as the "wisest fool in Europe." In domestic politics he sought to assert the theory of the divine right of kingship; in his foreign relations he strove to maintain peace at all hazards and attempted to promote a marriage between the future Charles I and the Infanta of Spain.

Jamy In *Henry V*, a Scottish captain.

Jaquenetta In *Love's Labour's Lost*, a country woman with whom Costard and Armado are in love.

Jaques In *As You Like It*, a philosophical companion of the exiled duke. He is usually spoken of as "the melancholy Jaques" and serves as a satirical commentator upon the extravagances of the others. At the end of the play he is the only character who does not desert the forest for the court.

Jaques [Also, Jaques de Boys (or de Bois)]   In *As You Like It*, an elder brother of Orlando and second son of Sir Rowland de Boys.

Jessica   In *The Merchant of Venice*, the daughter of Shylock. She elopes with Lorenzo, taking her father's jewels and money.

Joan of Arc [In the Dramatis Personae, Joan la Pucelle; also, La Pucelle]   In *1 Henry VI*, a leading character. She convinces the Dauphin of her marvellous powers, raises the siege of Orleans, persuades Burgundy to desert the English cause, and finally conjures up fiends to whom she offers herself in exchange for French victory. When captured by the English, she claims to be royal in blood and a virgin, but later states that she is with child, when she is sentenced to be burnt at the stake.

John, Don   In *Much Ado About Nothing*, the bastard brother of Don Pedro. It is he who causes Claudio to suspect Hero's chastity.

John, Friar   In *Romeo and Juliet*, a Franciscan friar sent by Friar Laurence to tell Romeo about Juliet's feigned death. He is prevented from reaching Mantua by an outbreak of plague, so Romeo does not find out that Juliet is merely sleeping and, upon arriving at the Capulets' tomb, believes her to be dead.

John of Gaunt, Duke of Lancaster   In *Richard II*, the father of Bolingbroke and uncle of the King. On his deathbed he utters the well-known speech in praise of England which begins "This royal throne of Kings, this sceptr'd isle" and warns Richard of the result of his careless practices (II.i).

John, King   The chief character of *King John*. Historically he was the youngest son of Henry II and seized the throne on the death of Richard I. In the play, the legitimacy of his claim to the throne is in doubt, and he plots to rid himself of a rival with a better claim, his nephew, the child Prince Arthur. He champions Engish unity against the papacy and the French. At the end of the play he dies of poison.

Jones, Inigo   (1573–1652) English architect and stage designer. He went to Italy to study painting and architecture and resided there many years. He returned to England in 1605. As court architect to Elizabeth I, and subsequently to James I and Charles I, he designed the sets and staging for the court masques by ►Jonson and other writers of the time. Among his works are the banqueting hall in Whitehall (1619–22), the Covent Garden Piazza, the famous gateway of St Mary's, Oxford (1632), the equally famous portico of old St Paul's and the reconstruction of that church (1631–41). He introduced to England the classical style of Palladio.

Jonson, Ben   (1572–1637) English actor, poet, dramatist, and essayist. His father was a clergyman and his stepfather, whose trade he followed for a short time, was a bricklayer. He studied at Westminster School but did not attend university, though he was awarded an honorary MA by Oxford in 1619. He served as a soldier in the Low Countries, but was in London about 1592 and began his connection with the theatre about 1595. Various entries in ►Henslowe's *Diary* indicate that Jonson worked for him in 1597. In 1598 he wrote *Every Man in His Humour*, in which Shakespeare acted; he was cited in *Palladis Tamia: Wits Treasury* by Francis ►Meres as "one of the best for tragedy"; and he fought a duel with, and killed, a fellow actor, Gabriel Spenser, for which he was imprisoned and was saved from hanging only by pleading benefit of clergy. His best-known plays are *Every Man in his Humour* (1598, revised 1616), *Every Man Out of His Humour* (1599), *Sejanus* (1603), *Volpone, or the Fox* (1606), *Epicoene, or the Silent Woman* (1609), *The Alchemist* (1610), and *Bartholomew Fair* (1614). Other plays include the comedies *Cynthia's Revels* (1600) and *The Poetaster* (1601), *The Devil is an Ass* (1616), *The Staple of News* (1625), *The New Inn* (1629), *The Magnetic Lady* (1632), and *A Tale of a Tub* (1633). *Catiline* (1611), like *Sejanus,* is a classical tragedy, closely based on historical sources. *The Hue and Cry After Cupid* (1608; unfinished), *The Masque of Queens* (1609), and *Oberon* (1611) are court masques, entertainments combining music, dancing, singing, with an allegorical and usually royalist plot. He wrote at least thirty of these masques. *Timber, or Discoveries Made upon Men and Matter* (published 1640) is an example of his prose. He also wrote poetry, in particular his tribute to Shakespeare, *To the Memory of My Beloved Master, Mr. William Shakespeare, and What He Hath Left Us* (written for and published in the 1623 first folio), and the lines *To the Reader* (also in the first folio). In 1616 he collected his best writings – plays, masques, epigrams, and the collection of poems called *The Forest* – and published them in a folio entitled *Works*, which occasioned some ridicule at the time on account of its apparent pretension. He made a number of enemies, including, later on in life, Inigo ►Jones, with whom he had collaborated on his earlier masques. But he also acquired many notable friends and patrons from amongst the aristocracy and the elite of his day, and after death was honoured with a commemorative volume of poetic tributes, *Jonsonus Virbius* (1638). Jonson is buried in Westminster Abbey, where his grave is marked by the inscription, "O Rare Ben Jonson." ►*Sejanus His Fall*.

Jourdain, Margery In *2 Henry VI*, a witch who summons a spirit for the Duchess of Gloucester (I.iv).

Julia In *The Two Gentlemen of Verona*, the woman who loves Proteus. She follows him to Milan, disguised as a page, and offers him her services.

Juliet In *Measure for Measure*, Claudio's betrothed. Claudio is sentenced to death when, through her pregnancy, it becomes known that he has seduced her. Later, she and Claudio are married.

Juliet The heroine of *Romeo and Juliet*. She is the daughter of Capulet and loves Romeo, the heir of the rival family of Montague, whom she sees first sees at a ball. She marries Romeo in secret, and after he has murdered her cousin Tybalt takes a sleeping potion so as to feign death and rejoin Romeo in exile after two days. But the plan goes wrong, Juliet awakes from the potion in the family vault to find Romeo dead beside her, and then stabs herself.

Julius Caesar [Full title, *The Tragedy of Julius Caesar*]   A historical tragedy by Shakespeare, written and produced *c.* 1599. It was seen by a Swiss visitor, Thomas Platter, at the ▸Globe theatre on 21 September 1599. There were humorous uses of the phrase "Et tu, Brute" soon after, one by Jonson in *Every Man out of his Humour* (V.vi). The play was printed in the first folio of 1623. Shakespeare's main source was North's translation of the lives of Marcus Brutus, Julius Caesar, and Marcus Antonius from Plutarch's *Lives of the Noble Grecians and Romans.* At some points he followed North very closely, as for instance in the scenes of Artemidorus preparing his petition (II.iii), the mob falling on Cinna the poet (III.iii), and especially that of Brutus with Portia (II.i), but elsewhere he modified his source considerably. Caesar's triumph for his victory over Pompey in fact took place four months before the feast of the Lupercal, but in I.i–ii Shakespeare puts them on the same day, together with the disrobing of Caesar's images by the tribunes, which took place still later. For dramatic effect, Shakespeare has the murder of Caesar followed on the same day by Antony's incitement of the mob, whereas in fact Antony's reading of the will took place a few days later, after a meeting of the senate. Antony's actual speeches at this crucial point in the play are Shakespeare's invention. Shakespeare also telescopes two battles at Philippi into a single encounter. The major figures were characterized in some detail by Plutarch, and Shakespeare makes much use of him; but he did make important changes. Shakespeare's Caesar is more noble than his original, and no references are made to his insults to the senate or his affair with Cleopatra; Shakespeare emphasizes his physical weakness. Plutarch's Brutus had more motivation for the assassination, since Caesar had shown clear signs of imperialist ambition; Shakespeare emphasizes Brutus's lack of judgment and his self-righteousness, as well as the idealism that is in Plutarch. Casca's character is mainly Shakespeare's invention. Several details of the play may have come from other sources. Appian's *Auncient Historie and exquisite Chronicle of The Romane Warres*, of which a translation was published in 1578, emphasized Antony's subtlety and command of rhetoric. Two plays, the anonymous *Caesar's Revenge*, published in 1607 but written earlier, and ▸Kyd's *Cornelia*, a translation of the Senecan play by Garnier, have also been suggested as sources. The treatment of the revenge theme in *Caesar's Revenge* may have influenced Shakespeare, especially in Antony's prophecy of civil war (III.i); Kyd's *Cornelia* also emphasized the horrors of civil war. Shakespeare's play may have started a fashion for the use of Roman themes in the popular theatre.

Dramatis Personae

Julius Caesar	Popilius Lena, *senator*
Octavius Caesar, *triumvir*	Marcus Brutus, *conspirator*
Mark Antony, *triumvir*	Cassius, *conspirator*
M. Aemilius Lepidus, *triumvir*	Casca, *conspirator*
Cicero, *senator*	Trebonius, *conspirator*
Publius, *senator*	Ligarius, *conspirator*

Decius Brutus, *conspirator*

Metellus Cimber, *conspirator*

Cinna, *conspirator*

Flavius *and* Marullus, *tribunes*

Artemidorus, *a sophist of Cnidos*

A Soothsayer

Cinna, *a poet*

Another Poet

Lucilius

Titinius

Messala

Young Cato

Volumnius

Varro

Clitus

Claudius

Strato

Lucius

Dardanius

Brutus's Servants

Pindarus, *Cassius's servant*

Calphurnia, *wife to Caesar*

Portia, *wife of Brutus*

Senators, Citizens, Guards, Attendants

The Story. Caesar's triumphal return to Rome (of which he has already been made dictator), after a series of military victories in Spain, brings to a climax the fear held by a faction of Roman leaders that the traditional freedoms of the republic may perish through Caesar's overweening ambition, and a plot to assassinate him begins to take shape. Cassius (the chief conspirator), Casca, Cinna, and others persuade Caesar's close friend Marcus Brutus to join their faction, and that night at Brutus's house they complete their plans. The night is disturbed, stormy, and full of portents of disaster. Caesar, despite both the warning from a soothsayer that he should beware the Ides of March and the ominous dream of his wife Calphurnia, goes to the Senate where, as planned by the conspirators, he is stabbed to death. Mark Antony, in a speech at Caesar's funeral, arouses the crowd to fury at the assassination. He then joins Octavius and Lepidus to form a governing triumvirate. The conspirators leave Rome and take refuge at Sardis. There, as Antony's army approaches, Cassius and Brutus quarrel, but they are reconciled when Brutus tells Cassius of the suicide of his (Brutus's) wife Portia. The ghost of Caesar then appears to Brutus in his tent, as a portent of disaster to come. In an unwise military move, the conspirators meet Antony's army on the plains of Philippi and are there defeated. Cassius and Brutus both die by suicide.

Junius Brutus ➤Brutus, Junius.

Juno In *The Tempest*, a character appearing in the masque celebrating the betrothal of Ferdinand and Miranda. In Roman mythology, the Queen of the gods and wife to Jupiter.

Jupiter In *Cymbeline*, an apparition that appears to Posthumus while he is asleep. Jupiter descends amid thunder and lightning, seated upon an eagle (V.iv). In Roman mythology, the King of the gods.

K

Katherina In *The Taming of the Shrew*, the "Shrew." The elder daughter of Baptista, she is married to Petruchio and is then tamed by his rough treatment. She concludes the play with a long speech advocating the total submission of wives to their husbands.

Katherine In *Henry V*, "fair Kate," daughter of Charles VI of France, whom Henry woos (V.ii). Henry insists on her hand as part of the peace treaty with France. The historical Catherine of Valois (1401–37) was the mother of Henry VI and after the death of Henry V married Owen Tudor; her grandson became Henry VII.

Katherine In *Henry VIII*, the historical Catherine of Aragon, first wife of King Henry. When she receives the news that Henry is divorcing her, her reaction is to regret the downfall of Wolsey, whom she has previously taken to be the source of her troubles. She dies, after seeing a vision of heavenly spirits.

Katherine In *Love's Labour's Lost*, a lady in attendance on the Princess of France. She is wooed by Dumain.

Kean, Edmund (*c.* 1787–1833) The greatest British actor of his time, who had his first success as Shylock (1814), and subsequently played Hamlet, Macbeth, Othello, and King Lear. He was much admired for his romantic and passionate acting, especially by Coleridge and Hazlitt.

Kemble, John Philip (1757–1823) British actor-manager, whose Shakespearean productions were among the earliest to attempt historical accuracy in sets and costumes. He played a number of Shakespearean roles, including Macbeth and Coriolanus, with his sister, Sarah ➤Siddons, as his leading lady.

Kemp, William [Also, Kempe] (*fl.* 1585–1603) English comic actor and dancer. One of the original shareholders in the ➤Lord Chamberlain's Men and in the ➤Globe theatre, he was also one of the principal actors listed in the first folio (1623) of Shakespeare's plays. He was known as a comic actor with the Earl of Leicester's Men and then with Lord ➤Strange's Men before joining the Chamberlain's company, where he played mostly fools and clowns. He seems to have favoured a physical style of clowning with extempore jesting, much like that of ➤Tarlton, and Shakespeare probably wrote such roles as Launce in *The Two Gentlemen of Verona*, Peter in *Romeo and Juliet*, and Dogberry in *Much Ado About Nothing* for him. He left the company in 1599, and the following year danced a marathon morris dance from London to Norwich, reported in his *Kemps Nine Daies Wonder* (1600). He may have returned to the Chamberlain's Men for a time in 1601, but left to act with other companies.

Kent, Earl of In *King Lear*, an honest counsellor to the King. He defends Cordelia to her father although this causes his banishment, and then returns in disguise to serve his master, even though he risks death in doing so. He stays with Lear throughout his sufferings on the heath, but never wins recognition from him. At the end of the play he refuses part rule of the country, saying that he must follow his master.

Kind-Hart's Dream [Full title, *Kind-Hart's Dreame. Conteining fiue Apparitions with their Inuectives against abuses raigning*] A pamphlet written by Henry ➤Chettle in 1592. In the preface is the first allusion to Shakespeare after that in Robert ➤Greene's ➤*Groatsworth of Wit*.

King John ➤John, King.

King John [Full title, *The Life and Death of King John*] A historical play by Shakespeare, written probably in 1596, and first printed in the 1623 first folio. The question of the play's sources is complicated by its relationship to the anonymous play *The Troublesome Raigne of John King of England*, printed in two parts in 1591. Because the edition of 1611 was published as "written by W.Sh." *The Troublesome Raigne* has sometimes been regarded as a later version derived from Shakespeare's play. However, it is now generally accepted to have been Shakespeare's principal source. *The Troublesome Raigne*, which was based on ➤Holinshed's *Chronicles* and Foxe's *Actes and Monuments of Martyrs*, is in many ways very close to *King John*, though for *King John* Shakespeare consulted Holinshed independently and made use of other historical material, including Hall's *The Union of the Two Noble and Illustre Famelies of Lancastre and Yorke* (1548) and possibly Radulph of Coggeshall's *English Chronicle*. Shakespeare's play is shorter and more compact than *The Troublesome Raigne*; it contains less comedy and it curbs the strong anti-Catholic bias in *The Troublesome Raigne*. The two plays differ in their presentation of John's right over that of his nephew Arthur to succeed Richard I as king, and Shakespeare emphasizes the case against John by making the bastard Philip Faulconbridge relate it (II.i) and by taking a sympathetic attitude to the rebel barons. The scene when Hubert prepares to blind Arthur (IV.i) is distinctly more pathetic in *King John*, where Arthur is a frightened child rather than, as in *The Troublesome Raigne*, an eloquent young man. But *King John* omits the scene in which John is poisoned by a monk. Both plays cover the whole reign of John (1199–1216) without any presentation of the signing of the Magna Carta, but *King John* has a rather different political emphasis. Shakespeare presents the barons' revolt against John as motivated not by John's efforts to curtail their rights but by disgust at his treatment of Arthur. Salisbury, Pembroke, and Bigot, the major rebels, are torn between their horror at John's crime and their equal horror at rebelling against their own king and country.

Dramatis Personae

King John

Prince Henry, *son to the King*

Arthur, Duke of Britain, *nephew to
the King*

Earl of Pembroke

Earl of Essex

Earl of Salisbury

Lord Bigot

Hubert de Burgh

Robert Faulconbridge

Philip the Bastard, *his half-brother*

James Gurney

Peter of Pomfret, *a prophet*

Philip, King of France

Lewis, the Dauphin

Limoges, Duke of Austria

Cardinal Pandulph, *papal legate*

Melun, *a French lord*

Chatillon, *ambassador from France*

Queen Elinor, *mother to King John*

Constance, *mother to Arthur*

Blanche of Spain, *niece to King John*

Lady Faulconbridge

*Lords, Ladies, Citizens of Angiers,
Sheriff, Heralds, Officers, Soldiers,
Messengers, and other Attendants*

The Story. John refuses the demand of King Philip of France that he surrender his throne to his youthful nephew Arthur, and invades France with an army under the leadership of Philip Faulconbridge (Philip the Bastard). After an indecisive battle at Angiers, a peace is arranged and sealed by the marriage of the Dauphin to John's niece, Blanche. However, the peace proves to be a short one; Pandulph, a papal legate, excommunicates John for not seating his (Pandulph's) choice as Archbishop of Canterbury, and orders Philip and the Dauphin to recommence the war. During the ensuing hostilities, Arthur is captured by the English. John orders his chamberlain, Hubert, to kill the boy and (although Hubert spares him) the English nobles suspect a murder when Arthur (who actually died escaping) is found dead. The disaffected nobles desert John and join the French army that, at Pandulph's insistence, has invaded England. To regain Pandulph's support, John surrenders his crown to the papal legate and receives it back in fief. During the battle at St Edmundsbury, Melun, a dying French lord, tells the English deserters that the Dauphin plans to execute them when John is defeated, and the nobles return to John. John dies of poison administered by a monk at Swinstead Abbey. An honourable peace follows and the English are united under the new King, Henry III.

King Lear ►Lear, King.

King Lear A tragedy by Shakespeare, written *c.* 1605, performed in 1606, and printed in 1608. The quarto of 1608 and first folio of 1623 differ in many ways, the former lacking about 100 lines which the latter has, but the folio having 300 lines of the quarto omitted. The quarto is described as a "Chronicle History" on the title-page, the folio text as a tragedy. Some editors now assume that the quarto text was Shakespeare's first version, the folio his own revision made a few years later, with changes that made the play more theatrical and may perhaps have reflected the demands of stage censorship. The story of the king who imposes a love-test on his daughters and ill-treats the one who loves him most is an old one and appears in many forms in European folklore. The story of Lear came into England first in Geoffrey of Monmouth's *Historia Regum Britanniae* (*c.* 1135), which Shakespeare probably used, perhaps in the original Latin. It was a popular story, and since many versions of it were available to him, Shakespeare seems to have taken details from a number of them. ➤Holinshed's *Chronicles* (second edition, 1587) supplied the names of Cornwall and Albany, but little else specifically; in William Harrison's story in his *Description of England* (printed in Holinshed's *Chronicles*) Shakespeare found a chapter on the religion of the ancient Britons, and in John Higgins's addition to *A Mirrour for Magistrates* (1574 and 1587) a detailed account of the reduction of Lear's retinue. It was ➤Spenser's account in *The Faerie Queene*, Book II Canto X, that provided the form of Cordelia's name and her death by hanging, since in the other sources she committed suicide. An earlier anonymous play on the Lear story, *The True Chronicle Historie of King Leir and his three daughters*, published in 1605 but probably written about 1590, is a more important source, although Shakespeare modified what he used of its plot very extensively. Shakespeare took material mainly from the earlier part of the play including the seven scenes which he condensed into I.i, the division of the kingdom, and a hint for Kent in the figure of Perillus who remains faithful to Leir throughout, though he is not banished, and Shakespeare also adapted from the old play the scene of Leir and Cordella symbolically kneeling towards the end. He changed the play's ending, in which Leir was restored to his throne and Cordella did not die, made Lear much older and more tragic than Leir, added the storm scene and Lear's madness. The Fool and the Gloucester subplot are both absent from the older play; the former is Shakespeare's invention, while the latter comes from an episode in ➤Sidney's *Arcadia*. In the *Arcadia*, the heroes meet the King of Paphlagonia, accompanied by his good son Leonatus, and hear how he was deceived by his bastard son Plexirtus, blinded, and cast out of his realm. The use Shakespeare makes of this story as a counterpart to that of Lear, comparing and contrasting the two fathers and the behaviour of good and bad children in each family, illustrates his skill in combining material from different sources. Two contemporary events seem also to have influenced the play. In 1603, an old knight, Sir Brian Annesley, who had three daughters, was reported unfit to look after his estate; his eldest daughter tried to have him declared insane, but his youngest, Cordell, defended her father and prevented his humiliation. He died in 1604, leaving most of his estate to Cordell; the eldest daughter and her husband disputed the will, but the Court of Chancery upheld it. No direct connection between this case and Shakespeare's play can be proved, although the similarity to Lear's situation is evident, but the other event, an apparent case of demoniac possession and the exposure of it as false in a pamphlet by Samuel Harsnett, *A Declaration of Egregious Popishe Impostures* (1603), is a direct source. The pamphlet describes how a group of household servants were encouraged to believe themselves possessed by devils and then "exorcised" by Jesuit priests. Shakespeare took from this the details of the language for Edgar's counterfeit madness, some descriptions for his storm scenes, and many words and phrases. Finally, the play was also influenced by Montaigne, especially by the language of ►Florio's translation of the *Essais* (1603). Nahum ►Tate, a dramatist of the Restoration period, adapted the play in 1679, and his version, with its happy ending but without the Fool, held the stage well into the eighteenth century.

Dramatis Personae

Lear, King of Britain	*Doctor*
King of France	*Fool*
Duke of Burgundy	*An Officer*
Duke of Cornwall	*Gentleman*
Duke of Albany	*A Herald*
Earl of Kent	*Servants to Cornwall*
Earl of Gloucester	Goneril, *daughter of Lear*
Edgar, *son of Gloucester*	Regan, *daughter of Lear*
Edmund, *bastard son of Gloucester*	Cordelia, *daughter of Lear*
Curan, *a courtier*	*Knights of Lear's train, Officers,*
Oswald, *steward to Goneril*	*Messengers, Soldiers, and Attendants*
Old Man, *Gloucester's tenant*	

The Story. Lear, intending to divide his kingdom between his three daughters, demands that they make public declarations of their love for him. When Cordelia declines to compete with her sisters, he disinherits her, banishes her supporter Kent, and divides the kingdom between his other daughters, Goneril and Regan, and their husbands, Albany and Cornwall. Goneril, with whom Lear first stays, treats him disrespectfully, and he goes to Regan, who refuses to admit him (and puts Kent, who, returning from banishment in disguise, has become a servant to Lear, in the stocks). Lear, driven to the point of madness by the behaviour of his daughters, rushes into a violent storm with Kent and the Fool. On the heath they meet Edgar, the legitimate son of the Duke of Gloucester (who has banished him because Edmund, the Duke's illegitimate son, has falsely persuaded the Duke that Edgar plans to murder him). Edgar is disguised as the mad Tom o'Bedlam. Lear has by this time utterly lost his mind; Gloucester has been blinded by Cornwall for aiding Lear. Lear, with Kent, and Gloucester, with Edgar, separately make their way to the coast to meet Cordelia, who is landing with the army of her husband, the King of France, to rescue Lear. There Edgar saves the life of his father and Cordelia tenderly cares for Lear, although they are taken prisoners by the English forces. Meanwhile, Regan and Goneril have fallen in love with Edmund, and the jealous Goneril poisons Regan and takes her own life when Edmund is killed by Edgar. It is revealed that Edmund has ordered Cordelia's execution, and Lear then enters carrying his dead daughter. Lear dies of a broken heart. Gloucester too has died moments after learning the identity of Edgar. The kingdom is left to Albany.

King of Antioch ►Antiochus.

King of Bohemia ➤Polixenes.

King of France In *All's Well That Ends Well*, the ailing King whom Helena cures and who later suspects Bertram of having murdered Helena. He speaks the Epilogue to the play.

King of France In *King Lear*, the husband of Cordelia. In the quarto text, he arrives with an army to rescue Lear and then returns to France, but he does not appear on stage after the first scene.

King of Naples ➤Alonso.

King of Navarre ➤Ferdinand.

King of Pentapolis ➤Simonides.

King of Sicilia ➤Leontes.

King of the Fairies ➤Oberon.

King's Men ➤Lord Chamberlain's Men.

Kozintsev, Grigori (1905–73) Russian film director, who made influential film versions of *Hamlet* (1964) and *King Lear* (1970).

Kurosawa, Akira (1910–98) Japanese film director, who made two influential films based on Shakespeare plays, *The Throne of Blood* (*Macbeth*, 1957) and *Ran* (*King Lear*, 1985).

Kyd, Thomas (1558–94) English playwright and member, with ➤Greene, ➤Nashe, and ➤Marlowe of the "University Wits". He translated *Cornelia* from the French of Garnier (published 1595), and may have written *Soliman and Perseda* (*c.* 1592). He is most famous for *The Spanish Tragedy* (*c.* 1587, staged 1592), which influenced *Hamlet*, and possibly also the hypothetical ➤*Ur-Hamlet*. He died having suffered torture and disgrace for his association with ➤Marlowe.

L

Laertes In *Hamlet*, the son of Polonius and brother of Ophelia. He cautions Ophelia against Hamlet's love. Later he seeks a duel with Hamlet (who has killed his father, Polonius, and whom he holds responsible for Ophelia's death) and falls in readily with Claudius's plot to ensure Hamlet's death by using a poisoned foil.

Lafew [Also, Lafeu] In *All's Well That Ends Well*, a sagacious old lord.

Lancaster, Prince John of In *1* and *2 Henry IV*, the younger brother of Prince Hal, and son of Henry IV. In *1 Henry IV*, he is at the battle of Shrewsbury, where he is commended for his conduct in battle by Hal (V.iv). In *2 Henry IV*, he leads an army against the rebels and executes them after he has promised them pardon if they disband. In *Henry V*, he appears as Duke of Bedford, and in *1 Henry VI*, as Regent of France, he captures Orleans and Rouen, where he dies (III.ii).

La Pucelle ➤Joan of Arc.

Lartius ➤Titus Lartius.

Launce In *The Two Gentlemen of Verona*, a clownish servant of Proteus, who appears with his dog Crab.

Laurence, Friar In *Romeo and Juliet*, a Franciscan friar, the confidant and adviser of Romeo and Juliet. He marries them in a secret ceremony in his cell.

Lavatch [Also, Lavache] A clown in *All's Well That Ends Well*.

Lavinia In *Titus Andronicus*, the daughter of Titus who marries Bassianus, son of the former Emperor of Rome. She is raped and mutilated by Tamora's sons, Demetrius and Chiron, and is finally killed by Titus.

Lear, King In *King Lear*, the protagonist, King of Britain. He tests the devotion of his daughters by requiring a public profession of their love for him, in return for which each will receive a third of his kingdom. This brings a gradual alienation from his family, as he first denies parental affinity with Cordelia, and then is rejected by both Regan and Goneril, who are by that time in possession of his kingdom. He invokes the curse of sterility upon Goneril, desiring that the storm "Crack nature's moulds, all germens spill at once / That make ingrateful man" (III.ii). As he wanders on the heath in the storm, accompanied by his Fool, he goes mad. He is assisted by the disguised Kent and by the Earl of Gloucester. In his sufferings, he comes to a new understanding of his own past follies and of injustice within society. He is reunited with Cordelia and returns to sanity, but dies, apparently of a broken heart, after Cordelia is hanged.

Le Beau　In *As You Like It*, a courtier in attendance on Frederick, the usurping duke.

Lena, Popilius　In *Julius Caesar*, a senator. His conversation with Caesar just before the assassination alarms the conspirators, who fear that their plan has been discovered.

Lennox　In *Macbeth*, a Scottish thane. Convinced of Macbeth's guilt (after the murder of Banquo and as a result of Macbeth's behaviour at the banquet), he joins the anti-Macbeth faction headed by Malcolm.

Leonardo　In *The Merchant of Venice*, the servant of Bassanio.

Leonato　In *Much Ado About Nothing*, the governor of Messina; the uncle of Beatrice and father of Hero.

Leonine　In *Pericles*, the attendant of Dionyza, employed to murder Marina. As he prepares to do so, he is attacked by pirates and runs off. However, he tells Dionyza that Marina is dead, and Dionyza poisons him.

Leontes　In *The Winter's Tale*, the King of Sicilia and husband of Hermione. He is based on the Pandosto of Robert ►Greene's *Pandosto*, from which the play was taken. He becomes convinced that his wife Hermione has committed adultery with Polixenes and has her put on trial. After sixteen years of penitence he is reunited with her.

Lepidus, M. Aemilius　In *Julius Caesar*, the historical Marcus Aemilius Lepidus, a Roman leader who becomes one of the triumvirate after Caesar's death. He witnesses the assassination and joins Octavius in the civil strife following. In *Antony and Cleopatra*, he attempts to serve as a moderator between his fellow triumvirs, Antony and Octavius, but is deposed and eliminated by Octavius.

Lewis, the Dauphin　[Also, Louis]　In *Henry V*, the son of Charles VI of France. He sends Henry a present of tennis balls to mock his claim upon the French throne. He later boasts of French prowess when preparations are being made for the battle of Agincourt.

Lewis, the Dauphin　In *King John*, the historical Louis (VIII), son of Philip II of France. To bring about peace with France a marriage is arranged between him and John's niece Blanche of Spain.

Lewis XI　In *3 Henry VI*, the historical Louis XI, King of France. He promises aid to Margaret in her fight against Edward IV, then turns against her when Warwick offers to arrange Edward's marriage to Lewis's sister-in-law, Lady Bona.

When Edward marries Lady Grey, Lewis is reconciled to Margaret and pledges arms to help restore Henry to the throne.

Lieutenant In *Coriolanus*, an officer in Aufidius's army, whose account of Coriolanus's popularity and superiority on the battlefield arouses Aufidius's jealousy (IV.vii).

Lieutenant In *3 Henry VI*, the Lieutenant of the Tower who apologizes to King Henry for having kept him prisoner (IV.vi).

Ligarius In *Julius Caesar*, one of the conspirators against Caesar. He does not, however, take part in the assassination.

Lincoln, Bishop of In *Henry VIII*, the historical John Longland. The King asks him to admit that he formerly advocated the divorce (II.iv).

Lion In *A Midsummer Night's Dream*, the part played by the joiner, Snug, in the interpolated play of *Pyramus and Thisbe*.

Lodge, Thomas (*c.* 1558–1625) English writer of a range of prose works, including *The Defence of Poetry, Music, and Stage Plays* (1580) in answer to Puritan attacks on the stage, and *Rosalynde* (1590), a pastoral romance used by Shakespeare as the basis for *As You Like It*. He also wrote poetry, including *Scylla's Metamorphosis* (1589), which was to initiate a fashion for Ovidian erotic narrative poems, followed by Shakespeare in *Venus and Adonis*. He subsequently became a doctor, travelled abroad on several occasions, and published medical works, as well as a number of translations.

Lodovico In *Othello*, a kinsman of Brabantio. He produces the letters (found in Roderigo's pockets) that incriminate Iago and, after Othello's death, vehemently denounces Iago.

Lodowick, Friar In *Measure for Measure*, the name assumed by the disguised Duke Vincentio.

London Prodigal, The A comedy performed by the King's Men at the ►Globe and published in 1605, attributed to Shakespeare at that time, and included by Chetwood in the second issue of the third folio (1664). It is not now considered to have been by Shakespeare.

Longaville In *Love's Labour's Lost*, one of the three lords attending the King of Navarre at his rural academy. He falls in love with Maria.

Lord Admiral's Men [Also, Admiral's Men; until 1585, Lord Howard's Company; after 1596, Earl of Nottingham's Company; after 1603, Prince Henry's Company; finally, Elector Palatine's Company, or Palsgrave's Company] Elizabethan and Jacobean theatrical company, led for a time by Edward ►Alleyn. This company and the ►Lord Chamberlain's Men were the two most important companies performing on the Elizabethan stage. ►Henslowe's *Diary* gives more information about this company than is available about any other. When their first patron, Charles Howard, became, in 1585, Lord High Admiral, they changed their name from Lord Howard's Company to the Lord Admiral's Men. For a time they joined ►Strange's Men and toured (1593–94) the provinces under the leadership of Edward Alleyn. In London after 1594, Henslowe (whose stepdaughter had married Alleyn) was the backer and manager of the company and received one half of the entrance money. They played at his ►Rose theatre every weekday from October to Lent and from Easter to midsummer, when they left to tour the provinces for three months. In 1596 they took the newest title of their patron as their name and were called the Earl of Nottingham's Company. After 1600 the company moved to the newly built ►Fortune theatre on the north side of the Thames. In the reign of James I they became known as Prince Henry's Company; later they were under the patronage of the Elector Palatine and were consequently called the Elector Palatine's Company, or, sometimes, the Palsgrave's Company.

Lord Chamberlain In *Henry VIII*, an official at Wolsey's feast and at the arraignment of Cranmer. He is in charge of the christening of the infant Elizabeth.

Lord Chamberlain's Men [Also, Chamberlain's Men; until 1594, Strange's Men or Derby's Men; after 1603, King's Men] Elizabethan theatrical company. They had formerly been Strange's Men, or Derby's Men (after Lord Strange became the Earl of Derby in 1572). This earlier company, in existence from the 1560s, was a group of travelling actors until they began to perform in the 1580s at court. In 1591 they played at the ►Curtain, in 1592 at the ►Rose. Their members included James and Richard ►Burbage, William ►Kemp, Thomas ►Pope, John ►Heminges, and Augustine ►Phillips. In the reorganization of companies during 1594, most of the members of Derby's Company formed a new company under the patronage of Henry Carey, who became Lord Chamberlain in 1585, and his son, George Carey, who became Lord Chamberlain in 1597. About 1594 Shakespeare and Richard Burbage joined the newly formed Lord Chamberlain's Men as shareholders as well as actors. Other members of the company included at various times Henry ►Condell, William ►Sly, Christopher Beeston, and John Duke. From that time on, Shakespeare wrote plays for no other company, and the company also performed many of ►Jonson's plays. They are thought to have performed at the ►Theatre, the playhouse in ►Newington Butts, the ►Curtain, and the ►Swan until the ►Globe was built in 1599. Between 1594 and 1603 they gave thirty-two performances at court. By the time they became the King's Men, in 1603, they had presumably acted Shakespeare's *As You Like It, The Comedy of Errors, Hamlet, Henry IV, Henry V, Henry VI, Julius Caesar, King John, Love's Labour's Lost, The Merchant of Venice, The Merry Wives of Windsor, A Midsummer Night's Dream, Much Ado About Nothing, Richard II, Richard III, Romeo and Juliet, Titus Andronicus, Twelfth Night,* and *The Two Gentlemen of Verona.* As the King's Men they continued acting at the Globe, and in 1609 they took ►Blackfriars theatre as their winter quarters. Between 1603 and 1616, they gave approximately twelve performances at court each year. Shakespeare is last mentioned as an actor in their performance of Jonson's *Sejanus*, first acted in 1603. In 1611 they performed *Cymbeline*, *Macbeth*, *The Winter's Tale*, and Jonson's *Catiline*. In 1619, when they were issued a new patent, some new shareholders, including Nathan ➤Field, joined them. The company dissolved in 1642 when the theatres were closed, but the actors of the Chamberlain's collaborated in publishing (1647) the first folio edition of ➤Beaumont and ➤Fletcher.

Lord Chancellor   In *Henry VIII*, the historical Sir Thomas Wriothesley. He is president of the Council arraigning Cranmer.

Lord Chief Justice   In *2 Henry IV*, the historical Sir William Gascoigne. In the play he warns Falstaff and orders him to repay Mistress Quickly. He later fears that Prince Hal as King may hold a grudge against him, because once Hal was imprisoned by his order. The new King, however, confirms his impartial justice and orders him to enforce the penalties against Falstaff and his followers.

Lord Howard's Company   ➤Lord Admiral's Men.

Lorenzo   In *The Merchant of Venice*, a Venetian gentleman in love with Jessica. He elopes with her, taking part of Shylock's treasure.

Lovel, Lord   In *Richard III*, a follower of Richard. He executes Hastings and brings in his head (III.v).

Lovell, Sir Thomas   In *Henry VIII*, a courtier in King Henry's confidence.

Lover's Complaint, A   Stanzaic poem in rhyme royal published with Shakespeare's Sonnets in 1609 as his work, though this attribution was long doubted. It is now accepted as Shakespeare's, written probably between 1602 and 1605, and recalling plays of that period, including *Hamlet* and *Troilus and Cressida*. It consists of the lamentation of a young woman who has been abandoned by her lover, overheard by the poet.

Love's Labour's Lost   A comedy by Shakespeare, first acted *c.* 1594–95, printed in quarto in 1598. The full original title (*A Pleasant Conceited Comedie called Love's Labour's Lost as it was presented before her Highness this last Christmas, Newly corrected and augmented by W. Shakespeare. Imprinted 1598*) marks the first appearance of Shakespeare's name on a play's title page. The earlier version, which some have thought to be implied by this title, probably does not exist. No literary source has been found for the plot, which is perhaps Shakespeare's invention, but the play's courtly characters have historical sources. The King of Navarre is based on King Henry of Navarre (King Henry IV of France in 1589) who established a philosophical academy. The Princess may well be Marguerite de Valois, Henry's estranged wife, who came on an embassy to him in 1578. John ➤Lyly was clearly an influence on the play's style, especially in the comic use of pedantry and the mockery of the language of logic and rhetoric, for instance in the dialogues of Armado and

Moth in I.ii and III.i and Armado's letter in IV.i. The treatment of characters such as the braggart Armado and the pedant Holofernes recalls the Italian *commedia dell'arte*. Many of the names in the play, including Berowne (or Biron), Longaville, Dumain, Boyet, and Mercade, were those of contemporary French noblemen, supporters of Henry of Navarre, whom Elizabeth at this time supported. *Love's Labour's Lost* was one of Shakespeare's most topical plays and numerous contemporary identifications have been suggested for the characters, for instance, ►Nashe for Moth, the scholar Gabriel Harvey for Armado or Holofernes, and figures from ►Raleigh's circle for various of the characters. The Muscovite masque in V.ii may well have been influenced by Shakespeare's recollection of the Christmas revelry at Gray's Inn in 1594–95, when Twelfth Night entertainment was provided by revellers dressed as ambassadors from Russia. After the closing of the theatres in 1642, there is no record of any performance for nearly two hundred years.

Dramatis Personae

Ferdinand, King of Navarre	Moth, *page to Armado*
Berowne	*A Forester*
Longaville	The Princess of France, *wooed by*
Dumain	Ferdinand
Boyet	Rosaline, *wooed by Berowne*
Marcade	Maria, *wooed by Longaville*
Don Adriano de Armado	Katherine, *wooed by Dumain*
Sir Nathaniel, *a curate*	Jaquenetta, *a country wench*
Holofernes, *a schoolmaster*	*Officers and Others, Attendants on the*
Dull, *a constable*	*King and Princess*
Costard, *a clown*	

The Story. It is a stylized play with a simple plot, hinging upon the revenge of Cupid on four men (Ferdinand, King of Navarre, and his attendant lords Berowne, Longaville, and Dumain) who have vowed to deny love for three years and devote themselves to study. The ladies (the Princess of France and her attendant ladies Rosaline, Maria, and Katherine), having come upon the academic retreat, are forbidden to enter, and thereupon determine to punish the lords by causing them to break their vows. This is accomplished (although not without some remorse on the part of each lord, but as Berowne argues, women in themselves provide a worthy subject of study and, in addition, forswearing their vows may be less dangerous than denying love's power), but when the lovers woo their ladies in Russian costume, the ladies confuse them by wearing masks and then exchanging them. In their own persons, the lovers then engage their ladies in a game of wit and sit with them to watch a pageant, but their revels are cut short by the news of the death of the father of the Princess. The ladies depart, and a year's penance is laid on each lover before he may have his lady. Contrast to the main plot concerning the courtly lovers is provided by the subplot of the rivalry of Armado and Costard for the affections of a country girl, Jaquenetta.

Love's Labour's Won   A title listed by Francis ►Meres in *Palladis Tamia* (1598) as that of a comedy by Shakespeare; it also appears in a bookseller's list of 1603. It may be a lost play or an alternative name for another play.

Lowin, John   (1576–1659) English actor of the Jacobean period. He is mentioned as one of the principal actors of Shakespeare's plays in the first folio (1623). It is recorded that he acted "with mighty applause" the parts of Falstaff, Volpone (in ►Jonson's comedy of that name), and Epicure Mammon (in Jonson's *The Alchemist*). Lowin ended his days keeping the Three Pigeons, a tavern at Brentford.

Luce   In *The Comedy of Errors*, a female servant to Adriana.

Lucentio   In *The Taming of the Shrew*, a young student from Pisa, who changes clothes with his servant Tranio. His wooing of Bianca forms the subplot of the play.

Lucetta   In *The Two Gentlemen of Verona*, a waiting-woman to Julia.

Luciana   In *The Comedy of Errors*, the sister of Adriana who is wooed by Antipholus of Syracuse.

Luciano   In *Hamlet*, a character in the play presented before the King. He is the murderer of his uncle, the sleeping Gonzago.

Lucilius   In *Julius Caesar*, a friend of Brutus and Cassius. He describes (IV.ii) the coldness with which Cassius received him as Brutus's emissary.

Lucilius   In *Timon of Athens*, a servant of Timon. One of Timon's generous acts is to give Lucilius enough money to win the girl he wants to marry.

Lucio   In *Measure for Measure*, a "fantastic" (i.e., profligate) and friend of Claudio who urges Isabella to intercede for Claudio. Not recognizing the Duke in a friar's disguise, he slanders the Duke and then reports that a friar has been maligning the Duke. The Duke finally orders him to marry a prostitute who has borne his child.

Lucius   In *Julius Caesar*, a boy, servant to Brutus.

Lucius   In *Timon of Athens*, a flattering lord; also, in the same play, a servant of this lord who is sent to recover a debt from Timon.

Lucius   In *Titus Andronicus*, a son of Titus. After his brothers are executed, his sister Lavinia raped, and his father mutilated, he joins the invading Goths. The emperor Saturninus is overthrown, Tamora and Aaron are killed, and Lucius becomes the ruler of Rome. He has a son who is also named Lucius.

Lucius, Caius   In *Cymbeline*, a Roman general who invades Britain. He discovers Imogen, disguised as a boy, and she follows his army. When Lucius and Imogen are captured by the Britons, Cymbeline recognizes his daughter and frees Lucius.

Lucullus   In *Timon of Athens*, a flattering lord.

Lucy, Sir William   In *1 Henry VI*, a leader who implores York and Somerset to go to Talbot's body after his defeat.

Lychorida   In *Pericles*, the nurse of Marina.

Lymoges   ➤Austria, Duke of.

Lyly, John   (*c.* 1554–1606) English writer of prose romances and plays. He was chiefly famous for *Euphues, the Anatomy of Wit* (1578), and *Euphues his England* (1580), didactic romances that popularized the elaborate and decorative prose style known as Euphuism. Its rhetorical bases are antithesis, alliteration, syntactic balance, and pseudo-scientific simile. Shakespeare often mocks the style, particularly in *Love's Labour's Lost* and *1 Henry IV*. Lyly also wrote comedies for the boys' companies between 1584 and 1590, and these too influenced Shakespeare.

Lysander   In *A Midsummer Night's Dream*, a young Athenian in love with Hermia. He runs off with her and while sleeping in the woods is mistaken by Puck for Demetrius. Puck squeezes in his eyes the juice of a magic herb, making him fall in love with Helena, and recriminations follow between him and Hermia. Oberon orders Puck to restore the lovers to their natural state, and Theseus then sanctions Lysander's marriage with Hermia.

Lysimachus   In *Pericles*, the governor of Mytilene.

M

Macbeth   The chief character of *Macbeth*. He is first of all Thane of Glamis and then inherits the title of Thane of Cawdor from an executed traitor. Instigated by a prophecy from three Witches that he will become King, and urged on by his wife, he murders Duncan, and has himself proclaimed King. To secure his position, he is driven to commit further criminal acts, and plunges his country into civil war. After he is killed in battle by Macduff he is described as a "dead butcher" (V.viii).

Macbeth [Full title, *The Tragedy of Macbeth*]   A tragedy by Shakespeare, probably written in 1605 or 1606. It was seen by Simon ➤Forman at the ➤Globe theatre on 20 April 1611, but is almost certain to have been first produced several years earlier. It was printed in the 1623 first folio, but there is some probability that cuts were made from the stage manuscript. The Hecate scenes, including the Witches' songs, are probably ➤Middleton's. In the Restoration period ➤Davenant made it into an opera. The play followed in the wake of the Gunpowder Plot, and there are various topical references, especially in the Porter scene (II.iii). Shakespeare's main source was ➤Holinshed's *Chronicles*, probably in the 1587 edition that he used elsewhere, although he may also have seen illustrations from the 1577 edition. He used Holinshed not only for the account of Macbeth's life but also for the story of the murder of King Duff by Donwald, and for the description of ancient Scottish life and customs. Shakespeare altered Holinshed's account of Macbeth's life in a number of ways; the involvement of Banquo, supposedly King James's ancestor, was omitted and Banquo's character generally whitewashed, while Macbeth was made more villainous. Holinshed's Duncan was a weak and unsatisfactory monarch whom Macbeth assassinated with the help of friends, and after the murder Macbeth ruled in a just and beneficent way for ten years before he was overcome by guilt and proceeded to further crimes. Holinshed's account of the murder of King Duff in fact bears more resemblance to the murder of Duncan in Shakespeare's play, although the subsequent career of Duff's murderer, Donwald, does not parallel Macbeth's. Holinshed describes Duff as a good king and Donwald as a kinsman whom he especially trusted; Donwald, urged on by his wife, secretly murdered Duff by cutting his throat while Duff was a guest in his home. After Duff's murder monstrous events took place in the kingdom. There were a number of other chronicles of Scottish history available to Shakespeare. He probably did not use William Stewart's *The Buik of the Chronicles of Scotland*, which was available in manuscript in King James's private library, although this has been disputed, but he may well have seen the *Rerum Scoticarum Historia* (1582) by George Buchanan, which contains a

Macbeth very similar in character to Shakespeare's and also describes the remorse felt by a royal murderer, King Kenneth, in much fuller terms than Holinshed. John Leslie's *De Origine Scotorum* (1578) supplied a Macbeth who killed Duncan without any assistance from Banquo, and Shakespeare may have seen this, although this, like Buchanan's work, was only available in Latin. James's interests were a significant consideration in the composition of *Macbeth*, and Shakespeare may well have read some of James's own work for it, especially the *Daemonologie* (1597), which could have provided hints for the treatment of the Witches. The chronicle sources for *Macbeth* provided Shakespeare with very little dialogue and few detailed encounters; these he may have derived from some of ➤Seneca's tragedies. *Medea* or *Agammemnon* may have suggested ideas for the characterization of Lady Macbeth, and both of these had been translated by John Studley. The atmosphere of concentrated evil is particularly Senecan and recalls Shakespeare's own earlier works, the poem *The Rape of Lucrece*, and *Richard III*. Finally, as might seem appropriate in a tragedy of damnation, Shakespeare drew heavily on the Bible.

Dramatis Personae

Duncan, King of Scotland
Malcolm, *son of Duncan*
Donalbain, *son of Duncan*
Macbeth, *general of the army*
Banquo, *general of the army*
Macduff, *Scottish nobleman*
Lennox, *Scottish nobleman*
Ross, *Scottish nobleman*
Menteith, *Scottish nobleman*
Angus, *Scottish nobleman*
Caithness, *Scottish nobleman*
Fleance, *son of Banquo*
Siward, Earl of Northumberland,
    general of the English forces
Young Siward, *his son*
Seyton, *officer to Macbeth*

Boy, son to Macduff
An English Doctor
A Scottish Doctor
A Sergeant
A Porter
An Old Man
Lady Macbeth
Lady Macduff
Gentlewoman to Lady Macbeth
Hecate, *and Three Witches*
Lords, Gentlemen, Officers, Soldiers,
    Murderers, Attendants, and
    Messengers
The Ghost of Banquo, and other
    Apparitions

The Story. Macbeth and Banquo, Scottish generals, are returning from a victorious campaign when they meet upon the heath three Witches who hail them, prophesying that Macbeth will be Thane of Cawdor and King hereafter, and that Banquo will beget kings. Part of the prophecy is immediately fulfilled when a messenger announces that Duncan, King of Scotland, has promoted Macbeth to Thane of Cawdor. Lady Macbeth, having learned of the Witches, plays upon her husband, already tempted by dreams of royal power, to kill the King, who falls into their hands when he arrives for a visit at the castle of Macbeth. But when the murder is done,

Macbeth is completely unnerved. Lady Macbeth returns to Duncan's room with the daggers that Macbeth has neglected to leave behind. Into this scene of horror comes the sound of knocking at the gate. The murder is discovered, and Macbeth puts the grooms to death to conceal his action. Duncan's sons, Malcolm and Donalbain, flee from Scotland, and Macbeth is crowned. He then hires murderers to kill Banquo and his son, Fleance, but the latter escapes. At a banquet given by Macbeth, the ghost of Banquo appears to him. Macbeth returns to consult with the Witches, who show him apparitions that tell him to beware Macduff, that "none of woman born / Shall harm Macbeth," and that he shall be safe until "Birnam Wood to high Dunsinane Hill / Shall come" (IV.i). However, he is then also shown a procession of future kings, all descendants of Banquo. Macduff, meanwhile, has gone to England to raise an army with Malcolm to defeat Macbeth and there learns that his wife and children have been killed at the order of Macbeth. Macbeth, preparing to meet the invading army, learns of Lady Macbeth's death. His response is that "She should have died hereafter" (V.v). The army advances, bearing branches cut from Birnam Wood for concealment, and Macduff who was "from his mother's womb / Untimely ripped" (V.vii) kills Macbeth. Malcolm is crowned King of Scotland.

Macbeth, Lady   In *Macbeth*, the wife of Macbeth. Hearing of the Witches' prophecy for her husband, she is eager for him to gain the throne at once, and spurs him on to murder Duncan. At first, her wifely support is vital to him, but eventually he makes his plans without her. She betrays her part in Duncan's murder in the sleepwalking scene. She dies, probably by suicide.

Macduff   In *Macbeth*, the Thane of Fife. He discovers the murdered Duncan and is the first to suspect Macbeth. He goes to England to beg Malcolm to return with him to fight Macbeth, and there hears of the slaughter of his wife and children. He was born by Caesarian section, and thus not naturally "of woman born" (V.iii). Therefore, according to the Witches' prophecy, he is the only agent capable of destroying Macbeth, whom he kills in battle.

Macduff, Lady   In *Macbeth*, Macduff's wife. She and her son are murdered on Macbeth's orders.

McKellen, Sir Ian   (1939–   ) British actor who has performed in many Shakespearean roles for several companies, including Richard II and Hamlet (Prospect Players, 1968–70, 1971), Edgar (Actors' Company, 1973), Coriolanus (National Theatre, 1984), Richard III (Royal National Theatre, 1990). He co-scripted and starred in a film version of *Richard III* (1996).

Macklin, Charles   (1699–1797) Irish actor and playwright, who came to fame in 1741 as Shylock in *The Merchant of Venice*, restoring Shakespeare's play to the stage in place of the adaptation by George Granville (1701). He continued to play the role until he was nearly ninety.

Macmorris   In *Henry V*, an Irish captain.

Macready, William   (1793–1873) British actor-manager who managed Covent Garden theatre from 1837 to 1839 and Drury Lane theatre from 1841 to 1848. He played most of Shakespeare's leading tragic roles, but is now more celebrated for restoring Shakespeare's own texts (particularly that of *King Lear*) to the stage in place of the adaptations written in the Restoration and eighteenth century.

Maecenas   In *Antony and Cleopatra*, a friend of Octavius who tries to reconcile the triumvirs. He later supports Octavius against Antony.

Malcolm   In *Macbeth*, elder son of Duncan. He flees to England when Duncan is murdered and is there approached by Macduff, who hopes he will return and claim the throne. To test Macduff's loyalty he represents himself as a man of disgraceful and vile character (IV.iii). At Macbeth's defeat he is crowned King of Scotland. Historically, he was Malcolm III, King of Scotland (1054–93); son of Duncan I. He ascended the throne on the defeat of the usurper Macbeth by Earl Siward of Northumbria on 27 July 1054, which was followed by his own victory at Lumphanan in Aberdeenshire, where Macbeth was slain.

Malvolio   In *Twelfth Night*, Olivia's steward, who is punished for his pomposity by the device of a forged letter, purporting to come from Olivia and declaring her love for him. He is humiliated by Sir Toby Belch, Maria, and Feste.

Mamillius   In *The Winter's Tale*, the young Prince, son of Leontes and Hermione. He gives the play its title, when he says, "A sad tale's best for winter" (II.i). His death is later reported.

Marcade   In *Love's Labour's Lost*, the messenger who brings the news of the death of the King of France.

Marcellus   In *Hamlet*, an officer on watch upon the battlements who has twice seen the Ghost (of Hamlet's father) when the play opens.

March, (5th) Earl of   ➤Mortimer, Edmund.

Marcius   [Also, Young Marcius]   In *Coriolanus*, the young son of Coriolanus who inherits his father's bellicose nature.

Marcus Andronicus   In *Titus Andronicus*, a tribune of the people and the brother of Titus. He tries to comfort Titus and to assist Lavinia after her mutilation, showing her how, in order to reveal the wrongdoers, to hold a stick in her mouth and write in the sand.

Mardian   In *Antony and Cleopatra*, a eunuch in attendance on Cleopatra. He is sent by Cleopatra to tell Antony that she is dead (IV.xiv).

Margarelon   In *Troilus and Cressida*, a bastard son of Priam, King of Troy.

Margaret In *1, 2,* and *3 Henry VI* and *Richard III*, the historical Margaret of Anjou, a protagonist against the Yorkist party. She is first depicted as a young girl, the daughter of Reignier, then after her marriage with Henry VI as a determined enemy of York and Gloucester and in love with Suffolk. In *3 Henry VI*, she is characterized as a strong woman fighting to keep the throne for her son. Her last appearance, in *Richard III*, is as an old woman who leads Queen Elizabeth and the Duchess of York in a chorus of cursing against Richard. This last is unhistorical.

Margaret In *Much Ado About Nothing*, a gentlewoman attending Hero, whom she impersonates in a pretended assignation with Borachio.

Maria In *Love's Labour's Lost*, a lady attending the Princess of France. She is wooed by Longaville.

Maria In *Twelfth Night*, Olivia's witty waiting-woman. She sets up the plot to humiliate Malvolio by writing a love letter in a hand like Olivia's.

Mariana In *All's Well That Ends Well*, a Florentine girl.

Mariana In *Measure for Measure*, a lady betrothed to Angelo, but after the loss of her dowry, rejected by him. She takes Isabella's place in Angelo's bed, and later the Duke orders him to marry her. It was in allusion to her that Tennyson wrote his *Mariana* and *Mariana in the South*.

Marina In *Pericles*, the virtuous and beautiful daughter of Pericles and Thaisa. Rescued by pirates from Dionyza, she is sold to the keeper of a brothel, where she keeps her virtue. She is finally reunited with Pericles and marries Lysimachus, Governor of Mytilene. In Gower's *Confessio Amantis*, from which Shakespeare got his plot, she is called Thaise.

Mark Antony [Also, Antony; Latin, Marcus Antonius] In *Julius Caesar*, one of the triumvirs with Octavius and Lepidus after Caesar's death. Brutus mistakenly believes him to be merely a minion of Caesar, and therefore allows him to deliver a funeral oration over Caesar's dead body as it lies in front of the Capitol. The famous speech beginning "Friends, Romans, countrymen, lend me your ears" (III.ii), although at first seeming to praise the conspirators, as Antony has promised, in fact turns the populace against them. With Octavius, he later defeats Brutus and Cassius at the Battle of Philippi (after dividing the rule of the Roman empire with Octavius). He appears as the hero of *Antony and Cleopatra*, which has its setting in the later years of his life. Despite his love for Cleopatra, he returns to Rome from Egypt on hearing of the death of his wife Fulvia and the threat of further civil war. After marrying Octavia as a political expedient to bind Octavius closer to him, Antony returns to Cleopatra in Egypt. As a result, war with Octavius breaks out. His fleet is defeated at Actium, and he stabs himself upon hearing a false report of Cleopatra's death.

Marlowe, Christopher (1564–93) English poet and dramatist, son of a shoe-maker, educated at Cambridge University. By 1587 he was attached to the ►Lord Admiral's Men as a playwright, enjoying the familiar acquaintance of Sir Walter ►Raleigh and other writers, adventurers, and men about town. He was the "gracer of tragedians" reproved for atheism by ►Greene in his ►*Groatsworth of Wit* (1592). ►Chettle is probably referring to him when he speaks of "one he cares not to be acquainted with." Marlowe freely avowed the heretical and even atheistic views for which eventually, in 1593, he was called to account. Information against him was lodged with the authorities, but before he could be brought to trial, he was slain by an Ingram Frizer in a tavern brawl at Deptford. This is the generally accepted circumstance of his death, although many other accounts have been circulated. Some have advanced the theory that Marlowe, secretly involved in politics (per-haps as a French agent), was the victim of a conspiracy. Even though the relative datings are often uncertain, his plays probably influenced Shakespeare's, though the opposite may in some cases be true. *Tamburlaine*, in two parts, probably first acted about 1587 and licensed for printing in 1590, is universally ascribed to him on in-ternal evidence alone. *Doctor Faustus* appears to have been first acted in 1588, but it was not entered on the Stationers' Register for publication until 1601. It is known to have been produced by ►Henslowe twenty-four times between 1594 and 1597, and subsequently it was performed frequently by English companies in several of the chief German cities. Two separate versions exist, printed in 1604 and 1616. *The Jew of Malta*, another tragedy, performed *c.* 1592, was frequently acted in England between 1591 and 1596, and was also given by English companies on the Conti-nent. Marlowe's historical play *Edward II* was entered on the Stationers' Register in 1593. About the same time, he collaborated with Thomas ►Nashe in writing *The Tragedy of Dido, Queen of Carthage*, and wrote *The Massacre at Paris* alone. He also wrote the unfinished erotic poem, *Hero and Leander*, and translated ►Ovid's *Elegies* and Lucan's First Book into English verse.

Marowitz, Charles (1934–) American theatre director, critic, and playwright. After working on the Theatre of Cruelty season at the ►Royal Shakespeare Com-pany with Peter ►Brook in the early 1960s, he began to produce radically rewrit-ten versions of Shakespeare, often in collage form. These included *Hamlet* (1965), *Macbeth* (1969), *Othello* (1972), and *The Taming of the Shrew* (1973).

Marston, John [Pseudonym, W. Kinsayder] (1576–1634) English dramatist, satirist, and divine. Under his pseudonym, he published *The Metamorphosis of Pig-malions Image, and certaine Satyres* (1598) and *The Scourge of Villanie* (1598), which were, with other satirical and erotic works, ordered to be burned (1599) by John Whitgift, Archbishop of Canterbury. Marston then began writing for the stage. *The History of Antonio and Mellida* (1599) and its sequel, *Antonio's Revenge* (1600), were both published in 1602. Ben ►Jonson attacked Marston in *The Poetaster* (1601), with the result that Marston, collaborating with Thomas ►Dekker, caricatured Jonson in *Satiromastix* (1602). Jonson and Marston subsequently became friends, however, and

Marston dedicated *The Malcontent* (1604) to Jonson. They collaborated (1605) with George ➤Chapman in *Eastward Ho*, and all three were imprisoned for a time for certain scenes in the play ridiculing the Scots. Among Marston's other plays are *What You Will* (1601), *The Dutch Courtezan* (1604), *Parasitaster, or the Fawn* (*c.* 1605), *The Wonder of Women, or the Tragedy of Sophonisba* (*c.* 1605), and parts of *Histriomastix* (*c.* 1599) and *Jack Drum's Entertainment* (*c.* 1600). He gave up writing for the stage in 1616 to become rector of Christchurch, Hampshire.

Martext, Sir Oliver In *As You Like It*, a country curate.

Martius In *Titus Andronicus*, one of the four sons of Titus.

Marullus In *Julius Caesar*, a tribune. He and Flavius fear the growing power of Caesar and attempt to stop a triumphal celebration from being held for him.

masque [Also, mask] A type of courtly dramatic entertainment originating from the silent entrance by masked figures into a banquet or gathering of distinguished guests, and completed by a dance between the masquers and those already present. ➤Lyly and ➤Jonson established the term in the French form "masque" in preference to "mask." The form started in Italy, where it received much of its original form and style at the court of Lorenzo de' Medici. Later it appeared in France, and appeared in England in the late fifteenth century, where there occurred a separation of the masquers and spectators. In the reign of Henry VIII the first masque was performed at court. In the time of Elizabeth an allegorical element was present to celebrate the Queen and her rule. The greatest development of the masque was under James I, partly because Queen Anne loved to participate in entertainments. Ben Jonson began to write masques (*The Masque of Blackness, The Masque of Queens, Hymenaei*) in collaboration with Inigo ➤Jones, which usually functioned as propaganda for the Stuart regime. They were elaborate and expensive stage spectacles in which courtiers, including Queen Anne and Prince Henry, took part. Jonson and Jones, who did the elaborate scenery and stage devices for court masques under James I and Charles I, could not agree over the primacy of their contributions: should the scenery be more important or the dialogue itself? Their collaboration came to an end, but each continued to work separately in the genre. The last Stuart court masque was ➤Davenant's *Salmacida Spolia* (21 January 1640), shortly before the downfall of Charles I.

Master Gunner of Orleans A minor character in *1 Henry VI*.

Mayor of London In *1 Henry VI*, he stops the fighting between followers of the Bishop of Winchester and those of the Duke of Gloucester. In *Richard III*, the Lord Mayor supports Richard's claim to the throne.

Mayor of York In *3 Henry VI*, Thomas Beverly, who reluctantly admits Edward IV into the town.

Measure for Measure A comedy by Shakespeare, acted at court, though not nec-
essarily on its first performance, on 26 December 1604; probably written earlier
the same year, and printed in the first folio of 1623. *Measure for Measure* was based
on a pre-existing play, *Promos and Cassandra* (1578) by George Whetstone, which
was itself based on an Italian source, a tale from Geraldi Cinthio's *Hecatommithi*
(1565). Cinthio also wrote a play on the same subject, *Epitia* (1583). Shakespeare
knew both Whetstone's play and Cinthio's collection of fables, which he also used
for the plot of *Othello*, and he may well have known *Epitia* too, since, like *Measure
for Measure* but less like *Promos and Cassandra*, it is very much concerned with the
nature of justice and authority, and contains characters who contrast in their atti-
tudes to justice much as Angelo and Escalus do. Other contemporary versions of
the story were contained in the second part of Thomas Lupton's *Siuquila* (1581),
an allegory about a kind of Puritan Utopia, and the narrative that Whetstone created out of his play and published in his *Heptameron of Civil Discourses* (1582). From
Promos and Cassandra Shakespeare took the story of a virtuous girl whose brother
is condemned to death for rape under severe new laws; the King's deputy, Promos
(Angelo), who has made the judgment, agrees to pardon the brother if his sister Cassandra (Isabella) will sleep with him. She does so, but afterwards Promos breaks his
promise and orders the young man to be executed. He is, however, secretly preserved by his jailer. Cassandra, believing him dead, reveals the story to the King and
asks him for justice; the King then orders Promos to marry Cassandra and afterwards be executed. But she has fallen in love with Promos, and begs for his life; at
first the King refuses, but when the brother is revealed alive he agrees, and all ends
happily. Shakespeare changed this plot in three important ways. Perhaps influenced
by the characterization of King Leonarchus in Barnaby ►Riche's pamphlet *The Adventures of Brusanus, Prince of Hungaria* (1592), he turned the minor figure of the King
into the ambiguous Duke Vincentio, who stage-manages the action of the play. He
made Isabella a novice, unlike any of the sources or analogues, thus giving her a
compelling reason for not agreeing to Angelo's demand and also a Christian motivation for forgiving him. Finally, he provided Mariana to substitute for Isabella
in Angelo's bed, and thus give a different emphasis to Angelo's character. The title
of the play and its theme of justice transcended by mercy perhaps came from Luke,
6:36–42.

Dramatis Personae

Vincentio, Duke of Vienna	Peter, *a friar*
Angelo, *his deputy*	*A Justice*
Escalus, *an ancient lord*	Varrius
Claudio, *a young gentleman*	Elbow, *a simple constable*
Lucio, *a fantastic*	Froth, *a foolish gentleman*
Two other Gentlemen	Pompey, *Mistress Overdone's servant*
Provost	Abhorson, *an executioner*
Thomas, *a friar*	Barnadine, *a dissolute prisoner*

Isabella, *sister to Claudio*
Mariana, *betrothed to Angelo*
Juliet, *beloved of Claudio*
Francisca, *a nun*

Mistress Overdone, *a bawd*
Lords, Officers, Citizens, Boy, and
Attendants

The Story. Vincentio, Duke of Vienna, realizing that stricter enforcement of laws is needed in the city, and wishing to test the probity of his deputy, Angelo, leaves Angelo in charge while he pretends to leave the city (really, however, he remains in the city, disguised as a friar). Angelo immediately arrests Claudio, who has made his fiancée, Juliet, pregnant, and sentences him to death. Claudio sends for his sister Isabella, who is about to enter a nunnery, to try to prevail upon Angelo for mercy. Angelo is at first adamant, but the beauty of Isabella arouses him and he offers to pardon Claudio if she will yield herself to him. She refuses indignantly and returns to the prison to tell Claudio, who begs her to sacrifice her chastity for his life. The Duke, still disguised as a friar, overhears the conversation and suggests that Isabella agree to Angelo's request but that they get Mariana, formerly the fiancée of Angelo, to substitute for Isabella at the assignation. Angelo sleeps, unknowingly, with Mariana, but then breaks his word and orders the execution of Claudio. However, the Provost of the prison prevents this by the substitution of a prisoner already awaiting execution for another offence and then sending Angelo the head of a prisoner who died of fever. The Duke then lays aside his disguise, hears the complaints, and straightens everything out; judgment is given upon Angelo (who still assumes that Claudio is dead) with the words: "An Angelo for Claudio, death for death! . . . and Measure still for Measure" (V.i). But Isabella, though still believing her brother to be dead, is prevailed upon to join Mariana in begging for Angelo's life. He is reprieved, and married to Mariana; Claudio is revealed to be alive; and the Duke proposes marriage to Isabella.

Melun In *King John*, a French lord who warns the English nobles who have deserted to the French side that the Dauphin intends to kill them when he has defeated John.

Menas In *Antony and Cleopatra*, a pirate who proposes to Pompey that they capture and kill the triumvirs as they are feasting on board ship.

Menecrates In *Antony and Cleopatra*, a pirate (associated with Pompey).

Menelaus In *Troilus and Cressida*, the husband of Helen.

Menenius Agrippa In *Coriolanus*, the talkative witty friend of Coriolanus. To calm the plebeians and tribunes, he tells them the fable of the belly and members; later he urges Coriolanus to control his wrath and to speak less arrogantly to the populace.

Menteith In *Macbeth*, a Scottish thane.

Merchant of Venice, The A comedy by Shakespeare, entered on the Stationers' Register in 1598, published in quarto in 1600, 1619, 1637, and 1652, and in the first folio in 1623. It was probably written in 1596 or 1597. To construct his play Shakespeare combined two stories, the Bond of Flesh and the Casket Choice, both of them with long traditions in folklore. The Bond of Flesh story involving Antonio, Bassanio, Portia, and Shylock seems to have originated in India, for a version is found in the *Mahabharata* (compiled between 500 and 200 BC), but Shakespeare's sources were probably tales from the *Gesta Romanorum*, a medieval compilation, and the collection of prose romances, *Il Pecorone* (1558), by Ser Giovanni Fiorentino. The Bond story in the *Gesta Romanorum* existed only in manuscript, and *Il Pecorone* must have been known to Shakespeare either in a manuscript translation or in Italian, since there was no published English translation known in his day. In the *Gesta Romanorum* the Bond story was linked with a tale of wooing, and here Shakespeare could have found several elements of the plot such as the triple love test, the disguising of the lady, and the lady's judgment that the flesh must be taken without loss of blood. The Shylock figure in this was not, however, a Jew. In the story from *Il Pecorone*, which is closer to the *Merchant of Venice*, a young man tries to woo the lady of Belmonte, a rich widow who has agreed to marry the first man that sleeps with her on condition that if he fail he must forfeit all his wealth. On two occasions he is given drugged wine and so prevented, and in consequence deprived of all his money; on the third occasion his godfather borrows a large sum from a Jew to equip him, and he is successful. He marries the lady, but he forgets to inform his godfather until the day for redeeming the Jew's bond is past; the lady sends him to Venice with the money, and herself follows disguised as a lawyer, but the Jew refuses it and demands instead his pound of flesh. The disguised lady steps forward, and all is resolved as in *The Merchant of Venice*, even down to the affair of the rings. Another version of the Bond of Flesh story that Shakespeare might have used is contained in *Zelauto* (1580) by Anthony Munday, although here the moneylender is no Jew but a usurer, and the forfeit demanded is the young man's eyes. There was also a contemporary ballad "shewing the crueltie of Gernutus a Jew," but this may be of later date than Shakespeare's play. The Caskets plot apparently derived from the *Gesta Romanorum*, and there was a translated version of this story made by Richard Robinson in 1595. Shakespeare interchanged the mottos on the gold and silver caskets in the original and completely changed that on the lead casket. The story of Jessica, Shylock, and Lorenzo was probably suggested by the elopement of the usurer's daughter in *Zelauto* and perhaps also by the treatment of Abigail, the Jew's daughter, in ►Marlowe's *The Jew of Malta*. Another probable source for Jessica's elopement was a tale in the fifteenth century collection *Il Novellino*, by Masuccio, in which a young man falls in love with the daughter of a miser, ingratiates himself with the old man, and borrows money from him, giving as security a slave; the slave then helps the daughter steal her father's wealth and elope with the young man. Shakespeare's decision to write a play centered on a Jew may have been influenced by the revivals of Marlowe's play in 1594 and 1596, and probably also by the trial and execution of Roderigo Lopez, a Portuguese Jew, for allegedly attempting to poison the Queen. A version of the play by George Granville, Lord Lansdowne, entitled *The Jew of Venice* was made in 1701, and it held the stage until 1741, when ➤Macklin restored Shakespeare's version.

Dramatis Personae

Duke of Venice
Prince of Morocco
Prince of Aragon
Antonio, *a merchant of Venice*
Bassanio, *his friend*
Gratiano
Solanio
Salerio
Lorenzo, *in love with Jessica*
Shylock, *a rich Jew*
Tubal, *a Jew, his friend*
Launcelot Gobbo, *a clown, Shylock's*
   servant

Old Gobbo, *father of Launcelot*
Leonardo, *Bassanio's servant*
Balthasar, *Portia's servant*
Stephano, *Portia's servant*
Portia, *a rich heiress*
Nerissa, *her waiting-maid*
Jessica, *daughter of Shylock*
Magnificoes of Venice, Officers of the
   Court of Justice, Jailer,
Servants to Portia, and other Attendants

The Story. Antonio, the merchant of Venice, is asked for a loan by his well-born but impecunious friend Bassanio in order that the latter may be enabled to pursue his courtship of the heiress Portia. Antonio, whose money is tied up in ships that have not yet returned to port, borrows 3,000 ducats from the Jewish usurer Shylock, who makes Antonio promise to forfeit a pound of flesh if he is unable to pay on the agreed date. Meanwhile, at Belmont, Portia has turned away two suitors, the Prince of Morocco and the Prince of Aragon, both of whom fail to pass the test (set by the terms of Portia's father's will) of selecting from three caskets (one each of gold, silver, and lead) the one containing Portia's portrait. Bassanio chooses the correct casket, the lead one, but as they are rejoicing in the thought of an early marriage, word comes that Antonio has been unable to pay his debt and that Shylock is demanding the pound of flesh. After a hasty wedding, Bassanio returns to Venice and, as soon as he has left, Portia and her maid, Nerissa (who has married Bassanio's friend Gratiano), leave also for Venice, disguised respectively as a lawyer and a clerk. In court, the disguised Portia first pleads with Shylock for mercy; rebuffed in this approach, she concedes the legality of Shylock's claim, but points out that if he exacts more than a pound of flesh, or if one drop of blood is shed, his life and lands are forfeit. Moreover, she points out, death is the penalty for conspiring against the life of a Venetian citizen. The Duke of Venice pardons Shylock from the death sentence, but orders that his fortune be divided between Antonio and the state. Antonio returns his share to Shylock, with the stipulation that he must leave it in his will to his daughter Jessica, disinherited when she eloped with Lorenzo, a Christian, and finally that Shylock himself must become a Christian. Portia and

Nerissa (whose real identity remains unknown to the others) will accept as payment only the rings Bassanio and Gratiano have received from their wives. Back at Belmont, the wives reproach their husbands for no longer having the rings, but, after much teasing, reveal the fact of their disguise. News comes that Antonio's ships have returned safely.

Mercutio In *Romeo and Juliet*, a friend of Romeo, slain in an encounter with Tybalt. He is remembered particularly for his Queen Mab speech (I.iv).

Meres, Francis (1565–1647) English author of *Palladis Tamia, or Wit's Treasury* (1598), an anthology of collective "wisdom" including a section on contemporary English writers that praises Shakespeare for his "sugred sonnets among his private friends". Meres calls Shakespeare "the most excellent" English playwright for comedy and tragedy, and gives a list of his plays, thus providing useful evidence as to which of them were in existence by this time.

Mermaid Tavern An Elizabethan literary gathering place, in Bread Street, Cheapside. Sir Walter ➤Raleigh, Ben ➤Jonson, Francis ➤Beaumont, John ➤Fletcher, John Selden, and, quite possibly, William Shakespeare were among the notable figures who frequented it. Its host, William Johnson, was named as trustee in the purchase of one of Shakespeare's property transactions.

Merry Wives of Windsor, The A comedy by Shakespeare, probably written *c.* 1597 and performed then in connection with ceremonies to do with the Order of the Garter. It was printed in the first folio of 1623 from an authoritative manuscript. In 1602 an imperfect and unauthorized version in quarto was printed (reprinted in 1619). This version seems to have been based on an actor's report (probably by one who played the Host) and has borrowings from *Henry V*. No major source has been found for the whole plot of this play, but various influences have been suggested for the four main components of it. The way in which Shakespeare interweaves elements of multifarious origin is very typical of the synthesizing process by which many of his plays were composed. The devices by which the amorous Falstaff is exposed to ridicule when he concurrently woos the two merry wives, Mistress Page and Mistress Ford, may well have come from the Italian novelle, in particular from Ser Giovanni Fiorentino's *Il Pecorone* (1558), Day 1, Novella 2, and G.F. Straparola's *Le Piacevoli Notti*, Night 4, Fable 4. In both stories the lover undergoes three ordeals and triumphs over the cuckolded husband; in *Il Pecorone* the lover is hidden by the wife under a pile of newly washed linen, which perhaps suggested the episode where Falstaff has to make his escape from Ford's house in a basket of dirty linen (III.iii). Straparola's story appeared in an English version in ➤Tarlton's *Newes out of Purgatorie* (1590), which Shakespeare undoubtedly knew. He also knew Barnaby ➤Riche's *A Farewell to the Militarie Profession* (1581) which contained the story of Mistress Doritie, who makes her two suitors, a doctor and a lawyer, look ridiculous. The situation of Anne Page in *The Merry Wives of Windsor*, who is wooed by two suitors chosen by her parents while herself preferring a third, owes something to *Casina*, a comedy by Plautus. In this play, a man and his wife propose different husbands for their slave-girl; a wedding is arranged, but a man takes the bride's place and she is enabled to escape and marry the man of her choice. The obscure references to visiting Germans who borrow horses but do not return them (IV.iii, v), to "cosen-garmombles" (IV.v, Q. text), and to the Ceremony of the Garter (V.iv), may relate to a matter of topical interest, the visit of Frederick Count Mompelgard of Würtemberg to England in 1592, his travels about the kingdom, and his persistent application to be admitted to the Order of the Garter, as he finally was in 1597. The fairy scene in Windsor Park where Falstaff disguises himself with a buck's head is related to the story of Actaeon from ►Ovid's ►*Metamorphoses*, ii. 138–252; Actaeon, a famous hunter, came upon the goddess Diana naked as she was bathing with her nymphs in a stream, and was punished by being changed into a stag and hunted to death. In Shakespeare's time "Actaeon" became a cant-name for a cuckold. John Dennis, an English critic of the early eighteenth century, maintained in his adaptation of it (1702) that this comedy was written at the request of Queen Elizabeth, who wanted to see Falstaff in love.

Dramatis Personae

Sir John Falstaff

Fenton, *a gentleman*

Shallow, *a country justice*

Slender, *cousin to Shallow*

Ford

Page

William Page, *son to Page*

Sir Hugh Evans, *a Welsh parson*

Doctor Caius, *a French physician*

Host of the Garter Inn

Bardolph, *follower of Falstaff*

Pistol, *follower of Falstaff*

Nym, *follower of Falstaff*

Robin, *page to Falstaff*

Simple, *servant to Slender*

Rugby, *Servant to Dr Caius*

Mistress Ford

Mistress Page

Anne Page, *her daughter*

Mistress Quickly, *servant to Dr Caius*

Servants to Page, Ford

The Story. Sir John Falstaff decides to pay court to Mistress Page and Mistress Ford, the merry wives of Windsor, hoping thereby to obtain some money (the two women are known to have charge of their husbands' purse strings). He sends identical notes to them and they, comparing them, decide to make a fool of the fat knight by appearing to encourage him. Meanwhile, Nym and Pistol, the cast-off cronies of Falstaff, inform the husbands of Falstaff's intentions (at this stage Ford himself is not confident of his wife's fidelity, and, in disguise, retains Falstaff to plead with her for him, as still another suitor). Mistress Ford, knowing all this, arranges an assignation with Falstaff, during which Ford returns, and Falstaff is hidden in a basket of dirty laundry and dumped in a muddy stream. At the second assignation, Ford again appears, and Falstaff tries to flee disguised as a woman ("the fat woman of Brentford"), but is beaten by Ford as a witch. Meanwhile, Anne Page, daughter of Mistress Page, has been courted by Slender, who is favoured by Page, by Dr Caius, who is favoured by Mistress Page, and by Fenton, whom Anne loves. Mistress Quickly, Dr Caius's servant, bears messages from all of them to Anne and encourages them all impartially. In the last act, everyone gathers in Windsor Forest: Falstaff to meet the wives, who leave him to be tormented by mock fairies; Slender to elope with Anne who, as Page tells him, is to be dressed in white; Caius also to elope with her, but thinking her to be dressed in green; and Fenton, who succeeds in carrying her off. Slender and Caius discover that they have eloped with boys disguised as fairies.

Messala   In *Julius Caesar*, a friend of Brutus and Cassius.

Metamorphoses   Poetical work by ➤Ovid, in fifteen books. The work is a collection of some 250 stories taken from Greek mythology, Latin folk tales, legends, and myths, including also some tales from the East. The unifying element in the collection is that all of the stories have to do with transformations: for an infinite variety of causes, gods, men, and animals are transformed in an infinite variety of ways. Ovid dexterously manoeuvered through intricate plots and relationships so that one story led almost imperceptibly to another, making the work a whole rather than a collection of separate, unconnected tales. The *Metamorphoses* is a treasury of myth and legend, gleaned by Ovid from the works of ancient poets and other writers and transformed by him into a masterpiece. His work has been a source of inspiration and influence for western European literature, as Ovid hoped it would be, for in the closing lines of the *Metamorphoses* he wrote: "My work is complete: a work which neither Jove's anger, nor fire nor sword shall destroy, nor yet the gnawing tooth of time... If there be any truth in poets' prophecies, I shall live to all eternity, immortalized by fame." It is a pervasive influence on Shakespeare's work, particularly on *Venus and Adonis*, *Titus Andronicus*, and *The Tempest*. He knew it both in the translation of Arthur Golding (1567) and in the original.

Michael   In *2 Henry VI*, a follower of Jack Cade.

Michael, Sir   In *1 Henry IV*, a priest or knight who is in the service of the Archbishop of York and is sent by him with letters to the rebels (IV.iv).

Middleton, Thomas   (1580–1627) English dramatist, poet, and pamphleteer, a possible collaborator with Shakespeare. His first publications were non-dramatic works, and he began his theatrical career collaborating with other playwrights, particularly ➤Dekker. He wrote many comedies but his best-known plays are the tragedies *Women Beware Women* (1621), *The Changeling* (with ➤Rowley, 1622), and the famous political satire, *A Game at Chess* (1624). He also wrote many masques and pageants for the City of London. He is now widely accepted as Shakespeare's collaborator on *Timon of Athens*, and *Macbeth* includes scenes with Hecate (III.v and parts of IV.i) long thought to be written by him. ➤*Second Maiden's Tragedy*.

Midsummer Night's Dream, A   A comedy by Shakespeare, written in 1594 or 1595, and certainly staged several times within the next four years, although the date of first performance is not known. It is mentioned by Francis ➤Meres in his *Palladis Tamia*, which was issued in 1598, was entered on the Stationers' Register 8 October 1600, and was first published in 1600. It is included in the first folio of 1623 with a few added stage directions but no scene markings. This is one of those plays for the plot of which Shakespeare depended on no one main source. There are five interwoven strands to the plot: (1) the marriage of Theseus and Hippolyta; (2) the quarrel between Titania and Oberon; (3) the assorted relationships of the four human lovers; (4) the adventures of Bottom; (5) the Pyramus and Thisbe play. No known source combines all these stories, and although Shakespeare took names and details for each of them from various subsidiary sources he did not rely heavily on the work of any other writer for any element of his play. Theseus and Hippolyta may have come from North's translation of Plutarch's *Life of Theseus* in which Theseus is depicted as a lawgiver and statesman, or perhaps from Chaucer's *The Knight's Tale*, where the marriage of the mature couple, Theseus and Hippolyta, is contrasted with the unhappy situation of the two young men who both love the same girl. It may also be that this love-triangle provided a starting point for the relationships between the human lovers of *A Midsummer Night's Dream*. Oberon and Titania are literary fairies and may be traced accordingly; Oberon comes from the romance *Huon of Bordeaux*, translated by Lord Berners (*c.* 1534), and perhaps also from Robert ➤Greene's *James IV*, while Titania comes from ➤Ovid's ➤*Metamorphoses*, iii. 173. But the main fairy background and the figure of Puck come from English folklore. Bottom's transformation and his brief love affair with Titania have various literary analogues but no specific sources: Midas and his ass's ears, the transformation of the amorous Apuleius in *The Golden Asse*, and various tales from Reginald Scot's *Discoverie of Witchcraft* (1584) may have contributed. Numerous sources have been discovered for the Pyramus and Thisbe play, which was very popular in Elizabethan times as a story of the misfortunes of thwarted love. Shakespeare undoubtedly read and was influenced by Golding's translation of Ovid's *Metamorphoses* (1567), iv. 67–201, which was written in the heavily-stressed fourteeners that readily lend themselves to parody. Other versions of the story that he may also have used include "A New Sonet of Pyramus and Thisbe" from the anthology *A Handfull of Plesant Delites* (1584), *A Gorgeous Gallery of Gallant Inventions* (1578), and perhaps Thomas Mouffet's didactic poem *The Silkewormes and Their Flies* (1599), which Shakespeare may have seen in manuscript.

Dramatis Personae

Theseus, Duke of Athens
Egeus, *father of Hermia*
Lysander, *in love with Hermia*
Demetrius, *in love with Hermia*
Philostrate, *Master of the Revels*
Quince, *a carpenter*
Snug, *a joiner*

Bottom, *a weaver*
Flute, *a bellows-mender*
Snout, *a tinker*
Starveling, *a tailor*
Hippolyta, Queen of the Amazons, *betrothed to Theseus*
Hermia, *in love with Lysander*

Helena, *in love with Demetrius*
Oberon, King of the Fairies
Titania, Queen of the Fairies
Puck, *or* Robin Goodfellow
Peaseblossom, *a fairy*
Cobweb, *a fairy*

Moth, *a fairy*
Mustardseed, *a fairy*
Other Fairies attending their King and
    Queen
Attendants on Theseus and Hippolyta

The Story. To the court of Theseus, Duke of Athens, who is about to marry Hippolyta, come Hermia and her father, Egeus, who insists that she marry Demetrius (who now loves Hermia, but who has earlier avowed love for Hermia's friend Helena, by whom he is still loved). Lysander also loves Hermia, and it is his suit that she favours. Theseus invokes the Athenian law, which gives her four days in which to agree to her father's request; if she persists after that time in her disobedience she must become a nun or be condemned to death. However, she and Lysander arrange to meet that night in a neighbouring wood, and plan to flee beyond the reach of Athenian law. She tells her plan to Helena, but Helena tells Demetrius, hoping thus to regain his love. Demetrius follows Hermia and Lysander into the wood, and Helena follows Demetrius. In the wood also, but unbeknownst to them, are fairies who have arrived from India for the wedding of Theseus and Hippolyta: Titania and Oberon, the Queen and King of the fairies, are quarrelling about the possession of a changeling boy left in Titania's care by his mother. Oberon, to spite Titania, drops on her eyelids as she sleeps a magic liquid squeezed from a certain flower so that when she awakens she will fall in love with the first creature she sees. This happens to be Bottom, a weaver, one of a group of Athenian artisans who have gone into the wood to rehearse a play in honour of the forthcoming marriage of Theseus and Hippolyta; Puck, Oberon's mischievous servant, has playfully given Bottom the head of an ass. Oberon, having overheard Demetrius berating Helena for following him, seeks to help them out of their difficulty by ordering Puck to anoint Demetrius so that he may fall in love with Helena. But Puck confuses Lysander with Demetrius, and drops the liquid on the eyes of the wrong man; Lysander, upon awakening, sees Helena, and loves her. Seeking to correct the mistake, Oberon himself now anoints Demetrius, who also first sees Helena upon awakening, so that both young men are now in love with Helena, exactly the reverse of the situation at the beginning. Neither Helena nor Hermia has any inkling of what has caused the situation; Hermia upbraids Helena (who, far from wanting the attentions of Lysander, has thought he was making a joke of her in offering them). Titania, meanwhile, has been entrapped by the unique (to her) beauty of Bottom's donkey's ears and velvet muzzle; never, in her bewitched eyes, has there been an object of such surpassing beauty. Oberon pities her humiliation and removes the spell; they are reconciled and she agrees to give up the changeling boy. Puck, by enclosing the human lovers in a mist, arranges that Lysander will awaken to love Hermia once more, and Demetrius to love Helena. Theseus and Hippolyta arrive in the wood, discover the couples, and arrange a triple wedding which takes place in the palace. At the ceremony, the artisans' play, the "most lamentable comedy" of Pyramus and Thisbe, is presented. After the lovers retire, the fairies dance through the palace to bless the human couples, leaving Puck to deliver the Epilogue.

Milan, Duke of   In *The Two Gentlemen of Verona*, the father of Silvia.

Milan, Duke of   ➤Antonio; ➤Prospero.

Miller, Jonathan   (1934–   ) British director who has worked at the National Theatre and the Old Vic, among other companies, and has staged many Shakespeare productions, including *The Merchant of Venice* (with Laurence Olivier, National Theatre, 1970), *The Tempest* (Mermaid, 1970, Old Vic, 1988), and recently *A Midsummer Night's Dream* (Almeida, 1996). He also directed several productions in the BBC television Shakespeare series.

miracle plays   ➤mystery plays.

Miranda   In *The Tempest*, the daughter of Prospero. She was born in Milan, but shipwrecked on the island with her father as a baby. She is loved by Ferdinand with whom she will contract a dynastic marriage.

Mirren, Helen   (1946–   ) British actress who has appeared in many Shakespearean roles, especially for the ➤Royal Shakespeare Company, including Cressida (1968), Lady Macbeth (1974), and Cleopatra (1982). She also took roles in the BBC television Shakespeare series, including Rosalind and Titania. Recently she has played Cleopatra at the Royal National Theatre (1998).

Mnouchkine, Ariane   (1939–   ) French theatre director and founder of the Paris-based ensemble company Theatre du Soleil (1964–   ). She specializes in production techniques drawing on many different traditions of theatre, particularly combining East and West. She has directed productions of *A Midsummer Night's Dream* (1969) and, in 1981, a season of *Richard III*, *Twelfth Night*, and *Henry IV*.

Montague   In *Romeo and Juliet*, the family name of Romeo. Montague is Romeo's father and a bitter enemy of Capulet. This feud between the houses of Montague and Capulet plays an important part in the separation of the lovers that leads to the eventual tragedy. The Montagues and Capulets are reconciled after Romeo and Juliet's deaths.

Montague, Lady   In *Romeo and Juliet*, the mother of Romeo.

Montague, Marquess of   In *3 Henry VI*, the historical John Neville, Marquis of Montague, a supporter of York who later joins the Lancastrians under Henry VI and is killed at the battle of Barnet.

Montano   The name of Reynaldo in the first quarto of *Hamlet*.

Montano   In *Othello*, the Governor of Cyprus.

Montgomery, Sir John   In *3 Henry VI*, a supporter of Edward, Earl of March. He urges Edward to fight for the throne (IV.vii).

Montjoy   In *Henry V*, a French herald who asks whether Henry will offer ransom before he is forced to engage in battle with the French army at Agincourt. Later he acknowledges French defeat.

Moonshine   In *A Midsummer Night's Dream*, the part played by Starveling, the tailor, in the interpolated play.

Mopsa   A shepherdess in *The Winter's Tale*.

morality plays [Also, moralities]   Plays developed in the early fifteenth century, having the didactic purpose of inculcating virtuous behaviour in their hearers. Generally speaking, the morality play presents abstract virtues and vices struggling for possession of a man's soul. There is usually a debate between Body and Soul in which the Soul moralizes against the Body, which has led it unwillingly down the road to damnation. Finally, after death, abstractions representing heavenly judgment decide whether Man shall be given mercy or harsh punishment. These heavenly abstractions are often the Four Daughters of God: Mercy and Peace (for salvation), Righteousness and Truth (for damnation). The earliest morality play is *The Pride of Life* (*c.* 1400), and others include *The Castle of Perseverance* (*c.* 1405), *Mind, Will, and Understanding* (*c.* 1460), *Mankynd* (*c.* 1475), and the well-known *Everyman* (late fifteenth century). ➤mystery plays.

Morgan   In *Cymbeline*, the assumed name of Belarius.

Morocco, Prince of   In *The Merchant of Venice*, an unsuccessful suitor of Portia. He chooses the golden casket as the one containing her portrait, and thus fails to win her.

Mortimer, Edmund   In *1 Henry IV*, a prisoner of Owen Glendower, whose daughter he marries. His sister is Hotspur's wife and he and Glendower join Hotspur against Henry IV. Shakespeare confused the historical Sir Edmund (1376–1409) with his nephew, Edmund, 5th Earl of March.

Mortimer, Edmund [Title, (5th) Earl of March]   In *1 Henry VI*, an old nobleman. He tells Richard that he is imprisoned by the Lancastrians because he is the real heir to the throne and Richard is his heir. Shakespeare apparently confused the historical Earl with his uncle, Sir Edmund Mortimer, or with another member of the family.

Mortimer, Lady   In *1 Henry IV*, the daughter of Owen Glendower and wife of Edmund Mortimer. She can speak only Welsh.

Mortimer, Sir John and **Sir Hugh**   In *3 Henry VI*, illegitimate sons of Roger Mortimer and uncles of Richard, Duke of York.

Morton   In *2 Henry IV*, the retainer who brings Northumberland news of Hotspur's death.

Morton, John   In *Richard III*, the Bishop of Ely, an adherent of Richmond after having escaped from Richard. The historical Morton became Archbishop of Canterbury in Henry VII's reign and Sir Thomas More lived in his house. More got material from him for his *History of King Richard III*, which Shakespeare used as a source for *Richard III*.

Moth   In *Love's Labour's Lost*, a witty page of Armado.

Moth   A fairy in *A Midsummer Night's Dream*.

Mouldy, Ralph   In *2 Henry IV*, a recruit whom Falstaff allows to purchase his freedom.

Mousetrap, The   ►*Hamlet*.

Mowbray   In *2 Henry IV*, one of the lords opposing Henry.

Mowbray, Thomas   In *Richard II*, the Duke of Norfolk. Bolingbroke accuses him of treason before Richard, and Mowbray, to defend his honour, challenges Bolingbroke to single combat. At the last moment, Richard calls off the tournament and banishes Bolingbroke for ten years and Mowbray for life. His historical counterpart was Thomas Mowbray, Earl of Nottingham, 12th Baron Mowbray, 1st Duke of Norfolk. (d. 1399). He was created Earl of Nottingham in 1383, earl marshal in 1384, and was one of the lord appellants of 1387, but afterwards joined the King. He was created Duke of Norfolk in 1397. Having been accused of treason by Henry Bolingbroke, Earl of Hereford (afterward Henry IV), in 1398, he challenged the latter to single combat, and the lists were set at Coventry in the presence of Richard II, who banished both disputants on the eve of the contest, Norfolk for life and Hereford for ten years.

Mucedorus   An anonymous play, printed in 1598 and reprinted with additions in 1610. It was erroneously assigned to Shakespeare by Edward Archer in 1656. It was a romance in a pastoral setting, and one of the most popular plays of the period.

Much Ado About Nothing   A comedy by Shakespeare, produced *c.* 1598. It was probably written in 1598 or 1599. It was first printed in 1600, and its registration that year marked the first appearance of Shakespeare's name in the Stationers' Register. The story of Hero and Claudio belongs to a long tradition dating back to a Greek romance and was available to Shakespeare in both dramatic and nondramatic versions. He probably knew Sir John Harrington's translation of the fifth canto of Ariosto's epic poem *Orlando Furioso*, which appeared in 1591, and the variant of this by Matteo Bandello in the twenty-second of his *Novelle*. Bandello's version was translated into French by François de Belleforest in his *Histoires Tragiques* (1574), but not into English in Shakespeare's lifetime. Edmund ►Spenser had included a version of this story in *The Faerie Queene* (1590), Book II, Canto IV, in the account of Phedon (Claudio) deceived as to the chastity of Claribella (Hero) by a plot between her maid and his best friend, which Shakespeare probably also knew, and there was a play, perhaps by Anthony Munday, called *Fedele and Fortunio* (1585) that contains a similar situation. Shakespeare took some of the names, notably Don Pedro and Leonato, and the setting in Messina, from Bandello, but he altered the situation so that Hero and Claudio were of the same rank, whereas in Bandello and several of the sources the Claudio figure was of higher rank and greater wealth. He also changed the circumstances of the deception so that evidence of Hero's guilt seemed greater and the censure of Claudio correspondingly less. But the parts of the play that are probably most attractive to modern audiences, the "merry war" between the reluctant lovers Beatrice and Benedick, and the comic misunderstandings of Dogberry and the Watch, are Shakespeare's own invention, as is the villainous Don John.

Dramatis Personae

Don Pedro, Prince of Arragon
Don John, *his bastard brother*
Claudio, *a young lord of Florence*
Benedick, *a young lord of Padua*
Leonato, *Governor of Messina*
Antonio, *his brother*
Balthasar, *servant to Don Pedro*
Borachio, *follower of Don John*
Conrade, *follower of Don John*
Dogberry, *a constable*

Verges, *a headborough*
Friar Francis
A Sexton
A Boy
Hero, *daughter of Leonato*
Beatrice, *niece of Leonato*
Margaret, *gentlewoman to Hero*
Ursula, *gentlewoman to Hero*
Messengers, Watch, Attendants

The Story. Claudio and Benedick, officers in the army of Don Pedro, Prince of Arragon, are with him when he visits Leonato, the Governor of Messina. Claudio falls in love with Hero, Leonato's daughter, and despite the scheming of Don John, the bastard brother of the Prince, the wedding is arranged. Meanwhile, Beatrice, the niece of Leonato, and Benedick bait each other in verbal skirmishes, each professing to oppose the very idea of love or marriage, but are tricked into love for each other when Claudio and Don Pedro contrive that each shall overhear a conversation touching on the love that the other is supposed to feel, but is unwilling to express, for the listener. In the affair of Claudio and Hero, however, things are somewhat less happy. Don John persuades Borachio to converse at midnight through a window with Hero's maid Margaret, who is dressed as Hero, and arranges that Claudio and Don Pedro shall witness the conversation and thereby be brought to suspect the virtue of Hero. The scheme succeeds, and at the wedding ceremony on the following day Claudio and Don Pedro denounce Hero, who swoons (whereupon Friar Francis, convinced of her innocence, persuades her father to announce her death). In the following scene the love of Beatrice and Benedick is declared, and Beatrice lays as a task on Benedick that he should kill Claudio for impugning her cousin Hero's virtue. However, Claudio is not to suffer for his mistrust; Borachio boasts of his exploit and is arrested by Dogberry and Verges. A repentant Claudio, believing Hero to be dead, agrees to marry Leonato's niece, who when she is unveiled turns out to be Hero. Benedick and Beatrice also marry, and word comes that Don John has been apprehended and is being returned for punishment.

Mustardseed   A fairy in *A Midsummer Night's Dream*.

Mutius   In *Titus Andronicus*, the youngest son of Titus. He is killed by his father as he attempts to protect Lavinia.

Myrmidons   In *Troilus and Cressida*, the soldiers of Achilles.

mystery plays [Also, miracle plays]   Plays developed in the fourteenth and fifteenth centuries for secular performance but with religious themes. They are the successors of earlier, simpler dramatizations of episodes in the Christian story that were presented in church. As such dramatic presentations grew more elaborate, they passed out of the church into the market place and the streets of the town and out of the hands of the clergy into those of the guilds. (The word "mystery" is used in the now archaic sense of a craft or trade.) In a number of larger towns cycles of such plays developed. They were often performed on "pageants," movable platforms that were wheeled through the streets. The great occasion for these performances was Corpus Christi Day, and most cycles were given then. The particular subjects were often assigned according to the association of a given guild with the event depicted. Thus the York cycle has the shipwrights' guild performing the story of Noah and his ark, the fishermen and mariners doing the ark's voyage, the bakers doing the Last Supper, the vintners performing the miracle of the wedding feast at Cana, and the cooks doing the harrowing of hell. At its peak, this cycle had fifty-seven pageants, more than that of any other town. There are four cycles preserved more or less fully, those of York (1415) with forty-eight plays, Wakefield (best known as the Towneley Plays, fifteenth century) with thirty-two plays, Chester (1328) with twenty-five plays, and the Hegge cycle (in a manuscript of 1468) with forty-two plays, as well as two Coventry plays and one each from Norwich and Newcastle. There are three plays in the Digby series (the Digby Plays) of the fifteenth century. The Beverley cycle of thirty-eight plays (1423) has vanished. The term "miracle play" has also been used to refer to this type of drama. The plays died out in the sixteenth century, and the last performance may have been of the Coventry cycle in 1580. Shakespeare is likely to have seen cycle plays in his youth. ➤ morality plays.

N

Nashe, Thomas [Also, Nash; pseudonym, Pasquil] (1567–*c.* 1601) English satirical pamphleteer, poet, and dramatist. He took the degree of BA at Cambridge (St John's College) in 1585. His earliest work is a preface to Robert ➤Greene's *Menaphon* (1589), which refers to the so-called ➤*Ur-Hamlet*. Using his pseudonym, he entered (1589) the Martin Marprelate controversy on the side of the bishops and is generally credited with writing *A Countercuffe to Martin Junior, Martins Months Minde*, and *Pasquils Apologie*, though no definite ascription is possible. In 1592 he began his long and scurrilous "paper war" with Gabriel Harvey in *Pierce Pennilesse, his supplication to the Devil*, which refers to "brave Talbot" in *1 Henry VI*. Nashe wrote a picaresque romance, *The Unfortunate Traveller or the Life of Jack Wilton* (1594), and, among other works, a satirical masque, *Summers Last Will and Testament* (1592). He may have collaborated on Christopher ➤Marlowe's play *Dido Queen of Carthage* (*c.* 1589). The lost play *The Isle of Dogs* (1597), written in collaboration with others, contained material considered seditious and slanderous, for which he was sentenced to the Fleet prison; however, he does not appear to have served his sentence.

Nathaniel In *The Taming of the Shrew*, one of Petruchio's servants.

Nathaniel, Sir A curate in *Love's Labour's Lost*.

National Theatre ➤Royal National Theatre.

Nerissa In *The Merchant of Venice*, the waiting-maid of Portia. When Portia disguises herself as a lawyer, Nerissa acts as a clerk.

Nestor In *Troilus and Cressida*, a Greek commander. Old and greatly venerated by the other warriors, he remarks that adversity is the test of valour (I.iii).

Neville The name of a family prominent in English history, several of whose members appear as characters in Shakespeare's historical plays, as follows: Anne Neville is Lady Anne in *Richard III*; John Neville is the Marquess of Montague in *3 Henry VI*; a Ralph Neville is the Earl of Westmoreland in *1* and *2 Henry IV* and in *Henry V*; another of the same name and title appears in *3 Henry VI*; a Richard Neville is the Earl of Salisbury in *2 Henry VI*; and another Richard Neville, the famous "Kingmaker," is the Earl of Warwick in *2* and *3 Henry VI*.

Newington Butts theatre A theatre in Newington, Surrey, on the south side of the Thames, in which plays were performed from about 1580 onwards.

New Place   The house of Shakespeare's (later) residence and death at Stratford-upon-Avon. The foundations still remain. It is now believed to have been built *c.* 1490. Shakespeare bought it for £60 in 1597. At that time there were two barns, two gardens, and two orchards belonging to it, and Shakespeare afterwards enlarged the gardens. He retired there permanently in 1610. The house was torn down in 1759, but the site was bought by subscription in 1861.

Nicanor   In *Coriolanus*, the Roman who chats with the Volscian and tells him of the banishment of Coriolanus (IV.iii).

Nielsen, Asta   (1881–1972) Danish actress on stage and screen, who in 1920 formed a film production company that brought out a silent version of *Hamlet*, in which she played the lead, as its first venture. In this film, Hamlet is a woman disguised as a man.

Ninagawa, Yukio   (1935–   ) Japanese theatre director who began directing Shakespeare with *Romeo and Juliet* in 1974. Many of his productions have been internationally acclaimed, including *Macbeth* (taken to the Edinburgh festival, 1985), *The Tempest* (1994), *A Midsummer Night's Dream* (1996), and *Hamlet* (1998). He draws on the conventions of traditional Japanese theatre but is also open to Western influences.

Nine Worthies   In *Love's Labour's Lost*, the masque presented before Ferdinand, King of Navarre, the Princess of France, and the rest of the court. In the masque, Costard is Pompey, Sir Nathaniel is Alexander, Moth is Hercules, and Armado is Hector.

Noble, Adrian   (1950–   ) British theatre director who has worked with the ►Royal Shakespeare Company since 1981, becoming artistic director in 1991. Recent productions have included *Hamlet* (1992), *A Midsummer Night's Dream* (1994, filmed 1995), *Cymbeline* (1997), and *The Tempest* (1998).

Norfolk, Duke of   In *3 Henry VI*, a supporter of the Yorkist (White Rose) faction.

Norfolk, (1st) Duke of   In *Richard II*, ►Mowbray, Thomas.

Norfolk, (1st) Duke of   In *Richard III*, the historical John Howard, a supporter of the King. He is killed at Bosworth.

Norfolk, (2nd) Duke of   In *Henry VIII*, the historical Thomas Howard, a strong opponent of Wolsey. He appears as the Earl of Surrey, son of the 1st Duke of Norfolk, in *Richard III*.

Northumberland, Earl of   In *Macbeth*, ►Siward.

Northumberland, (1st) Earl of   In *Richard II*, the elder Henry Percy, who joins Bolingbroke on his return to England and later orders Richard to Pomfret and his

Queen to France. In *1 Henry IV*, he pretends illness to avoid committing himself against Henry IV (Bolingbroke) in battle and is not present at Shrewsbury when his son Hotspur is killed. In *2 Henry IV*, he encourages Archbishop Scroop to rebel but then flees to Scotland. Later it is announced that he has been defeated.

Northumberland, (3rd) **Earl of**   In *3 Henry VI*, the historical Henry Percy, grandson of Hotspur, a supporter of the King and of the Lancastrian (Red Rose) faction. He is killed at Towton.

Northumberland, Lady   In *2 Henry IV*, the wife of the (1st) Earl of Northumberland. She advises her husband to flee to Scotland.

Nunn, Trevor   (1940–   ) British theatre director who has worked with the ►Royal Shakespeare Company (artistic director, 1968–86) and is currently artistic director at the ►Royal National Theatre (1997–   ). He has directed a large number of Shakespeare's plays over a period of nearly thirty years, notably *Hamlet* (1970), *The Comedy of Errors* (in a musical version, 1976), *Macbeth* (1976), *All's Well that Ends Well* (1981), and more recently *Othello* (1989, filmed 1990), and *Measure for Measure* (1991).

Nurse   In *Romeo and Juliet*, Juliet's wet-nurse, a comic go-between during the early romance who later (after Romeo is banished) urges Juliet to forget him and marry Paris.

Nurse   In *Titus Andronicus*, a witness of the birth to Tamora of Aaron's bastard son, killed by Aaron.

Nym   In *The Merry Wives of Windsor*, a thief and low-life character, the companion of Falstaff. He also appears with Pistol and Bardolph in *Henry V*. It has been thought that he may be a parody of characters in the Jonsonian humour comedies, since he is constantly referring to his "humour."

O

Oberon In *A Midsummer Night's Dream*, the King of the Fairies, who quarrels with his wife Titania. It is the magic liquid that he drops into her eyes (and thus causes her to fall in love with the first creature she sees on awakening), and that Puck drips into the eyes of various human participants in the play, that makes possible the various misunderstandings and misdirected affections upon which the plot depends.

Octavia In *Antony and Cleopatra*, the wife of Antony. She accepts marriage with Antony in an effort to reconcile him and her brother Octavius, but Antony deserts her for Cleopatra.

Octavius Caesar In *Julius Caesar*, one of the triumvirs after Caesar's death and a victorious general in the civil war against Cassius and Brutus. In *Antony and Cleopatra* he marries off his sister Octavia to Antony, rids himself of Lepidus, the other triumvir, and makes war on Cleopatra and Antony after the latter has deserted Octavia and fled to Egypt. Having defeated Antony at Actium, he invades Egypt and after the suicides of Antony and Cleopatra is left in control of the Roman Empire. The historical Octavius (63 BC–AD 14), better known under his later title of Augustus, was Caesar's nephew and became emperor of Rome in 27 BC.

Old Lady In *Henry VIII*, a companion to Anne Bullen (II.iii).

Old Man In *King Lear*, one of Gloucester's tenants. He leads the blinded Earl and is sent by him for clothes for Tom o'Bedlam (IV.i).

Old Man In *Macbeth*, a minor character who describes the unnatural events that have taken place after the death of Duncan (II.iv).

Oliver In *As You Like It*, the elder brother of Orlando. He plots to kill Orlando, who flees to the forest. Later Oliver is saved from a lion, repents, and marries Celia. In ➤Lodge's *Rosalynde*, from which the plot is taken, he is called Saladyne.

Olivia A principal character in *Twelfth Night*. She is wooed by Orsino, but falls in love with the disguised Viola, whom Orsino uses as his proxy. She marries Viola's twin brother, Sebastian.

Olivier, Laurence, Baron (1907–89) British actor and director, one of the major figures in twentieth-century theatre. He played a huge range of leading roles in Shakespeare, making his first stage appearance at the Shakespeare Festival Theatre, Stratford-upon-Avon, in a special boys' performance of *The Taming of the Shrew*

(1922), in which he played Katherine. In the 1930s he played Romeo, Hamlet, Sir Toby Belch, and Henry V; in the 1940s, Richard III, Hotspur, and King Lear; in the 1950s, Antony, Titus Andronicus, and Malvolio; in the 1960s, Othello (filmed 1965); in the 1970s, Shylock. He directed and starred in film versions of *Henry V* (1944), *Hamlet* (1948), and *Richard III* (1955). He was founder-director of the National Theatre (1963–70). His last Shakespearean role was as King Lear in a television version (1982).

Ophelia   In *Hamlet*, the daughter of Polonius. She obeys her father and repulses Hamlet's overtures. Hamlet's subsequent cruelty to her and the shock of her father's death combine to drive her mad, and she drowns herself.

Orlando   In *As You Like It*, the younger brother of Oliver and lover of Rosalind. He escapes the court and flees to the Forest of Arden with the old retainer, Adam. There he meets Rosalind, in male disguise, and woos her as Ganymede.

Orléans, Duke of   In *Henry V*, the historical Charles d'Orléans, the cousin and close companion of the Dauphin. He brags of the French superiority, but is captured at Agincourt.

Orsino   In *Twelfth Night*, the Duke of Illyria. He believes himself to be in love with Olivia and woos her using the disguised Viola as his intermediary. Eventually he comes to love Viola.

Osric   In *Hamlet*, an affected courtier.

Ostler, Williams   (*fl.* 1601–14) English actor. Initially a boy player with the ►Children of the Revels, he left them in 1608 to join the King's Men. He is one of the performers listed in the first folio (1623) of Shakespeare's plays.

Oswald   In *King Lear*, Goneril's steward. He angers Lear and is struck by him. He is called a "serviceable villain" (IV.vi) by Edgar, who kills him.

Othello   The hero of the tragedy *Othello*. He is a Moor who has won a high reputation as a soldier in the service of Venice. All of his experience has been in the military world, so that he comes to his marriage in middle age innocent of women and of civilian life. He falls victim to the plotting of Iago, and gradually his trust in his wife and his confidence in himself are totally eroded. When he realizes that he has been tricked into murdering his innocent wife, he immediately executes justice on himself by committing suicide.

Othello   [Full title, *The Tragedy of Othello, the Moor of Venice*]   A tragedy by Shakespeare, probably written in 1603–04, but maybe earlier, first acted in 1604 (and performed before the King on 1 November 1604), and printed in 1622 in a quarto and in 1623 in the first folio. The relationship between the two texts has been much disputed, but some editors now believe both to be derived from Shakespearean manuscripts, with the folio version representing Shakespeare's own revisions. The play's main source was Giraldi Cinthio's *Gli Hecatommithi*, Decade 3, Story 7, first published in 1565, which Shakespeare perhaps read in the French translation made by Gabriel Chappuys in 1584, no English version being known until 1753. Shakespeare alters both the circumstances of the story and the characterization. In Cinthio, the Moor and his wife Disdemona have been married for several years before the story starts, and all the events take place over a much longer period of time than in Shakespeare's play. The Ensign (Iago) is motivated by thwarted love for Disdemona; he steals her handkerchief while she is caressing his child. The murder of Disdemona is contrived to look like an accident; the Moor and the Ensign beat her to death with a stocking filled with sand and then cause the ceiling of the room to collapse, thus burying the body. After her death the Moor becomes half mad with grief and misery; he dismisses the Ensign, who thereupon plots with the Corporal (Cassio) to bring him to trial for murder. Finally, all is revealed and God avenges Disdemona's death. In this account the Moor is a totally passive and ignoble victim of the malicious Ensign. No character corresponding to Shakespeare's Roderigo appears. Shakespeare may also have used Geoffrey Fenton's translation of a story from Belleforest's *Histoires Tragiques*, adapted from the Italian *Certaine Tragicall Discourses* by Matteo Bandello, published in 1567. This story tells of a soldier husband who becomes needlessly jealous of his young wife a month after their marriage and stabs her in bed in a paroxysm of fury. The wife does not die immediately but survives her husband, who commits suicide. After his death she pardons him. The ending of this perhaps suggested Desdemona's last words to Emilia. Some details of the background of the Venetian–Turkish war in *Othello* may have been drawn from Richard Knolles's *History of the Turks* (1603) and perhaps also from William Thomas's *History of Italy* (1549) and Sir Lewis Lewkenor's *The Commonwealth and Government of Venice*, translated in 1599 from Contarini's *De Magistratibus et Republica Venetorum* of 1543. In his play, Shakespeare concentrates on the betrayal of a good man by a completely wicked man. Iago links Cassio's innocent activities with the supposed faithlessness of Desdemona and thus builds in Othello's mind a structure of suspicion. He works towards this by a strategy of disingenuous indirection, leaving Othello always with the suspicion that he (Iago) knows more than he has hinted at. The play moves at a rapid pace, an effect produced in part by the double time scheme, by which the stage events occur within the compass of two days whereas the actual sequence of time for the plot development is several months.

Dramatis Personae

Duke of Venice	Iago, *Othello's ancient*
Brabantio, *a senator*	Roderigo
Other Senators	Montano, *Governor of Cyprus*
Gratiano, *Brabantio's brother*	Clown, *Othello's servant*
Lodovico, *Brabantio's kinsman*	Desdemona, *Othello's wife*
Othello, *a noble Moor*	Emilia, *Iago's wife*
Cassio, *Othello's lieutenant*	Bianca, *Cassio's mistress*

Sailor	Gentlemen, Musicians, and
Messengers, Herald, Officers,	*Attendants*

The Story. Othello, a Moorish general in the service of Venice, has secretly married Desdemona, a Venetian gentlewoman. While he is explaining their love to her father, Brabantio, and the Senate, news comes that war has broken out in Cyprus, and he must leave immediately. Desdemona follows him, accompanied by Othello's ensign, Iago, who is angry that a promotion has been given to Cassio rather than himself. This is the initial motive for the course of treachery he immediately starts to follow. Iago manages to get Cassio drunk and consequently demoted for disorderly behaviour; then suggests to him that he approach Othello through Desdemona for reinstatement. At the same time, Iago manages to suggest to Othello that Desdemona and Cassio are having an affair. Then, obtaining from Emilia (his wife) a handkerchief that Desdemona inadvertently drops, he contrives that Cassio should give the handkerchief to his mistress Bianca and that Othello should see them arguing over it. The handkerchief itself has magic in it, Othello tells Desdemona, and it is more than a mere incriminating clue, as it links together all the play's main characters. In the last act, Othello is a ruthless avenger, bent (as he now thinks) on taking up the cause of all deceived husbands, and also preventing Desdemona from betraying other men. Just as he has always done his duty on the field of battle, Othello must do his duty now. He asks Iago to kill Cassio; the deed is attempted by Iago's dupe Roderigo but fails, and Iago kills Roderigo to avoid betrayal. Othello goes to Desdemona and smothers her in her bed. But his love for her is not dead, and at this climactic moment he is overwhelmed by a realization of his loss. At the same time, he does not yet suspect the perfidy of Iago but Emilia questions Iago and instantly perceives the truth, crying "Villainy, villainy!" (V.ii). Meanwhile, letters have been found on Roderigo's body that incriminate Iago. After trying, and failing, to kill Iago, Othello recalls the service he has done on the battlefield and asks that Cassio and the others remaining do him the justice of reporting things honestly as they have happened. He then stabs himself and, falling on the bed, dies.

Overdone, Mistress· In *Measure for Measure*, a bawd who is sent to prison.

Ovid [Full name, Publius Ovidius Naso] (43 BC–AD 18) Roman poet, one of the leading writers of the Augustan age. He lived at Rome, and was exiled for an unknown reason to Tomi on the Euxine (Black Sea) in Moesia, about AD 9. His chief works are elegies and poems on mythological subjects, ➤*Metamorphoses, Fasti, Ars Amatoria, Heroïdes*, and *Amores*. Shakespeare drew on the *Metamorphoses* and the *Fasti*. Ovid had a high reputation in the Renaissance and influenced many writers.

Oxford, Earl of In *3 Henry VI*, the historical John de Vere, a supporter of Margaret and the Lancastrians. He is captured at the battle of Tewkesbury. In *Richard III*, he joins Richmond and fights at Bosworth.

P

Page   In *The Merry Wives of Windsor*, the husband of Mistress Page.

Page to Falstaff   In *2 Henry IV*, a small boy who serves Falstaff. In *Henry V*, he is the "Boy" who serves Bardolph, Nym, and Pistol, upon whose antics he comments caustically. He is killed by the French while guarding the army supplies of the English. ➤Robin.

Page, Anne   In *The Merry Wives of Windsor*, the daughter of the Pages, wooed and finally won by Fenton. She rejects both Slender and Dr Caius, her parents' choices.

Page, Mistress   In *The Merry Wives of Windsor*, one of the married women to whom Falstaff professes love. She fools him into believing that she responds but in fact devises the Windsor Forest incident, the climax of all the pranks played on Falstaff.

Page, William   In *The Merry Wives of Windsor*, the young brother of Anne Page given a Latin lesson in IV.i.

Palace of Pleasure, The   A collection of tales published in two volumes (a third was projected, but never written) by William Painter in 1566–67. Translations of the stories of Livy, Boccaccio, Bandello, and Margaret of Navarre appear here (Painter originally intended to translate only from Livy, but changed his plan and added the later French and Italian stories). The two volumes contain a hundred tales, making this the largest prose work between *Morte d'Arthur* and North's *Plutarch*, and it is a source for the plots of many Elizabethan dramas, including *All's Well that Ends Well*.

Palamon   In *The Two Noble Kinsmen*, one of the principal characters, the cousin and friend of Arcite. Originally a character in Chaucer's *The Knight's Tale*.

Palsgrave's Company   ➤Lord Admiral's Men.

Pandarus   In *Troilus and Cressida*, the uncle of Cressida, an older and more corrupt character than Chaucer's Pandarus in *Troilus and Criseyde*. At the end of the play he predicts his own death and bequeaths his diseases to the audience.

Pander   In *Pericles*, the owner of the brothel in Mytilene to which Boult brings Marina. His trade is nearly lost when she persuades his clients to desist from their vice.

Pandulph, Cardinal   In *King John*, the papal legate who forces the French king to break his peace with John. He persuades the Dauphin to invade England, but then vainly tries to make him withdraw when John accepts the Pope's (and Pandulph's) candidate for Archbishop of Canterbury.

Panthino   In *The Two Gentlemen of Verona*, the servant of Antonio.

Paris   In *Romeo and Juliet*, a nobleman to whom Capulet has betrothed his daughter Juliet, against her will.

Paris   In *Troilus and Cressida*, a son of Priam and lover of Helen. He opposes Hector's suggestion that Helen be returned to the Greeks so that the war may end, and fights with Menelaus, Helen's former husband (V.vii).

Parolles   In *All's Well That Ends Well*, a comic braggart. When exposed, he takes his dishonour calmly and decides to make use of his talents: "There's place and means for every man alive" (IV.iii).

Pasquil   Pseudonym of ➤Nashe, Thomas.

Patroclus   In *Troilus and Cressida*, a Greek commander. He urges his lover Achilles to stop sulking and rejoin the war, but it requires his death at Trojan hands finally to rouse Achilles to action.

Patience   In *Henry VIII*, a gentlewoman to Queen Katherine.

Paulina   In *The Winter's Tale*, the wife of Antigonus who speaks out in Hermione's defence. She brings Leontes the baby Perdita and announces Hermione's death. Years later she produces Hermione before Leontes and there is a reconciliation. Antigonus having died, Leontes persuades Paulina to marry Camillo.

Peaseblossom   A fairy in *A Midsummer Night's Dream*.

Pedant   In *The Taming of the Shrew*, an old man who pretends to be Vincentio, the father of Lucentio, and is useful in arranging Lucentio's marriage to Bianca.

Pedro, Don   In *Much Ado About Nothing*, the Prince of Arragon. He arranges for the marriage of Claudio and Hero, but by the scheme of his bastard brother, Don John, is convinced of Hero's unfaithfulness. Later he makes amends when the truth is discovered.

Pembroke, Earl of   In *3 Henry VI*, the historical William Herbert, a Yorkist whom Edward IV orders to secure men for his cause against King Henry.

Pembroke, (1st) Earl of   In *King John*, the historical William Marshal, 1st Earl of Pembroke and Striguil. He disapproves of submission to the Pope and later joins the other English lords in their defection to the French after Arthur's supposed murder. When these lords find that the French have sworn to kill them after defeating John, they return to his side.

Pembroke, (3rd) **Earl of** ➤Herbert, William.

Pembroke's Men Theatrical company under the patronage of William ➤Herbert, 3rd Earl of Pembroke; active in the early 1590s but in financial troubles in 1593. They played *Titus Andronicus*, and the bad quartos of 2 and 3 *Henry VI* were among the plays they owned. The young Shakespeare may have been a member of the company.

Pennington, Michael (1943–) British actor who worked with the ➤Royal Shakespeare Company (1964–81) before forming (1985) the ➤English Shakespeare Company with Michael ➤Bogdanov, for which he has both acted and directed. Major roles have included Hamlet (1980), Coriolanus, Leontes (1990), and Macbeth (1992).

Percy, Henry In the history plays, three characters based on historical figures appear under the name of Henry Percy: the (1st) Earl of Northumberland, father of Hotspur, in *Richard II* and 1 and 2 *Henry IV*; Hotspur, in 1 *Henry IV*; and the (3rd) Earl of Northumberland, grandson of Hotspur, in 3 *Henry VI*.

Percy, Lady In 1 *Henry IV*, the wife of Hotspur and sister of Mortimer. In a domestic scene she pleads with Hotspur to tell what plans he has in hand. In 2 *Henry IV*, she urges Northumberland to be avenged for his son's death at Shrewsbury.

Percy, Thomas, Earl of Worcester ➤Worcester, Thomas Percy, Earl of.

Perdita In *The Winter's Tale*, the daughter of Leontes and Hermione. Leontes orders that she be abandoned as a baby in some desert place, but she is rescued and raised as a shepherdess. Florizel falls in love with her, and she is finally restored to her mother and penitent father.

Pericles The Prince of Tyre, the hero of *Pericles*. He undergoes much suffering, losing both wife and daughter, but is eventually rewarded when they are miraculously restored to him.

Pericles [Full title, *Pericles, Prince of Tyre*] A play by Shakespeare, possibly in collaboration with George ➤Wilkins, written probably in 1607 or 1608. It was published in 1609, in quarto, in a corrupt and probably unauthorized text, and again in quarto in 1611, 1619, 1630, and 1635. The number of quartos testifies to the play's contemporary popularity. Not in the first folio of 1623, it appeared first in folio in 1664. It is now generally agreed that Shakespeare did not write the entire play, and it was probably not included in the folio of 1623 for that reason. It has been suggested that Shakespeare took two acts by another playwright, probably George Wilkins, and added three more (except possibly for the Gower choruses). The main sources for the play are the story of Apollonius of Tyre from Book VIII of John Gower's *Confessio Amantis* (1343) and Laurence Twine's romance, *The Patterne of Painefull Adventures* (c.1594), a version of story 153 from the medieval Latin collection *Gesta Romanorum*. Material from Gower and Twine is interwoven throughout the play. In Gower, the hero's name is Apollinus, and in Twine, the more usual Apollonius; Shakespeare's name Pericles has been thought to come from Pyrocles in ➤Sidney's *Arcadia* (1590), whose adventures are to some extent similar, and other suggestions for its source have included North's translation of Plutarch's *Lives*, which also contains the names Cleon and Lysimachus. Marina's name is perhaps Shakespeare's invention, for she is called Thaise in Gower and Tharsia in Twine, a name that Shakespeare or his coauthor adapted for her mother. The relationship of *Pericles* with its main sources is somewhat complicated by the existence of George Wilkins's novel, *The Painfull Adventures of Pericles, Prince of Tyre*, published in 1608, a year before the play; this is mainly founded on Twine's book, which was reissued in 1607, and, apparently, on a *Pericles* performed by the King's Men. This *Pericles* may have been the one Shakespeare partly wrote, an earlier version of it, or a completely different play that Shakespeare too used as a source. The Shakespearean *Pericles* differs from Gower and Twine in the addition of the character Gower, who acts as a chorus or presenter. The play omits details of Antiochus's incest with his daughter, adds a test enforced by Simonides to prove Pericles's love for Thaisa, and generally strengthens the contrast between the different father–daughter relationships. The brothel scenes are elaborated and made more sordid in the play, although Lysimachus's character is made purer so that he may be a fitting husband for Marina. It is difficult to generalize on the use of the sources in this play, since Shakespeare's part in it is still not certain and the text is corrupt.

Dramatis Personae

Antiochus, King of Antioch
Pericles, Prince of Tyre
Helicanus, *a lord of Tyre*
Escanes, *a lord of Tyre*
Simonides, King of Pentapolis
Cleon, *Governor of Tarsus*
Lysimachus, *Governor of Mytilene*
Cerimon, *a lord of Ephesus*
Thaliard, *a lord of Antioch*
Philemon, *Cerimon's servant*
Leonine, *Dionyza's servant*
A Pander
Boult, *the Pander's servant*

Marshal
Daughter of Antiochus
Dionyza, *wife of Cleon*
Thaisa, *daughter of Simonides*
Marina, *daughter of Pericles*
Lychorida, *Marina's nurse*
A Bawd
Lords, Ladies, Knights, Gentlemen, Sailors, Pirates, Fishermen, and Messengers
Diana
Gower, *as Chorus*

The Story. Pericles discovers early in his courtship of the daughter of Antiochus of Antioch that the father and daughter are entangled in an incestuous romance, and is therefore placed in peril of his life by Antiochus. Deputing his loyal minister, Helicanus, to rule Tyre in his stead, he boards ship for Tarsus, but is cast up on the shores of Pentapolis, the sole survivor of a shipwreck. He participates in a tourney for the hand of Thaisa, daughter of King Simonides of Pentapolis, and their marriage follows shortly on the heels of his victory. Thus far, in the first two acts (which Shakespeare is believed not to have written), the play follows a very straightforward plot, but at this point complications are introduced. Pericles is informed by Helicanus of the death of Antiochus, and the hero therefore sets out at once for Tyre with his wife, who is now pregnant. A violent storm arises, and the terrified Thaisa gives birth to a daughter and, a few moments later, appears to die. Pericles, believing her dead, places her in a chest and casts the chest into the sea. Thaisa is washed ashore at Ephesus and restored to consciousness by Cerimon. Convinced that her husband has perished, she enters the temple of Diana as a votaress. Pericles, meanwhile, leaves the daughter, Marina, in Tarsus with Cleon and his wife Dionyza. Sixteen years later Dionyza, violently jealous of this child, now become a woman more beautiful than her own daughter Philoten, seeks to rid herself of Marina by ordering a servant to kill her. The servant is frightened off by pirates, however, and Marina is carried off to a brothel in Mytilene. Humbled by her chastity and virtue, the patrons of this establishment leave her untouched, and one of them, Lysimachus, governor of the city, buys her freedom. Meanwhile, Pericles sees Marina's tomb in a dream-vision and sets out to visit it. Believing her to be dead, he vows never to wash his face or cut his hair, and refuses to speak. He is cast ashore at Mytilene, and confronted with Marina, who woos him back to life. In a vision he sees the goddess Diana, who directs him to Ephesus, where Thaisa awaits and the family is reunited.

Peter In *Measure for Measure*, a Friar, confidant of Vincentio, the Duke of Vienna.

Peter In *Romeo and Juliet*, the servant of Juliet's nurse.

Peter of Pomfret In *King John*, a prophet who predicts that John will yield up his crown before Ascension Day. He is hanged for this.

Peto In *1* and *2 Henry IV*, an associate of Falstaff.

Petruchio In *The Taming of the Shrew*, a Veronese gentleman who, attracted by her dowry, determines to wed and tame the shrew, Katherina. By asserting his dominance (in such ways as arriving late and in old clothes for the wedding, refusing to let her stay for the dinner, taking her food and new clothes from her, and making her call the sun the moon) he forces her (or enables her to take on) the role of submissive wife.

Phebe In *As You Like It*, a shepherdess loved by Silvius. She falls in love with the disguised Rosalind but finally marries Silvius.

Philario In *Cymbeline*, an Italian gentleman, the friend who tries to prevent Posthumus and Iachimo from making their wager.

Philemon In *Pericles*, a servant of Cerimon.

Philip, King of France In *King John*, the historical Philip II, who supports Arthur's claim to the English throne.

Philip Faulconbridge ➤Faulconbridge, Philip.

Philip the Bastard ➤Faulconbridge, Philip.

Phillips, Augustine (d. 1605) English actor and musician. He was one of the original shareholders in the ➤Lord Chamberlain's Men (formed 1594) and of the ➤Globe (1599) and is listed as a principal actor in the first folio (1623) of Shakespeare's plays.

Philo In *Antony and Cleopatra*, a friend of Antony.

Philostrate In *A Midsummer Night's Dream*, Theseus's master of the revels.

Philoten In *Pericles*, the daughter of Cleon and Dionyza who does not appear on stage.

Philotus In *Timon of Athens*, a servant to one of Timon's creditors.

Phoenix, the An indoor playhouse near Drury Lane. It was altered (1617), possibly to a surviving design by Inigo ➤Jones, from a pit for cock-fighting and it was often known as the Cockpit. It was pulled down in 1649 by the Puritans but not completely destroyed.

Phoenix and the Turtle, The A poem generally accepted as being by Shakespeare, first published in an appendix to a book called *Love's Martyr*, by Robert Chester, in 1601. It is an elegy, celebrating the faithful love of a couple beyond death.

Phrynia In *Timon of Athens*, a mistress of Alcibiades.

Pinch In *The Comedy of Errors*, a schoolmaster who believes Antipholus and Dromio of Ephesus to be mad and orders them confined.

Pindarus In *Julius Caesar*, a servant to Cassius. When Cassius thinks the battle is lost at Philippi, he makes Pindarus assist in his suicide.

Pirithous In *The Two Noble Kinsmen*, an Athenian general and loving friend of Theseus.

Pisanio In *Cymbeline*, the servant of Posthumus. When he receives his master's letter ordering him to kill Imogen, he disguises her as a boy and bids her join the Roman army.

Pistol In *2 Henry IV*, in *The Merry Wives of Windsor*, and also in *Henry V*, a bully and swaggerer, a companion of Falstaff. He is a version of the stock type of Italian comedy, the "Thrasio" or cowardly boaster. In *Henry V* he is married to Mistress Quickly, and after her death he decides to become a pimp.

Plantagenet, Lady Margaret In *Richard III*, a young daughter of Clarence who mourns his death.

Plantagenet, Richard ➤York, (3rd) Duke of.

Players In *Hamlet*, the company that comes to play at the court. They travel because they could not find city employment owing to a "late innovation" (II.ii). This is a Shakespearean reference to contemporary conditions in the London theatrical world, either to the child companies whose popularity had temporarily surpassed that of the adult companies or to the banning of plays in London because of ➤Essex's recent rebellion (1601). They perform the "Murder of Gonzago" (the play that Hamlet refers to as *The Mousetrap*).

Players In the Induction to *The Taming of the Shrew*, the company represented as about to enact the play itself, for the entertainment of Christopher Sly.

plays In all, there are now some thirty-eight plays that are generally attributed to Shakespeare, with John ➤Fletcher as co-author of *Henry VIII* and *The Two Noble Kinsmen*, and the first two acts of *Pericles* and parts of *1 Henry VI* written by others (in the former case most probably George ➤Wilkins). Scenes from the anonymous *Edward III* are thought by many to be written by Shakespeare, and some recent scholars ascribe the whole play to him. He is also thought to have written a scene in *Sir Thomas More* (?1593), an attribution suggested by analysis of the handwriting of the manuscript in which the play survives. The dates of composition of the plays can be given only tentatively, since many were written some time before they were registered or printed, and the probable revision of some of the plays makes the problem even more difficult. In some cases letters, journals, and other sources have aided in a closer determination of when the plays were first acted, and parodies of various lines or references to some of the plays in other plays of the period have also aided in dating the plays. In many cases, internal evidence, such as references to contemporary events, has also proved helpful. The following is an alphabetical listing of the plays, with tentatives dates of composition:

All's Well That Ends Well (c. 1603–04)
Antony and Cleopatra (c. 1606)
As You Like It (1599–1600)
The Comedy of Errors (1592–93)
Coriolanus (1607–08)
Cymbeline (1609–10)
Hamlet (1600–1601)
1 Henry IV (c. 1597)
2 Henry IV (c. 1598)
Henry V (1598–99)
1 Henry VI (1589–91)
2 Henry VI (1589–91)

3 Henry VI (1589–91)
Henry VIII (1612–13)
Julius Caesar (c. 1599)
King John (1596)
King Lear (c. 1605)
Love's Labour's Lost (1594–95)
Macbeth (1605–06)
Measure for Measure (1603–04)
The Merchant of Venice (1596–97)
The Merry Wives of Windsor (c. 1597)
A Midsummer Night's Dream
  (1594–95)

Much Ado About Nothing (c. 1598)
Othello (1603–04)
Pericles (1607–08)
Richard II (1595)
Richard III (1592–93)
Romeo and Juliet (1594–95)
The Taming of the Shrew (1592–93)
The Tempest (1611)

Timon of Athens (1605–08)
Titus Andronicus (1592–93)
Troilus and Cressida (1601–02)
Twelfth Night (1600–01)
The Two Gentlemen of Verona
  (1591–93)
The Two Noble Kinsmen (1613)
The Winter's Tale (1609–11)

Poel, William   (1852–1934) British theatre director and actor, who founded (1894) the Elizabethan Stage Society, a non-commercial company with the aim of presenting the plays of Shakespeare and his contemporaries in conditions approximating to those of the Elizabethan stage. The Society's first production was *Twelfth Night* in St George's Hall, London (1895). Its last was *Romeo and Juliet* (1905).

Poins   In *1* and *2 Henry IV*, a witty companion of Prince Henry and Falstaff.

Polixenes   In *The Winter's Tale*, the King of Bohemia, father of Florizel.

Polonius   In *Hamlet*, the father of Ophelia, and the King's chamberlain. He believes Hamlet, who makes a fool of him, to be mad for love of Ophelia. He is killed by Hamlet when hiding in Gertrude's chamber to spy on her encounter with her son.

Polydore   In *Cymbeline*, the name under which Guiderius is raised by Morgan (actually Belarius).

Pompey   [Also, Sextus Pompeius]   In *Antony and Cleopatra*, a leader of the rebellion against the triumvirate. When Antony returns from Egypt, Pompey makes peace with him and Octavius and entertains them on his galley. In the war between Antony and Octavius, he sides with Antony. In history he was the younger son of Pompey the Great.

Pompey   In *Measure for Measure*, the comic servant of Mistress Overdone.

Pope, Thomas   (fl. 1586–1603) English actor, comedian, and acrobat. He is first recorded as acting at Elsinore in 1586. He is listed in the first folio (1623) of Shakespeare's plays as a principal actor and was an original shareholder in the ▶Lord Chamberlain's Men (formed 1594).

Porter   In *Macbeth*, the drunken doorman who admits Macduff and Lennox to Macbeth's castle just as Macbeth has murdered Duncan.

Portia   In *Julius Caesar*, the wife of Marcus Brutus. She goes insane from anxiety over her husband, and her death (from swallowing fire) is reported (IV.iii).

Portia In *The Merchant of Venice*, an heiress in love with Bassanio. Portia (disguised as Balthasar, a learned doctor of law) delivers the famous speech beginning "The quality of mercy is not strain'd" (IV.i), a plea for Shylock to show mercy. In her adherence to the exact letter of the law she beats Shylock at his own game and brings about his ruin.

Posthumus Leonatus In *Cymbeline*, the husband of Imogen. He wagers on her fidelity with Iachimo, and is deceived into believing her unfaithful, after which he attempts to have her murdered. After much suffering they are reunited in the last scene.

Priam In *Troilus and Cressida*, the King of Troy. He debates with his sons about returning Helen to the Greeks and later pleads with Hector not to fight Achilles.

Prince Henry's Company ➤Lord Admiral's Men.

Prince of Bohemia ➤Florizel.

Prince of Verona ➤Escalus.

Princess of France In *Love's Labour's Lost*, a visitor to the "little Academe" (I.i) of the King of Navarre. The King falls in love with her and thus breaks his vow to deny love for three years.

Proculeius In *Antony and Cleopatra*, a friend of Octavius. He is sent to capture Cleopatra at the end of the play but is frustrated in his purpose when she kills herself.

Prospero In *The Tempest*, the rightful Duke of Milan. He is a learned magician living in exile on an island with his daughter Miranda. Through his use of magic he makes Ferdinand fall in love with Miranda, after having caused the shipwreck that brought Ferdinand to the island, and thwarts the plan of Caliban, Stephano, and Trinculo to murder him. He renounces his magic when he has brought his enemies to repentance. In IV.i he speaks the well-known lines beginning "Our revels now are ended" in which life is compared to a stage spectacle.

Proteus In *The Two Gentlemen of Verona*, one of the "two gentlemen." He is faithless to Julia, his betrothed, and betrays his friend Valentine, but repents.

Provost In *Measure for Measure*, the prison custodian. He sympathizes with Claudio and agrees to execute Barnardine in his stead, but finally sends Angelo the head of another prisoner who has already died.

Publius In *Julius Caesar*, a senator who is astonished by the conspiracy against Caesar.

Publius In *Titus Andronicus*, the son of Marcus Andronicus.

Puck [Also, Robin Goodfellow]   In *A Midsummer Night's Dream*, the servant of Oberon. He plays many pranks in the woods near Athens, including changing the head of Bottom to that of an ass. Puck was a mischievous household spirit of English folklore.

Pyramus   In classical legend, a Babylonian youth, lover of ➤Thisbe. The lovers were forbidden to see each other by their parents, but continued secretly to talk together through a crack in the wall that separated their gardens. They finally planned to meet at a certain tomb. Thisbe, who arrived first, was terrified by a lion and fled, dropping her cloak. Pyramus arrived a few minutes later, found the cloak bloodstained from the lion's mouth, believed Thisbe dead, and killed himself. When Thisbe returned and found her lover dead, she too killed herself. Their story is celebrated by ➤Ovid in his ➤*Metamorphoses*, and Shakespeare introduces it in the interlude of *A Midsummer Night's Dream*, presented by Bottom, Flute, and the other artisans in honour of the marriage of Theseus and Hippolyta. Various elements of their story are reminiscent of that of Romeo and Juliet, especially the feuding families and the double deaths at the tomb.

Q

Queen In *Cymbeline*, the wife of Cymbeline and the mother of Cloten by a former husband. In her efforts to secure the throne for her son, she tries to marry him to Imogen, then attempts to poison Imogen, Cymbeline, and Pisanio. She goes mad and confesses her crimes before she dies.

Queen In *Richard II*, the historical Isabel of France, Richard's Queen. She overhears a gardener talking about an orchard and contrasting his husbandry with that of Richard. She bids farewell to Richard as he goes to the Tower.

Queen Elizabeth's Men [Also, The Queen's Company] A theatrical company under the patronage of Queen Elizabeth, formed in 1583 from twelve of the best players then performing. Its members included Richard ➤Tarlton. It dominated the London stage for the next five years.

Queen of the Amazons ➤Hippolyta.

Queen of the Fairies ➤Titania.

Queen of the Goths ➤Tamora.

Quickly, Mistress In *The Merry Wives of Windsor*, the housekeeper of Dr Caius. She assists Anne Page's suitors and later plays the Queen of the Fairies. In *1* and *2 Henry IV* and *Henry V* she is the garrulous Hostess of the Boar's Head, the tavern that Falstaff and his friends frequent. In *2 Henry IV*, she claims that Falstaff has promised to marry her, and that he owes her £100. Later she goes to prison with Doll Tearsheet for beating up a man. In *Henry V*, she has married Pistol. In a speech of comic pathos, she describes the death of Falstaff (II.iii).

Quince, Peter In *A Midsummer Night's Dream*, a carpenter. He is stage manager and speaks the Prologue in the interpolated play confusing all the punctuation.

Quintus In *Titus Andronicus*, one of the four sons of Titus.

R

Raleigh, Sir Walter [Surname as he preferred to spell it, Ralegh] (*c.* 1552–18) English courtier, colonizer, and poet, a great favourite of Queen Elizabeth throughout the 1580s. He introduced cultivation of the potato, in Munster, on lands he was granted by the Queen; he is also credited with introducing tobacco into England. In 1588 he took an active part against the Armada. During this period he became a friend of Edmund ➤Spenser, whom he had met in Ireland some years earlier. He introduced Spenser to Elizabeth and persuaded him to publish *The Faerie Queene*. Raleigh became the centre of a group of poets and scientists, known as the "school of night," that included Christopher ➤Marlowe, Thomas Harriot, George ➤Chapman, Walter Warner, and Matthew Royden, among others. On the accession of James in 1603, Raleigh was stripped of his honours and estates and tried for treason. He was sentenced to death but the sentence was not carried out. A prisoner in the Tower until 1616, Raleigh devoted himself to chemical experiments and the writing of his *History of the World*, which was left unfinished when he was released. He commanded another expedition to Guiana and the Orinoco, but it was a failure from the start. On his return, when the Spanish ambassador made an official complaint about the destruction of a Spanish town by Raleigh, an old sentence was invoked, and Raleigh was executed. In addition to the incomplete *History of the World*, he wrote a number of other prose works, including accounts of the Azores fight and the discovery of Guiana, and he was the author of several poems, the longest of which is the fragmentary *Cynthia*.

Rambures In *Henry V*, the Master of the Crossbows and one of the French lords who boast about the power of the French army before the battle of Agincourt.

Rape of Lucrece, The [Also, *Lucrece*] A narrative poem by Shakespeare, published in 1594. It was dedicated to the Earl of ➤Southampton and was perhaps the "graver labour" promised to him in Shakespeare's dedication of *Venus and Adonis* (1593). The poem was popular in its time and went through six editions before Shakespeare's death. The form is that of rhyme royal (seven-line pentameter stanzas, rhyming *ababbcc*), and the genre that of Ovidian complaint, a hybrid mode combining a narrative of the downfall of one in high estate with the decorative rhetorical manner and sensuous subject matter of ➤Ovid. The poem recounts Tarquin's arrival in Collatium, his stealthy nocturnal visit to Lucrece's room, her pleas for pity, and the rape; afterwards, Lucrece laments at length, summons her husband, Brutus, by letter, and, after telling him what has happened, commits suicide. Brutus vows vengeance, and the Tarquin family is permanently banished from Rome. Shakespeare divides the interest of the poem between Tarquin and Lucrece. She is presented through elaborate rhetorical display, which generalizes her situation in abstract terms; in Tarquin, Shakespeare explores the rapist's dilemma, caught between "frozen conscience and hot-burning will", in terms that recall both Macbeth and Iachimo. The poem also has affinities with *Titus Andronicus* in its preoccupation with lust, bloodshed, and violated chastity.

Ratcliff, Sir Richard   In *Richard III*, a follower of the King who leads Richard's various victims to execution. He is killed at Bosworth with Richard.

Ratsey's Ghost [Also, *Ratseis Ghost*]   A pamphlet published in 1605, which mentions the play *Hamlet* by name during a discussion of Ratsey's criminal career as a highwayman.

Red Bull, the   An inn in Clerkenwell (now part of London), formally converted into a public playhouse about 1604. It was probably similar to the ▶Globe and the ▶Swan in its stage fittings, but was used to present plays requiring considerable spectacle.

Redgrave, Sir Michael   (1908–85) British actor known for his many Shakespearean roles, particularly for the Old Vic company and at the ▶Shakespeare Memorial Theatre, Stratford-upon-Avon. His first professional performance was as the King of Navarre in *Love's Labour's Lost* (Old Vic, 1936); other roles included Orlando (Shakespeare Memorial Theatre, 1936), Macbeth (Shakespeare Memorial Theatre, 1947), Berowne and Hamlet (Shakespeare Memorial Theatre, 1949–50), Shylock, King Lear, and Antony (Shakespeare Memorial Theatre, 1953), and Claudius (National Theatre, 1963).

Redgrave, Vanessa   (1937–   ) British actress, daughter of Sir Michael ▶Redgrave. She has performed many Shakespearean roles since 1959, when she first appeared at the ▶Shakespeare Memorial Theatre, Stratford-upon-Avon, as Helena and Valeria. Other roles have included Rosalind and Katherine (Shakespeare Memorial Theatre, 1961), Imogen (▶Royal Shakespeare Company, 1962), and Cleopatra (1986, 1995).

Regan   In *King Lear*, the second daughter of Lear; like her sister Goneril, she flatters Lear in order to win his land. She is cruel towards Gloucester, and encourages her husband Cornwall to blind him. Finally she finds herself in competition with Goneril for the favours of Edmund and dies of poison at her sister's hand.

Reignier, Duke of Anjou   In *1 Henry VI*, the supporter of the Dauphin and Joan of Arc, and the assumed King of Naples, Sicily, and Jerusalem. He agrees to the marriage of Margaret, his daughter, with Henry in return for the territories of Maine and Anjou.

Revels Office An official body existing in England from about the middle of the sixteenth century to the late seventeenth century, headed by the Master of the Revels and charged with supervising court performances of plays and other entertainments.

Reynaldo In *Hamlet*, a servant to Polonius. In the first quarto he is called Montano.

Rice, John (*fl.* 1607–20). English actor, who appeared in Shakespeare's plays and is mentioned as a principal actor in the first folio (1623) of Shakespeare's works.

Richard, Duke of Gloucester ➤Gloucester, Richard, Duke of.

Richard, Duke of York ➤York, Richard, (5th) Duke of.

Richard II In *Richard II*, the King of England, a weak monarch. Historically, he was a grandson to Edward III and the last Plantagenet king. In the play he is intensely conscious of his status as anointed monarch, but his misuse of his power creates enemies, and he is instrumental in bringing about his own downfall and usurpation by Henry Bolingbroke.

Richard II [Full title, *The Tragedy of King Richard the Second*] A historical play by Shakespeare, produced probably in 1595, and published in 1597. The deposition scene carried particular significance for Queen Elizabeth (whose right to the throne was questioned by a fair number of her subjects for most of her reign) and it was omitted in the first quarto (1597); however, by the time of the fourth quarto (1608) it was restored. It was probably this play which was given a special performance at the ➤Globe theatre on 7 February 1601, the day before ➤Essex started his rebellion. It was paid for by Essex's supporters, but none of the actors was punished for putting it on. Shakespeare took material for the play from a number of sources but his main source was ➤Holinshed's *Chronicles* (second edition, 1587), from which he took most of the names and events in his play, following, with certain alterations, Holinshed's account of the end of Richard's reign from April 1398 to March 1400. In several instances he telescoped and rearranged the sequence of events for greater dramatic effect; the death of Gaunt, Richard's departure for Ireland, and the return of Bolingbroke from banishment all take place in a single scene (II.i), whereas in Holinshed they happen over a matter of months, and the events of Act IV are also compressed. The accusations of Bagot and Fitzwater were made on separate occasions in October 1598 after the actual abdication of the king, which was in September, and the Abbot of Westminster's plan for conspiracy was not formed until December. Other changes from Holinshed reflect on Shakespeare's planning of the characterization in his play. He omits an episode in which Northumberland tricked Richard into an ambush on the way to Flint Castle that might have reflected badly on Bolingbroke, and he totally changes the ages of Northumberland's son, Henry Percy (Hotspur), and Bolingbroke's son, the future Henry V. Hotspur was in fact two years older than both Richard II and Bolingbroke, whereas in *Richard II* he is a youth; and Bolingbroke's son was only twelve in 1399, when Shakespeare has Bolingbroke speak of him as a dissolute young gallant. He used another chronicle, *The Union of the Two Noble and Illustre Famelies of Lancastre and Yorke* (1548) by Edward Hall, for the point of departure of his play, since Hall's account of Richard II's reign also begins with the quarrel between Mowbray and Hereford, but for little otherwise. He knew the anonymous contemporary play, *Woodstock*, which deals with events from 1382 to 1399 and especially with the life of Richard II's uncle, Thomas of Woodstock, Earl of Gloucester, who is referred to several times in *Richard II*, although critics have differed as to how far this play influenced him. Shakespeare also knew *A Mirrour for Magistrates* (1599) in which Richard II is presented as a proud and tyrannous king, a classic example of the idea that "lawles life, to lawles death ey drawes." Froissart's *Chronicles*, translated by Lord Berners in 1525, was also available to him, and from this he may have taken hints for the conception of Gaunt as a wise but rejected counsellor, for the important part Northumberland played in calling back Bolingbroke, and for Bolingbroke's popularity with the people, although he could have found these elsewhere. Two other French chronicles, the *Chronicque de la Traison et Mort de Richard Deux Roy Dengleterre* and the *Histoire du Roy d'Angleterre Richard II* by Jean Créton, both known to Holinshed and Hall, may have been used independently by Shakespeare. The *Traison* is evidence of a tradition more favourable to Richard II than that of the Tudor chronicles, and it may have helped Shakespeare to form his relatively sympathetic portrait of Richard II, especially in the account of Richard's leave-taking from his Queen, although in the *Traison* the event takes place before Richard's departure for Ireland. From Créton may have come the comparison between Richard's betrayal and that of Christ. The *Traison* and Créton's account also influenced Samuel ►Daniel in his poem *The First Fowre Bookes of the Civile Wars* (1595), which it is likely that Shakespeare knew and used. Many parallels between *Richard II* and Daniel's poem may be incidental, but Shakespeare seems to owe to Daniel the conception of the Queen—she was in fact a child of nine at the time—and he may also have used Daniel for the account of the contrasted entries of Richard and Bolingbroke into London (V.ii). Finally, ►Marlowe's *Edward II* may well have provided some ideas and inspiration in its treatment of the fall of a weak monarch.

Dramatis Personae

King Richard II	Lord Berkeley
John of Gaunt	Bushy
Edmund of Langley, Duke of York	Bagot
Henry Bolingbroke, Duke of	Green
Hereford, *later* Henry IV	Earl of Northumberland
Duke of Aumerle	Henry Percy (Hotspur)
Thomas Mowbray, Duke of Norfolk	Lord Ross
Duke of Surrey	Lord Willoughby
Earl of Salisbury	Lord Fitzwater

Bishop of Carlisle	Duchess of Gloucester
Abbot of Westminster	Duchess of York
Lord Marshal	*Lady attending on the Queen*
Sir Stephen Scroop	*Lords, Heralds, Officers, Soldiers,*
Sir Pierce of Exton	*Gardeners, Keepers, Messenger,*
Captain of a band of Welshmen	*Groom, other Attendants*
Queen to King Richard	

The Story. In the presence of the King, Bolingbroke accuses Mowbray of causing the death of the Duke of Gloucester. It is agreed that each man may defend his honour in a tournament, but just as each is about to attack the other, the King halts the proceedings and banishes them both. Shortly afterwards, upon the death of John of Gaunt (Bolingbroke's father), Richard seizes his estates in order to finance an Irish campaign. This additional evidence of Richard's disregard for the rights of his nobles arouses the ire of both York and Northumberland, and the latter, with other nobles, goes to join Bolingbroke (who has returned, despite his exile, to claim his dukedom). When Richard returns from Ireland, he learns that his army has dispersed and his favourites, Bushy and Green, have been executed by Bolingbroke. Richard takes refuge in Flint Castle, and when Bolingbroke meets him there (ostensibly to claim his estates) submits to being taken as a prisoner to London. Before Parliament, he is forced to confess his crimes against the state, and despite the protests of the Bishop of Carlisle, he hands over his crown to Bolingbroke, who is already acting as King. Aumerle, the son of York, has meanwhile plotted against the new ruler. When York discovers this he hastens to inform Bolingbroke, but Aumerle and his mother, York's wife, plead for and are granted clemency. Richard is imprisoned in Pomfret Castle, where he is murdered by Sir Pierce of Exton (who believes that Bolingbroke wishes Richard's death). Bolingbroke expresses regret for the murder and vows to lead a crusade to ease his conscience. In its theme, the play explores an issue which was to tear England apart half a century later: the basis of royal authority, whether derived directly from God or from the consent of the people and the effective exercise of power.

Richard III ►Gloucester, Richard, Duke of.

Richard III [Full title, *The Tragedy of King Richard the Third*] A historical play, written by Shakespeare in 1592–93. It was printed anonymously in quarto in 1597; in a 1598 quarto Shakespeare's name appears; other quartos were published in 1602, 1605, 1612, and 1622; it appears also in the first folio of 1623. In 1700, ►Cibber produced an alteration, using parts of other Shakespeare plays, that was long considered the only acting version of the text. Shakespeare's main sources were the two prose chronicles, ►Holinshed's *Chronicles* (second edition, 1587) and *The Union of the Two Noble and Illustre Famelies of Lancastre and Yorke* (1548) by Edward Hall, which Holinshed had used as a source, although Shakespeare consulted it independently. Both Hall and Holinshed had the story of the fiend-like Richard, which owes more to Tudor propaganda than to historical fact, from chronicles composed in the reign of Richard's successors Henry VII and Henry VIII, especially Sir Thomas More's *History of King Richard III*, printed in English in 1557 and in Latin in 1566, and also Polydore Vergil's *Historia Angliae* (1534). Shakespeare might have consulted More or Vergil himself, but he is more likely to have come to their work through the medium of Hall and Holinshed. As was usual in his history plays, Shakespeare had to select from, rearrange, and compress events taking place over a considerable period of time, in this instance fourteen years, from Henry VI's death in May 1471 to the Battle of Bosworth in August 1485. For instance, in the play the arrest of the Duke of Clarence takes place before the burial of Henry VI and his execution before the death of his brother Edward IV, whereas in fact Henry was buried in 1471, Clarence was executed in 1477, and Edward died in 1483. As well as using Hall and Holinshed for the major events of the play and the characterization of the hero, Shakespeare took various minor details from their accounts; the bleeding of Henry VI's corpse during the funeral procession comes from Holinshed, the two murderers of Clarence from Hall's account of the murder of the Princes in the Tower, the demise of the credulous Hastings (III.iv) from Hall, and the contrasting orations of Richmond and Richard before the battle from both. Other details were taken from sixteenth-century plays and poems. From *A Mirrour for Magistrates* (1559) Shakespeare took the idea of the ghosts of Richard's victims appearing at his bedside the night before the battle and also the account of Clarence's wretched death; the *Mirrour* was the first work to suggest that Richard was in part responsible for Clarence's death. He may have found a precedent for his use of the women characters from the Latin tragedy *Richardus Tertius* (1579) by Thomas Legge; in *Richard III* the women are distinctly more significant than in Shakespeare's earlier histories and Queen Margaret, who in fact never came back to England after she was ransomed but died in 1383 in France, is unhistorically introduced into several scenes to prophesy and curse. Legge used various Senecan plays such as *Hercules Furens*, translated by Jasper Heywood in 1561, for some of Queen Elizabeth's part, and Shakespeare may also have drawn on ►Seneca, either in the original or in one of the contemporary translations. The relationship of Shakespeare's *Richard III* to the anonymous play, *The True Tragedy of Richard III*, published in 1594 but written earlier, is not clear; but the plays have many features in common, especially in their fusion of elements from the Senecan revenge play with the English chronicle play.

Dramatis Personae

King Edward IV

Edward, Prince of Wales, *son to King Edward, afterwards* King Edward V

Richard, Duke of York, *son to King Edward*

George, Duke of Clarence

Richard, Duke of Gloucester, *afterwards* King Richard III

A young Son and Daughter of Clarence

Henry, Earl of Richmond, *afterwards* King Henry VII

Cardinal Bourchier

Thomas Rotherham, Archbishop of
York
John Morton
Duke of Buckingham
Duke of Norfolk
Earl Rivers
Marquess of Dorset, *son to Queen
Elizabeth*
Lord Grey, *son to Queen Elizabeth*
Earl of Oxford
Lord Hastings
Lord Stanley (Earl of Derby)
Lord Lovel
Sir Thomas Vaughan
Sir Richard Ratcliff
Sir William Catesby
Sir James Tyrrel
Sir James Blunt

Sir Walter Herbert
Sir Robert Brackenbury
Christopher Urswick, *a priest*
Another Priest
Tressel *and* Berkeley
Lord Mayor of London
Sheriff of Wiltshire
Elizabeth, *Queen to King Edward IV*
Margaret, *widow of King Henry VI*
Duchess of York, *mother to King
Edward IV, Richard, Duke of
Gloucester, and George, Duke of
Clarence*
Lady Anne
*Lords and other Attendants, a
Pursuivant, Scrivener, Citizens,
Murderers, Messengers, Soldiers*
Ghosts of those murdered by Richard III

The Story. Richard, Duke of Gloucester, having determined to obtain the crown, sets out to dispose of every obstacle that may stand in his way. He contrives to get his elder brother, the Duke of Clarence, imprisoned by the dying Edward IV, and orders his murder in the Tower. As the funeral procession of Henry VI passes by, he greets Lady Anne, the widow of Henry's son, and is soundly cursed by her; nevertheless, he proposes marriage to her and is accepted. Margaret the widow of Henry VI, Elizabeth the widow of the now dead Edward IV, and the Duchess of York, the mother of Edward, Clarence, and Richard, all curse Richard and mourn the loss of their loved ones. While appearing to arrange the coronation of young Edward (whom he has imprisoned with his younger brother in the Tower), Richard executes Hastings, Rivers, Grey, and Vaughan, supporters of Elizabeth and her son. Buckingham, Richard's supporter, goes to the Guildhall and persuades the citizens to offer Richard the crown. When he is crowned he disposes of all who might oppose him, including the young princes in the Tower. His henchman, Buckingham, having refused to kill the princes, flees to join Richmond but is murdered on the way. Meanwhile Richmond has landed and marches toward London, and at Bosworth Field the two forces meet. On the eve of the battle, Richard sees the ghosts of all his victims, and the following day he is slain by Richmond, who is then crowned Henry VII, the first Tudor king.

Richardson, Ian   (1934–   ) British actor who has appeared in many Shakespearean roles, mostly for the ►Royal Shakespeare Company; they include Oberon (1962), Ford (1964, etc.), Coriolanus and Bertram (1976), Prospero (1970), and Richard II and Bolingbroke (alternately with Richard Pascoe, 1973–74).

Riche, Barnaby (*c.* 1540–1617) English pamphleteer and soldier, who wrote a large number of prose works, including military tracts, romances, satirical pamphlets, and accounts of the state of Ireland, where he was for a time stationed. His pamphlet *Riche His Farewell to Military Profession* (1581), contains eight narratives including *Apollonius and Silla*, one of the main sources for *Twelfth Night*.

Richmond, Henry Tudor, Earl of In *3 Henry VI*, a young boy who Henry prophesies shall be King one day. In *Richard III*, he lands with an army, bent on dethroning the tyrannical Richard. He defeats Richard at Bosworth and is proclaimed Henry VII. His reign is foreseen as bringing peace to England. The historical Henry VII, first of the Tudor dynasty, unified the Lancastrians and Yorkists by his marriage with Edward IV's daughter, Elizabeth.

Rinaldo In *All's Well That Ends Well*, the steward of the Countess of Roussillion.

Rivers, Earl In *3 Henry VI*, the brother of Elizabeth, Lady Grey, who is later the Queen of Edward IV. In *Richard III*, he is executed on Richard's order because he has urged the coronation of young Prince Edward.

Robin In *The Merry Wives of Windsor*, Falstaff's page. He may be the same person as the Page who appears in *2 Henry IV* with Falstaff and in *Henry V* with Bardolph, Nym, and Pistol.

Robin Goodfellow ➤Puck.

Robinson, Richard (d. 1648) English actor, celebrated as a player of women's roles. He appears in the lists of actors of the Shakespeare (1623) and ➤Beaumont and ➤Fletcher (1647) folios. He is known to have acted in ➤Jonson's *Catiline* (1611) and Fletcher's *Bonduca* (1611).

Roderigo In *Othello*, a foolish gentleman in love with Desdemona. Iago uses him to involve Cassio in a quarrel, hoping the latter will be killed, but then stabs Roderigo while he is scuffling with Cassio. The letters incriminating Iago in the plot to play upon Othello's jealousy are found on Roderigo's body.

Rogero In *The Winter's Tale*, a gentleman of Sicilia.

Romeo The hero of *Romeo and Juliet*. Initially, he suffers from an unrequited passion for Rosaline, but falls deeply in love with Juliet when he first sees her at the Capulets' ball. He is forced against his will into a duel with Tybalt whom he kills, and from then on his premonitions of misfortune are tragically realized.

Romeo and Juliet [Full title, *The Tragedy of Romeo and Juliet*] A tragedy by Shakespeare, printed in an unauthorized edition in 1597, which is 800 lines shorter than the quarto of 1599, and known to have been produced before 1597. It was probably written in 1594–95. Shakespeare's main source was a long narrative poem in fourteeners called *The Tragical Historye of Romeus and Juliet* by Arthur Brooke, published in 1562, from which he had already taken a few phrases for his poem *Venus* *and Adonis.* Brooke's poem was in turn based on a French translation by Pierre Boiastuau of an Italian novella by Matteo Bandello. The story of two young lovers who persist in their romance despite the enmity of their families only to come to a tragic conclusion had long been popular in Renaissance Italy in several forms, the earliest known version being the story of Mariotto and Gianozza of Siena told by Masuccio in *Il Novellino* (1476). In Luigi da Porto's *Istoria novellamente ritrovata di due Nobili Amanti* (*c.* 1530), for the first time the story is set in Verona, the lovers are aristocrats, and the feuding families are the Montecchi and the Cappelleti. Shakespeare did not know the Italian versions of the story and probably not Boiastuau's French one, but apart from Brooke's poem he may also have known William Painter's translation of Boiastuau in his ➤*Palace of Pleasure* (1567). Brooke, in his preface to the reader, says that he has seen the story "lately set foorth on stage," but no stage version before Shakespeare's is known. It is clear that the story of Romeo and Juliet was popular in Elizabethan England. Brooke's poem was reprinted in 1582, and reissued in 1587. Shakespeare followed it quite closely. Romeo's former love, the meeting of Romeo and Juliet at the ball, the helpful intervention of Friar Laurence, the clandestine marriage, Romeo's fight with Tybalt and subsequent banishment, Juliet's sleeping potion, the ill-luck with the messenger sent to Romeo, the suicide of Romeo followed by the immediate revival of Juliet and her death, are all essential features of Shakespeare's play to be found in Brooke. Shakespeare alters his source principally by speeding up the action and filling out the characters. In Brooke, the story takes place at a leisurely pace over several months; in Shakespeare the lovers meet, mature, and die in a few hectic days. The characters of Mercutio and Tybalt are developed from the briefest descriptions; their enmity and their opposition to the world of the lovers are entirely Shakespeare's invention. The lovers are younger than in the source; in Brooke, Juliet is sixteen, in Shakespeare only fourteen. Brooke says his aim is to describe "a couple of unfortunate lovers, thralling themselves to unhonest desire, neglecting the authorities and advise of parents and frendes ... and by all meanes of unhonest lyfe, hastyng to most unhappye deathe." His is a moral tale, emphasizing the rashness of youth and the inconstancy of fortune. Shakespeare takes from him the theme of ill-luck and "inauspicious stars," but his emphasis is rather on the beauty and pathos of Romeo and Juliet's sacrificial passion than on their "unhonest lyfe." *Romeo and Juliet* was adapted by Otway in 1680 as *Caius Marius*.

Dramatis Personae

Escalus, Prince of Verona	Benvolio, *friend to Romeo*
Paris, *kinsman to the Prince*	Tybalt, *nephew to Lady Capulet*
Montague	Friar Laurence
Capulet	Friar John
Cousin to Capulet	Balthasar, *servant to Romeo*
Romeo, *son to Montague*	Sampson, *servant to Capulet*
Mercutio, *friend to Romeo*	Gregory, *servant to Capulet*

Peter, *servant to Juliet's nurse*
Abraham, *servant to Montague*
An Apothecary
Three Musicians
Page to Paris; *another Page*
An Officer
Lady Montague
Lady Capulet

Juliet, *daughter to Capulet*
Nurse to Juliet
Citizens of Verona, *Kinsfolk*
of both houses, Masquers,
Guards, Watchmen, and
Attendants
Chorus

The Story. In Verona live the feuding families of Montague and Capulet. Romeo, the son of Montague, is infatuated with Rosaline, Capulet's niece. Learning that she is invited to a ball at Capulet's, he joins with some masquers and attends, in disguise, but there falls in love with Juliet, the daughter of Capulet. That night he steals into Capulet's orchard and, standing under Juliet's balcony, hears her declare her love for him, "O Romeo, Romeo wherefore art thou Romeo? … be but sworn my love, / And I'll no longer be a Capulet" (II.iii). At this, he steps forward and declares his love for her, and they plan to be secretly married the following day. Romeo arranges with Friar Laurence for the marriage, and with the aid of Juliet's nurse, the two are wed at the Friar's cell. That same afternoon, in a chance meeting with Tybalt, a Capulet, Romeo is challenged to a duel, but he refuses, knowing Tybalt is Juliet's cousin. Romeo's friend Mercutio accepts the challenge and is killed, at which Romeo avenges his death by killing Tybalt. Since such fighting had been declared unlawful, Romeo is banished by the Prince, and after one night with Juliet he leaves for Mantua, reassured by Friar Laurence that in time all will be reconciled. Meanwhile, Juliet's parents announce that she is to be married immediately to Paris, a kinsman of the Prince. Her parents refuse to postpone the marriage, and her nurse advises that a handsome and noble second husband in Verona is of more use than a first husband in banishment. Now alone with her dilemma, Juliet obtains from Friar Laurence a sleeping potion that will make her seem as if dead, for forty-two hours, during which time he will send a message to Romeo, who will come and free her from the tomb. However, Friar John, with the message for Romeo, is delayed by constables who think he may be infected with the plague, so Romeo hears only of Juliet's death. He returns to Verona, fights with and kills the mourning Paris at Juliet's tomb, then enters the tomb, drinks poison, and dies at Juliet's side. Juliet awakens as Friar Laurence, who has just heard of his plans going awry, enters the tomb to rescue her. On seeing the dead Romeo, she refuses to leave the tomb, and when the Friar is frightened away, she first tries to poison herself with the remains of Romeo's poison, then stabs herself. Alerted by Paris's page, the watch arrives, discovers the bodies, and captures Friar Laurence, who tells of the secret marriage, the sleeping potion, and the double death. At this tragedy, Montague and Capulet repent of their enmity.

Rosader   In Thomas ➤Lodge's *Rosalynde*, the younger brother of Torrismond the Usurper, and lover of Rosalynde. He became Orlando in Shakespeare's adaptation of the story, *As You Like It*.

Rosalind   In *As You Like It*, the daughter of the exiled Duke, in love with Orlando and the heroine of the play. She assumes male disguise to go into exile in the Forest of Arden. She is a vigorous and witty character who controls the romantic action of the play and contrives the reunions and marriages in the final scene. Rosalind satirizes the extravagance and artifice of romantic love while herself falling a victim to it.

Rosaline   In *Love's Labour's Lost*, an attendant to the Princess of France. Berowne falls in love with her.

Rosaline   In *Romeo and Juliet*, a Capulet with whom Romeo is in love at the beginning of the play. She does not appear.

Rose, the   An Elizabethan playhouse on the ➤Bankside close to the ➤Globe, built in 1587 by Philip ➤Henslowe and his partner John Cholmley. Shakespeare may have acted there in his early days with the ➤Admiral's Men. The excavation of part of its foundations in 1989 reveals it to have been a polygonal structure, originally with a raked floor in the yard sloping toward the stage, which was tapered at the front, and erected to the north-north-west of the theatre. It probably had a thatched roof and walls of timber and plaster with a lower section of brick. It was rebuilt by Henslowe in 1592 to enlarge and level the yard, and to relocate the stage, possibly providing a roof over it. It was demolished in 1606.

Rosencrantz   In *Hamlet*, an old schoolfellow of Hamlet, sent for, along with Guildenstern, by the King to spy upon Hamlet. He is killed when Hamlet substitutes his and Guildenstern's names for his own in instructions sent by Claudius.

Ross   In *Macbeth*, a Scottish thane who must tell Macduff that his wife and children have been killed on Macbeth's orders.

Ross, Lord   In *Richard II*, one of the noblemen who join Bolingbroke when he comes to claim his estates.

Rotherham, Thomas   In *Richard III*, the Archbishop of York. He resigns when he hears that Rivers and Grey have been imprisoned.

Roussillion, Countess of   [Also, Rosillion]   In *All's Well That Ends Well*, the mother of Bertram and the guardian of Helena, who tries to bring Bertram back when he abandons Helena.

Rowe, Nicholas   (1674–1718) British dramatist and poet, appointed (1715) Poet Laureate. He was Shakespeare's first editor. His edition (1709) contained the first formal biography of Shakespeare and a collection of traditions and anecdotes, which even if of doubtful veracity, have been influential on Shakespearean biography. Rowe also used his knowledge of the stage to divide the plays into acts and scenes, to indicate exits and entrances, to add a *dramatis personae* to each play, and to amend spelling and punctuation in the text.

Rowley, William   (*c.* 1585–1626) English dramatist. He is mentioned as an actor in the Duke of York's Company in 1610, and also acted with Princess Elizabeth's Company at the ►Cockpit theatre in 1623. In 1621 he was writing for this latter company, both alone and with Thomas ►Middleton. He joined the ►King's Men in 1625 and did his last work for them. A play in which he collaborated, *The Birth of Merlin* (printed 1622), bore Shakespeare's name as co-author when it was printed, but it is now generally thought that not Shakespeare but possibly Middleton collaborated on it. He worked with Middleton on several plays, including *The Changeling* (acted 1624, published 1653). With John Ford and Thomas ►Dekker he wrote *The Witch of Edmonton* (acted 1623, printed 1658); with Dekker, *Keep the Widow Waking* (now lost); with John Webster, *A Cure for a Cuckold* (printed 1661); and with Thomas Heywood, *Fortune by Land and Sea* (printed 1655). He may also have worked on some of the plays attributed to ►Beaumont and ►Fletcher.

Royal National Theatre   A theatre designed by Denys Lasdun and erected on the South Bank of the Thames in London in 1976. Although efforts had been made to found a National Theatre in London since the early years of the twentieth century, it was not until 1963 that the National Theatre company began operations, under the direction of Sir Laurence ►Olivier at the Old Vic. The first production was *Hamlet*. Subsequent Shakespeare productions included *Othello* (1964) and *The Merchant of Venice* (1970). Peter ►Hall became director in 1973 and served until 1988, when Richard ►Eyre took over; he was succeeded by Trevor ►Nunn in 1997. The company moved to its permanent home on the South Bank in 1976. It received the title Royal National Theatre in 1988.

Royal Shakespeare Company   The name given in 1961 to the semi-permanent company performing at the ►Shakespeare Memorial Theatre, Stratford-upon-Avon, then under the direction of Peter ►Hall. The following year Hall was joined by Michel Saint-Denis and Peter ►Brook as co-directors. The subsequent directors have been Trevor ►Nunn (1968–86), Terry ►Hands (1986–91), and Adrian ►Noble (1991–   ). The company also performed at the Aldwych Theatre, London, until 1982, when it acquired two purpose-built theatres (the main house and the smaller Pit) in the Barbican as its London base. It is the major British company performing Shakespeare.

Rugby, John   In *The Merry Wives of Windsor*, a servant to Dr Caius.

Rumour   In the Induction to *2 Henry IV*, a stage direction reads "Enter Rumour painted full of tongues." He brings false news to Northumberland of Hotspur's victory at Shrewsbury. Rumour was a common figure in masques.

Rutland, Edmund, Earl of   In *3 Henry VI*, a son of the Duke of York, killed by Clifford to avenge the death of his father.

Rylance, Mark   (1960–   ) British actor and director. As artistic director of the ►International Shakespeare Globe Centre (1996–   ), he both acts in and directs Shakespearean productions in conditions designed to approximate to those of the Elizabethan theatre. He has played Hamlet (1988), and Romeo (1989) for the ►Royal Shakespeare Company, and at the Globe, Proteus (1996), Henry V (1997), and Bassanio (1998).

S

Salisbury, Earl of   In *2 Henry VI*, the historical Richard Neville. He is the enemy of Suffolk, whom he has banished, and also of Cardinal Beaufort whose death he witnesses. He joins the Duke of York and fights at St Albans.

Salisbury, (3rd) Earl of   In *King John*, the historical William de Longespée (or Longsword), illegitimate son of Henry II. Disapproving of John's second coronation and suspecting him of responsibility for Arthur's death, he resolves to join the Dauphin, but on learning of the French treachery returns to John.

Salisbury, (3rd) Earl of   In *Richard II*, the historical John de Montacute (or Montagu), a loyal supporter of Richard. He tries to keep Richard's Welsh troops in order, and later he rebels against Henry IV but is captured and executed.

Salisbury, (4th) Earl of   In *Henry V*, the historical Thomas de Montacute (or Montagu). He is present at Agincourt. In *1 Henry VI*, he is killed by a cannon blast.

Salisbury Court   A private theatre in the Whitefriars district of London, which was built in 1629 and became one of the principal playhouses. It was destroyed in 1649.

Sampson   In *Romeo and Juliet*, a servant of Capulet.

Sandys, Lord   [Also, Sir William Sandys (or Sands).]   In *Henry VIII*, a courtier.

Saturninus   In *Titus Andronicus*, the son of the late emperor of Rome. When Titus withdraws from the election, Saturninus is chosen emperor. He marries Tamora, Queen of the Goths. Discovering the body of his brother Bassianus, he orders Titus's sons executed for his murder. He kills Titus and is himself killed by Lucius.

Say, Lord   In *2 Henry VI*, the Lord Treasurer. Cade captures him and accuses him of various crimes against the populace. He is executed and his head put on a pole.

Scales, Lord   In *2 Henry VI*, the commander of the Tower who is solicited for aid during the rebellion of Cade. In *1 Henry VI*, a messenger reports that he has been captured at Patay.

Scarus   In *Antony and Cleopatra*, a friend of Antony. He describes the flight of Cleopatra's fleet at Actium and remains loyal to Antony.

Scofield, Paul   (1922–   ) British actor who has performed in many Shakespearean roles since the 1940s, many of them at Stratford-upon-Avon. His first

Shakespearean roles were Vincentio and then Tranio in *The Taming of the Shrew* for ENSA in 1941; subsequently he has played Don Armado, Lucio, and Mercutio (1946–47), the Bastard in *King John*, Hamlet and the Clown in *The Winter's Tale* (1948), King Lear (1962–63), and Timon of Athens (1965), all at the ➤Shakespeare Memorial Theatre, Stratford-upon-Avon, and Othello (National Theatre, 1980). More recently he has played Shakespearean roles only on film, including the French King in *Henry V* (1989) and the Ghost in *Hamlet* (1990).

Scroop, Lord   In *Henry V*, a traitor who, with Cambridge and Grey, plots to murder the King. He is discovered and given a warrant for his death.

Scroop, Richard   In *1* and *2 Henry IV*, the historical Richard le Scrope, Archbishop of York. He joins Hotspur's rebellion in *1 Henry IV* but is not present at the crucial battle. In *2 Henry IV*, he is tricked into making an armistice and dismissing his forces, after which he is arrested.

Scroop, Sir Stephen   In *Richard II*, a supporter of Richard who reports the death of Bushy and Green.

Sea Captain   In *Twelfth Night*, the captain of the ship wrecked on the Illyrian coast. He promises to present Viola, disguised as a page, to Orsino, the Duke.

Seacole   In *Much Ado About Nothing*, the Second Watchman, who arrests Borachio and Conrade.

Sebastian   In *The Tempest*, the brother of Alonso, King of Naples. He is ready to murder Alonso for his power, but is easily prevented by Ariel.

Sebastian   In *Twelfth Night*, the twin brother of Viola, who, much to his surprise, finds himself married to Olivia.

Second Maiden's Tragedy, The   A play of unknown authorship, at various times attributed to ➤Chapman, Massinger, Webster, Tourneur, and also to Shakespeare but now thought, on the basis of internal evidence, to be by ➤Middleton.

Sejanus His Fall   A tragedy by Ben ➤Jonson, acted in 1603 and published in 1605. Shakespeare's name appears in the list of actors, printed in the folio of 1616.

Seleucus   In *Antony and Cleopatra*, the treasurer of Cleopatra, who reveals that she has not been open with Caesar about the extent of her wealth.

Sempronius   In *Timon of Athens*, one of the lords who refuse to help Timon.

Sempronius   In *Titus Andronicus*, a kinsman of Titus.

Seneca, Lucius Annaeus   (*c.* 4 BC–AD 65) Roman statesman, philosopher, and dramatist. He lived during the reigns of Caligula and Nero, and was eventually obliged to commit suicide. He was the author of nine tragedies, all translated into English by 1581 and familiar to Elizabethan writers. They were violent and sensational plays on mythological themes, intended for reading and recitation rather than for stage performance. Shakespeare was strongly influenced by both their themes and their style, especially in *Titus Andronicus*, *Richard III*, *Hamlet*, and *Macbeth*.

Servilius   In *Timon of Athens*, one of Timon's servants.

Setebos   A supposed Patagonian god, mentioned by Caliban in *The Tempest*, and by Browning in "Caliban upon Setebos".

Sextus Pompeius   ►Pompey.

Seyton   In *Macbeth*, an officer attending Macbeth. He reports the death of Lady Macbeth.

Shadow, Simon   In *2 Henry IV*, a man pressed into military service by Falstaff.

Shakespeare Memorial Theatre   [Also, Royal Shakespeare Theatre]   A theatre in Stratford-upon-Avon that serves as the home of the ►Royal Shakespeare Company (RSC). The present building, which was opened in 1932, stands on the site of an earlier Shakespeare Memorial Theatre that was built in 1879 but burned down in 1926. During the period 1879 to 1926, festival performances were given for a few months only each year. During the 1940s, however, the prestige of the Shakespeare festival increased considerably, and the theatre came to rival, then overtake, the Old Vic as a centre for Shakespeare productions. In the 1950s the company expanded, and developed a tradition of touring. In 1960 Peter ►Hall became director and a year later the company was named the ►Royal Shakespeare Company. There are now three theatres in the complex at Stratford-upon-Avon; the main house, the Swan Theatre (built in 1986), and the Other Place. Performances are given all the year round.

Shallow   A country justice in *The Merry Wives of Windsor* and *2 Henry IV*. He has fictitious memories of a riotous youth. In *2 Henry IV*, when Hal denounces Falstaff, Shallow loses both his hope of advancement and his loan of £1,000 to Falstaff. In *The Merry Wives*, he threatens a suit against Falstaff for his tricks and tries to secure the hand of Anne Page for Slender, his cousin.

Shank, John   (d. 1636) English actor who played clown roles. A member of ►Pembroke's, ►Queen Elizabeth's, and the ►King's Men (1613), he is also mentioned as a principal actor in the (1623) folio of Shakespeare's plays.

Shaw, Fiona   (1958–   ) Irish-born actress who has played many Shakespearean roles, especially for the ►Royal Shakespeare Company, including Celia (1985), Katherine (1987), Beatrice (1987), and Portia (1987). At the ►Royal National Theatre she has played Richard II (1995). She has published several books on acting, including *Players of Shakespeare* (1987).

Shepherd   In *1 Henry VI*, the father of Joan of Arc.

Shepherd, Old In *The Winter's Tale*, he finds the baby Perdita on the shore of Bohemia, and brings her up as his daughter. He is condemned to death by Polixenes for permitting Florizel's infatuation with her and flees with the lovers to Sicilia.

Sher, Antony (1951–) South African-born actor who is also a writer and painter. He has played major roles in Shakespeare including the Fool in *King Lear* (1982), Richard III (1984), and Shylock and Malvolio (1987), all for the ➤Royal Shakespeare Company. More recently he has played Titus Andronicus for the Market Theatre, Johannesburg (1995), a production also televised. He has written about the experience of preparing for the roles of Richard III (*The Year of the King*, 1995) and *Titus Andronicus* (*Woza Shakespeare*, 1996).

Shipmaster [Also, Sea Captain] In *2 Henry VI*, the captor of the Duke of Suffolk.

Shylock In *The Merchant of Venice*, a Jew, one of the principal characters. He lends Bassanio 3,000 ducats on condition that if they are not repaid at the promised time he shall be allowed to cut a pound of flesh from the body of Antonio, Bassanio's friend and surety. He claims the forfeiture in court but is defeated by Portia, who reminds him that he loses his life if he sheds one drop of blood or takes more or less than his lawful pound of flesh. Shakespeare's handling of racial otherness in this play is often compared with ➤Marlowe's in *The Jew of Malta*.

Sicinius Velutus In *Coriolanus*, a tribune of the people. Junius Brutus is the other.

Siddons, Sarah (1755–1831) British actress famous for tragic roles, especially her Lady Macbeth, which was praised by Hazlitt; she also played Desdemona, Ophelia, Volumnia, Constance, Queen Katherine, Rosalind, and Hermione. She was sister to John Philip ➤Kemble, with whom she acted.

Sidney, Sir Philip (1554–86) English soldier, statesman, poet, and critic, brother of Mary Herbert, Countess of Pembroke. Knighted in 1583, he was a favourite, at various times, of Queen Elizabeth. He was appointed (1585) governor of Flushing, and was shot (22 September 1586) at the Battle of Zutphen, He was given a hero's funeral in St Paul's Cathedral. His literary works include the prose romance *Arcadia* (written 1580–83, published 1590), *Apologie for Poetrie* (published 1595, in two editions, one entitled *Defense of Poesie*), and *Astrophel and Stella* (1591), a series of eleven songs and 108 sonnets addressed to Penelope Devereux (wife of Robert Rich). The *Arcadia*, written for his sister's amusement, was used by Shakespeare, ➤Spenser, ➤Beaumont and ➤Fletcher, and many others, as source material.

Silence In *2 Henry IV*, a country justice who contributes to Justice Shallow's reminiscences in his orchard.

Silius In *Antony and Cleopatra*, an officer under Ventidius.

Silvia In *Two Gentlemen of Verona*, the daughter of the Duke of Milan, loved by Valentine.

Silvius In *As You Like It*, a shepherd in love with Phebe.

Simonides In *Pericles*, the King of Pentapolis and father of Thaisa. He calls Pericles a traitor to test him before he consents to his marriage to Thaisa.

Simpcox, Saunder In *2 Henry VI*, an impostor who pretends to be lame until he is whipped and runs away. His wife is also present and is whipped with him.

Simple In *The Merry Wives of Windsor*, a servant of Slender.

Sinklo In *3 Henry VI*, one of the keepers; Humphrey is the other. The name derives from that of John Sincler, an actor of Shakespeare's day, who is indicated by the stage directions in the folio of 1623 to have played the part.

Sir Thomas More A chronicle play that has survived in manuscript form, written in 1592–93. It is now regarded as a collaborative work, originally by Anthony Munday and perhaps Henry ►Chettle and Thomas ►Dekker, with revisions by others, including probably Shakespeare. Shakespeare's handwriting is thought to be that known as "Hand D" in the manuscript, and these pages thus constitute his only known literary manuscript to survive. His contribution to the play is a scene of three pages depicting More dealing with a May Day rebellion by apprentices (which took place in 1517) against foreigners in London. The manuscript shows traces of censorship by Edmund Tilney, Master of the Revels, probably dating from between 1593 and 1595.

Siward [Title, Earl of Northumberland; sometimes called Siward the Strong.] In *Macbeth*, he leads an army of 10,000 English soldiers sent by Edward the Confessor against Macbeth. His son, Young Siward, is killed in a fight with Macbeth. Historically, he was a Danish soldier in England, who died in 1055.

Slender In *The Merry Wives of Windsor*, a foolish gentleman, cousin to Shallow, and suitor to Anne Page, favoured by her father.

Sly, Christopher A tinker in the Induction to *The Taming of the Shrew*. He is found in a drunken sleep by a nobleman, who has him taken to his own home, as a jest. When he wakes he is made to believe that he is the lord of the manor, just recovered from fifteen years of insanity. The "Taming of the Shrew" is played for his entertainment.

Sly, William (d. 1608) English actor. He is listed as a principal actor in the 1623 folio of Shakespeare's plays and may have joined the ►Lord Chamberlain's Men at their formation in 1594. He was an original shareholder in the ►Blackfriars theatre.

Smith the Weaver In *2 Henry VI*, a follower of Jack Cade.

Snare   In *2 Henry IV*, one of the two sheriff's officers (Fang is the other) sent to arrest Falstaff in Mistress Quickly's suit.

Snout, Tom   In *A Midsummer Night's Dream*, a tinker who is cast in the part of the father of Pyramus in the interpolated play. However, he finally plays the part of the Wall.

Snug   In *A Midsummer Night's Dream*, a joiner who plays the part of the Lion in the interpolated play.

Solanio and Salerio   [Also, Salanio and Salarino]   Two minor characters in *The Merchant of Venice*. They play roles in incidents involving Lorenzo and Antonio.

Solinus   In *The Comedy of Errors*, the Duke of Ephesus.

Somerset, (2nd) Duke of   In *2 Henry VI*, the historical Edmund Beaufort, brother of John Beaufort. He carries on a fight with the Duke of York, begun by his brother. Made Regent of France, he later reports that he has lost the English territories. He is killed at St Albans.

Somerset, (4th) Duke of   In *3 Henry VI*, the historical Edmund Beaufort, son of the 2nd Duke. He joins Warwick against Edward IV, sends Richmond to Brittany for security, and is captured and executed at the battle of Tewkesbury.

Somerset, Earl of   In *1 Henry VI*, John Beaufort, who later becomes Duke. He tries to maintain peace between Gloucester and the Bishop of Winchester but quarrels with the Duke of York.

Somervile, Sir John   In *3 Henry VI*, a supporter of the Yorkist faction.

Sonnets   Shakespeare's sonnets, 154 in number, were published in 1609, together with the poem "A Lover's Complaint". They were dedicated by the publisher, Thomas Thorpe, to "Mr ➤W. H." Two of them, numbers 138 and 144, had been published earlier, in slightly different forms, in a collection called *The Passionate Pilgrim* (1599). Shakespeare was known as a writer of sonnets by 1598, when a reference to his "sugred sonnets among his private friends" appeared in Francis ➤Meres's book *Palladis Tamia*. The exact date of composition of Shakespeare's sonnets is unknown, but the main vogue for sonnet cycles was in the 1590s and for this and other reasons they are thought to have been written during this decade. It has been widely believed that the publication was unauthorized, and that Shakespeare had no hand in it. In part, this is because no other edition appeared until that of John Benson in 1639 (dated 1640), which is surprising in view of Shakespeare's high reputation in and after 1609; it is possible, although it would be strange, that the 1609 text was not widely known. But some scholars now think it unlikely that Thorpe, a reputable publisher, would have jeopardized his reputation, or his relationship with Shakespeare's acting company, the ➤King's Men, by publishing without legal authority to do so.

The great majority of the sonnets (excepting only 99, 126, and 145) are in the form known as the "Shakespearean" or "English" sonnet, consisting of twelve pentameter lines rhyming alternately *ababcdcdefef*, and concluding with a couplet. In this respect, they are less innovative formally than other sequences, such as ►Sidney's *Astrophel and Stella*. It is not entirely easy to construct a narrative out of the sequence, and some rearrangements have been attempted; but most of the sonnets (perhaps 1 to 126) can be said to be concerned with the poet's feelings towards a young man of higher social status than himself, and the remainder with a woman (known as the "Dark Lady") who has an adulterous relationship with the poet, and also an affair with the young man.

Identifications for these figures (along with that of the "Rival Poet" of sonnets 78–86) have been frequently proposed, and a web of biographical speculation has been woven around the sonnet sequence. The most common suggestions for the rival poet are ►Marlowe and ►Chapman, and for the young man Henry Wriothesley, the Earl of ►Southampton, who was Shakespeare's patron for *Venus and Adonis* and *The Rape of Lucrece*, and William ►Herbert, the Earl of Pembroke, to whom the first folio was dedicated. The identity of the "Dark Lady", variously proposed as Luce Morgan (or Black Luce), Mary Fitton, and Emilia Lanier, is most problematic. While it is not unlikely that some of the sonnets have biographical origins, it is clearly a misconception to think, as Wordsworth did, that "with this key, Shakespeare unlocked his heart".

Soothsayer In *Antony and Cleopatra*, a seer who tells Charmian and Iras that they will outlive Cleopatra.

Soothsayer In *Cymbeline*, he foretells success to the Romans and interprets Posthumus's vision.

Soothsayer In *Julius Caesar*, an old man who warns Caesar to "beware the Ides of March" (I.ii).

Southampton, (3rd) **Earl of** [Title of Henry Wriothesley] (1573–1624) English politician and soldier, a friend and patron of William Shakespeare, who dedicated to him *Venus and Adonis* and *The Rape of Lucrece*. He has often been regarded as the "Mr W. H." to whom the Sonnets are dedicated, and though there is no strong evidence to support this claim, he seems now to be regarded as the most likely contender. He was a patron also of several other writers, including Thomas ►Nashe and John ►Florio. He accompanied Robert Devereux, 2nd Earl of ►Essex, on the expeditions of 1596 and 1597, and in 1598 married Essex's cousin, Elizabeth Vernon, a marriage that angered Queen Elizabeth. He sponsored the performance of what was probably Shakespeare's *Richard II*, just before the ill-fated rebellion of Essex (1601) and, being otherwise implicated in the plot, was sentenced to death. The sentence was commuted to life imprisonment, and he was released (1603) on the accession of James I. He was deeply interested in colonization and was a member of the council of the Virginia Company, whose expedition (1605) he helped to finance. He was treasurer of the company from 1620 to 1624.

Southwell, John   In *2 Henry VI*, a priest who conjures up a spirit for the Duchess of Gloucester.

Speed   In *The Two Gentlemen of Verona*, a servant of Valentine.

Spenser, Edmund   (1552–99) English poet. He was educated at the Merchant Taylors' School, London, and at Pembroke College, Cambridge (1569–76), where he associated with Gabriel Harvey and other men of note. Afterwards, he became intimate with Sir Philip ►Sidney, Robert Dudley, 1st Earl of Leicester, and Sir Walter ►Raleigh. In 1580 he went to Ireland as secretary to Lord Grey of Wilton. He returned to London with Raleigh in 1589 with the first three books of *The Faerie Queene*, which he published in 1590, dedicating the work to Queen Elizabeth. The second three books were published in 1596, after Spenser had returned to Ireland. In 1598 his house was burnt down by the Irish, and he was forced to flee to England, where he died soon after. His first poems, translations from Petrarch and Joachim du Bellay, were published in John van der Noodt's *Theatre of Voluptuous Worldlings* (1569). His chief poems are *The Shepherd's Calendar* (1579), *The Faerie Queene* (1590–96), *Daphnaida* (1591), *Complaints* (1591), *Colin Clout's Come Home Again*, in which there may be a reference to Shakespeare as Aetion, *Astrophel, Amoretti*, and *Epithalamion* (1595), and *Four Hymns* and *Prothalamion* (1596).

Stafford, Lord   In *3 Henry VI*, a supporter of the Yorkist faction.

Stafford, Sir Humphrey and **William**   In *2 Henry VI*, brothers, members of an armed force that tries to stop the rebel, Jack Cade, and his men. The two Staffords are killed.

Stanley, Lord   In *Richard III*, a lord attending Richard. He is mistrusted by Richard because his wife is the mother (by Henry Tudor) of Richmond. Richard keeps Stanley's son, George, as hostage when Richmond lands in England, and on the eve of Bosworth, Stanley tells Richmond he cannot openly help him. However, he also refuses to help Richard. In one quarto and the folio he is called the Earl of Derby.

Stanley, Sir John   In *2 Henry VI*, the escort of the Duchess of Gloucester when she goes into exile.

Stanley, Sir William   In *3 Henry VI*, a member of the Yorkist faction.

Starveling, Robin   In *A Midsummer Night's Dream*, a tailor who is cast in the part of the mother in the interpolated play. He actually has no lines to speak and plays Moonshine instead.

Stein, Peter   (1937–) German theatre director of international acclaim, founder of the Schaubuhne am Halleschen Ufer, Berlin (1970), where he has directed *As*

You Like It (1977), *Titus Andronicus* (1992), *Julius Caesar* (1992), and *Antony and Cleopatra* (1994). He is known particularly for his appropriations of classic plays for contemporary political purposes.

Stephano   A messenger in *The Merchant of Venice*.

Stephano   In *The Tempest*, a drunken butler who plots with Caliban to murder Prospero.

Stephens, Sir Robert   (1931–95) British actor who played various Shakespearean roles: for the National Theatre he played Horatio (1963) in the company's inaugural production and Benedick (1965), and for the ►Royal Shakespeare Company Falstaff (1991) and King Lear (1993–94), his last stage role.

Stevenson, Juliet   (1956–   ) British actress who has played many Shakespearean roles for the ►Royal Shakespeare Company, beginning with small roles in her first season (1978–79) but subsequently including Hippolyta/Titania (1981), Isabella (1983), and Rosalind and Cressida (1985).

Stowe, John   (1525–1605) English historian and antiquary. He published an edition of Chaucer (1561), which Shakespeare probably used, and his *Chronicles of England* (1580, reissued as *Annals* in 1592) was an important source. He also wrote *A Survey of London* (1598, enlarged 1603 and subsequently).

Strange's Men   ►Lord Chamberlain's Men.

Stratford-upon-Avon   [Also: Stratford-on-Avon, Stratford]   A market town in central England, famous as the birthplace of Shakespeare. It contains the Church of the Holy Trinity, with the tomb of Shakespeare; the house where it is thought that Shakespeare was born; and ►New Place, the site of the house built by Sir Hugh Clopton in the time of Henry VII and bought by Shakespeare in 1597. Shakespeare's supposed birthplace is now the property of the Shakespeare Birthplace Trust and has been restored. A Shakespeare Museum has been formed in the house. The ►Shakespeare Memorial Theatre (built by popular subscription from the USA and Britain) now contains the Swan Theatre, built in 1986. The Shakespeare fountain was erected in 1887 by George W. Childs.

Strato   In *Julius Caesar*, a servant of Brutus. He is the only one who will consent to hold the sword on which Brutus kills himself (V.v).

Strehler, Giorgio   (1921–97) Italian theatre director of international acclaim, who founded the Piccolo Teatro, Milan (1947) and the Théâtre de l'Europe, Paris (1983). He directed Shakespeare productions for over thirty years, including *Richard III*, *The Tempest*, and *Romeo and Juliet* (1948), *Macbeth* and *Coriolanus* (1952), *1, 2,* and *3 Henry VI* (1955), *Coriolanus* (1957), *King Lear* (1972), and *The Tempest* (1978). His work was strongly influenced by that of Brecht and the Berliner Ensemble.

Suffolk, (1st) **Duke of** In *Henry VIII*, the historical Charles Brandon. He is present in a number of scenes including the coronation of Anne, the arraignment of Cranmer, and the christening of Princess Elizabeth.

Suffolk, (4th) **Earl of** In *1 Henry VI*, the historical William de la Pole, a Lancastrian supporter who captures Margaret at Angiers. He arranges her marriage with Henry and becomes her lover. In *2 Henry VI*, he is created (1st) Duke and attains greater power, managing the imprisonment of Gloucester and the banishment of the Duchess of Gloucester. He himself is banished, and later killed by Walter Whitmore.

Surrey, (1st) **Duke of** In *Richard II*, the historical Thomas Holland, also 3rd Earl of Kent. He defends Aumerle against a charge of treason, joins the rebellion against Henry IV, and is captured and killed. He is also referred to in the play as Kent (V.vi).

Surrey, Earl of In *2 Henry IV*, the historical Thomas Fitzalan, a supporter of the King.

Surrey, Earl of In *Henry VIII*, the historical Thomas Howard, a gentleman of the court. He opposes Wolsey and avenges the death of Buckingham.

Surveyor In *Henry VIII*, the surveyor to the Duke of Buckingham. He swears that his master threatened Henry's life.

Suzman, Janet (1939–) South African-born actress and director who played many roles for the ►Royal Shakespeare Company during the period 1963 to 1972, including Rosaline, Portia, and Ophelia (1965), Katherine and Celia (1967), Beatrice and Rosalind (1968), and Cleopatra and Lavinia (1972). She directed *Othello* for the Market Theatre, Johannesburg in 1988.

Swan, the A London playhouse built in 1596 on the ►Bankside, on the south bank of the Thames. A well-known drawing of the Swan by a visitor, Johannes de Witt, one of the very few in existence of an Elizabethan theatre, shows a circular building with three galleries of three tiers each. A forestage extends into the pit yard, and halfway back columns support the roof of the stage. Above the stage were six boxes, probably for "gentlemen" spectators, and possibly including one for musicians. After 1620, it was used for prize fights, and by 1632 a contemporary source referred to it as "fallen to decay."

Sycorax A witch, the mother of Caliban in *The Tempest*; she does not appear in the play.

T

Tailor In *The Taming of the Shrew*, a character who brings a dress for Katherina that is refused by Petruchio.

Talbot, John In *1 Henry VI*, the son of Lord Talbot, who dies heroically in battle.

Talbot, Lord In *1 Henry VI*, the commander of the English army. He is captured at Patay through Fastolf's cowardice, escapes from the Countess of Auvergne, and with his son is surrounded and killed near Bordeaux.

Taming of the Shrew, The A comedy by Shakespeare, printed in the first folio of 1623. It is difficult to discuss the source of *The Taming of the Shrew* since its exact relationship to a very similar play, *The Taming of a Shrew*, is not known. The date of Shakespeare's play is uncertain since it was neither published nor mentioned before the folio of 1623. *A Shrew* was printed in 1594, at about the same time or just after *The Shrew* is thought to have been written. Four possible relationships between the two plays have been conjectured: that *A Shrew* was a separate earlier play and *The Shrew* was derived from it; that *A Shrew* is an earlier version, or "bad quarto," of *The Shrew*; that both plays derive from a common, but lost, original; or, as most editors now believe, that *The Shrew* was the source for *A Shrew*, which means that Shakespeare's play must date from no later than 1594, when *A Shrew* was published. Both plays are constructed from the same three main elements, the Induction and scenes with Sly the Tinker, the wooing and taming of Katherina, and the contrasted wooing of her sister. In *A Shrew* the Sly episode is filled out, with the Tinker making several interruptions to the play and finally going home to tame his own wife, whereas in Shakespeare's play, although the character of Sly is more developed and the preparation for the play more subtly done, the story is never completed, for Sly disappears from the action at the end of the first act. The taming of the shrew, a story long known in fabliaux, is similarly dealt with in both plays, except that Katherina and her husband Petruchio are more fully characterized in Shakespeare's play. The two versions of the Bianca plot differ considerably. In *A Shrew* Kate has two sisters who are wooed by two friends; like Bianca they cannot marry until their sister is provided for, so they produce a husband for her, but the disguises and intrigues of their suitors are not very similar to those in the subplot of Shakespeare's play. Shakespeare took his subplot partially from the classical comedy *Supposes* (1566) by George Gascoigne, a prose version of Ariosto's *I Suppositi* (1509), which has a willing girl wooed by rivals, her real suitor having disguised himself as his servant to get access to her, as Lucentio does in *The Taming of the Shrew*. The substance of *A Shrew* is combined with a number of elements from *Supposes* in Shakespeare's play to produce a witty comedy of love and marriage.

Dramatis Personae

A Lord

Christopher Sly, *a tinker*

Hostess, Page, Players, Huntsmen, and
    Servants

Baptista Minola *of Padua*

Vincentio, *an old gentleman of Pisa*

Lucentio, *son to Vincentio, in love with*
    Bianca

Petruchio, *gentleman of Verona, suitor*
    to Katherina

Gremio, *suitor to Bianca*

Hortensio, *suitor to Bianca*

Tranio, *servant to Lucentio*

Biondello, *servant to Lucentio*

Grumio, *servant to Petruchio*

Curtis, *servant to Petruchio*

A Pedant

Katherina, *the shrew, daughter to*
    Baptista

Bianca, *daughter to Baptista*

Widow

Tailor, Haberdasher, and Servants

The Story. In the Induction, Christopher Sly is found in a drunken sleep by a nobleman who decides to play a joke on him. Sly is taken to the nobleman's house, treated lavishly, and persuaded (with some difficulty) that he is himself a nobleman just recovered from fifteen years of insanity. For his entertainment a group of strolling players present "The Taming of the Shrew": Baptista Minola has two daughters, the hot-tempered Katherina, and the docile Bianca. Baptista will not allow the younger to wed until Katherina has found a husband. Petruchio resolves to woo her, partly to help his friend Hortensio gain Bianca, and partly for Katherina's large dowry. At their first meeting she rails at him, but he pretends that he finds her soft-spoken and gentle, and commences his taming of her. He arrives late at the wedding, riding on a tired nag and dressed in disreputable clothes. He embarrasses her at the ceremony, refuses to let her stay for the wedding dinner, takes her to his country house, where his cruelty to his servants forces her to defend them, gives her nothing to eat, tosses in bed all night so that she can get no sleep, and sends her new clothes away. After these and other pranks she is so exhausted and bewildered that she is quite submissive. Meanwhile young Lucentio, in the guise of a tutor, has won Bianca; Hortensio, the disappointed rival, consoles himself with a rich widow. At Lucentio's wedding feast, Petruchio easily wins a wager that he has the most docile and obedient wife of any husband in the room and Katherine makes a long speech in praise of patriachal marriage.

Tamora In *Titus Andronicus*, the Queen of the Goths. Taken prisoner by Titus, with her three sons, she plots with her lover, Aaron, to avenge the sacrifice of her eldest son. Titus, in turn, avenges the death of his sons, the rape and mutilation of his daughter, and the loss of his own hand, first by serving Tamora a pie in which her sons' bodies have been baked, and then by killing her.

Tarlton, Richard.(d. 1588) English clown and comic actor, enrolled (1583) as one of the twelve members of ►Queen Elizabeth's Men. He was celebrated for his extemporaneous rhymes and for his "jigs" (comic songs with a dance), which he invented. He was the author of a play entitled *The Seven Deadly Sins* (1590), the second part of which survives in the form of a "plot", summarizing episodes, listing actors names, and providing a cue sheet. He was at one time commonly identified with "poor Yorick", the dead clown in *Hamlet*.

Tate, Nahum (1652–1715) English dramatist and poet, chiefly remembered now for his notorious adaptation of *King Lear* (1681), which provided a happy ending, omitted the Fool, and ousted Shakespeare's play from the stage until 1756. Tate also adapted *Richard II* as *The Sicilian Usurper* (1680) and *Coriolanus* as *The Ingratitude of a Commonwealth* (1680). He adapted plays by Shakespeare's contemporaries, translated the *Psalms of David*, and became Poet Laureate in 1692.

Taurus In *Antony and Cleopatra*, Octavius's commander at Actium.

Taylor, Joseph (d. 1652) English actor. Originally in the ►Children of the Revels, he joined the ►King's Men in 1619 after the death of Richard ►Burbage. He was the successor of Burbage in *Hamlet* and *Othello*. John Downes in *Roscius Anglicanus* (1708) says that Shakespeare personally instructed him in the playing of *Hamlet*, and the remembrance of this performance enabled ►Davenant, who had seen it, to perpetuate the Shakespearean tradition when he instructed ►Betterton in the role in 1663.

Tearsheet, Doll In *2 Henry IV*, a whore, Falstaff's mistress. She quarrels with Pistol (II.iv). Later she is taken to prison.

Tempest, The A play by Shakespeare, written and first performed in 1611 and first printed in the first folio of 1623. It was his last play as a solo writer. No source has been discovered for the plot or characters, although there are several analogues. It is clear that Shakespeare was interested in the colonization of America, and in particular in the shipwreck of a colonizing vessel, the *Sea-Adventure*, that took place off the coast of Bermuda in 1609, and this incident may have provided some ideas for the play. He read three accounts of it, Sylvester Jourdain's *Discovery of the Bermudas* (1610), the Council of Virginia's *True Declaration of the State of the Colony in Virginia* (1610), and William Strachey's letter, known as the *True Repertory of the Wracke*, dated 1610 and published in 1625. Strachey's letter, which Shakespeare must have read in manuscript, and Jourdain's pamphlet supplied details for the storm at sea as described by Ariel (I.ii), the conversations of Alonso and his fellows in II.i, and Stephano's and Trinculo's scattered remarks about their preservation. The *True Declaration* emphasizes the idea that providence was responsible for the safety of the shipwrecked colonists, a notion that Shakespeare makes into an important theme in his play. Shakespeare had also read Montaigne's essay "On Cannibals" in Florio's translation, which influenced Gonzalo's description of the ideal commonwealth, and perhaps also the general contrast between civilized and natural manners and societies in the play. Prospero's speech renouncing his magic powers (V.i) was partly based on ►Ovid's ►*Metamorphoses*, vii 197–209, for which Shakespeare probably used the original Latin as well as the translation made by William Golding in 1587. It is also likely that Virgil's *Aeneid*, particularly books 1–6, shaped something of the plot and themes. Contemporary folklore contributed something to Ariel as did the tradition of the wild man and ideas about the native inhabitants of America to Caliban, but little otherwise can be said with any certainty of Shakespeare's sources for this play; it seems that both the plot, which in its major lines and ideas resembles the plots of his other late plays, and the strange and original characters of Ariel and Caliban came largely from Shakespeare's own imagination. The play was adapted as *The Enchanted Island* by ►Davenant and ►Dryden (1667), and this extremely successful version held the stage for more than a century. *The Tempest* has inspired a large number of other works, including Browning's poem "Caliban upon Setebos" and Auden's poem sequence *The Sea and the Mirror*.

Dramatis Personae

Alonso, King of Naples	Master of a ship
Sebastian, *his brother*	Boatswain
Prospero, *the right* Duke of Milan	Mariners
Antonio, *his brother, the usurping*	Miranda, *daughter to Prospero*
Duke of Milan	Ariel, *an airy spirit*
Ferdinand, *son to the King*	Iris, *a spirit*
Gonzalo, *an honest old counsellor*	Ceres, *a spirit*
Adrian, *a lord*	Juno, *a spirit*
Francisco, *a lord*	Nymphs, *spirits*
Caliban, *Prospero's slave*	Reapers, *spirits*
Trinculo, *a jester*	Other Spirits attending on Prospero
Stephano, *a drunken butler*	

The Story. Prospero, whose brother, Antonio, with the aid of Alonso, King of Naples, has usurped his rightful claim to the duchy of Milan and set him adrift in a boat with his daughter, Miranda, is now, twelve years later, living with Miranda on an island. Through the exercise of his magical powers, Prospero has released the airy spirit Ariel, who had been imprisoned in a tree, and obliged the brutish Caliban, son of the witch Sycorax, to serve him. Learning that his former enemies are sailing near the island, Prospero summons a tempest to force them into his power, and they reach the shore from their wrecked ship in separate groups. Ferdinand, the son of the King of Naples, wanders to the cave of Prospero and there, under the spell of Prospero's magic, meeting Miranda, falls in love with her, and she with him. Meanwhile, most of the other survivors (who believe Ferdinand to be dead) are lulled to sleep by Ariel's music, but Antonio and Sebastian, Alonso's brother, remain awake and plot the murder of Alonso. Ariel, however, prevents this by awakening the others just in time. Another group from the ship, Stephano, a drunken butler, and Trinculo, a jester, have met Caliban and have given him some of their liquor. Caliban offers to serve them, suggesting that they should murder Prospero and seize the island, and that Stephano should then marry Miranda. But Ariel has overheard these plotters too, and warns Prospero, who, with Ariel's aid, sets out to punish and reward all according to their just deserts. To punish Alonso and Antonio, Prospero and Ariel set before the hungry men a magnificent banquet that vanishes when they try to eat. Ariel, disguised as a harpy, then rebukes Alonso for his crimes against Prospero. Prospero next presents a graceful masque before the now betrothed Ferdinand and Miranda, but suddenly interrupts it when he remembers Caliban's plot. These conspirators, however, are easily distracted by the gaudy clothes Ariel has hung upon a line, and run away howling as spirits in the shape of dogs chase them around the island. The other group of conspirators is now led by Ariel's music to the cave of Prospero, where Prospero reveals his identity and demands the return of his dukedom. He shows the repentant Alonso Ferdinand and Miranda playing chess; the other conspirators return, sore from the pinching they have received; Prospero renounces his magic, setting free Ariel and Caliban, who says he will try to be wiser and to seek for grace. The entire group plans to sail for Naples with "calm seas, auspicious gales" (V.i) on the following day. Because *The Tempest* is Shakespeare's final comedy, critics in the past often interpreted the role of Prospero as Shakespeare bidding farewell to his own art, although he went on to write at least two more plays in collaboration. Many of Shakespeare's earlier themes are reworked in this play, and it resembles very strikingly his other romances *Pericles*, *Cymbeline*, and *The Winter's Tale*.

Terry, Dame Ellen   (1848–1928) British actress who often performed in Shakespearean roles with Sir Henry ➤Irving, for example playing Portia to his Shylock. Other roles included Beatrice, Ophelia, Desdemona, Juliet, Viola, Lady Macbeth, Imogen, Queen Katherine, Volumnia. Her correspondence with Bernard Shaw was published in 1931.

Thaisa   In *Pericles*, the daughter of Simonides and wife of Pericles.

Thaliard   In *Pericles*, a lord of Antioch.

Thane of Cawdor   ➤Cawdor, Thane of.

Thane of Fife   ➤Macduff.

Thane of Glamis   ➤Glamis, Thane of.

Theatre, the   The first purpose-built London theatre. It was a wooden building erected by James ➤Burbage, in 1576–77, on the site of the priory of St John the Baptist, Shoreditch, which had been destroyed during the Reformation. It was taken down in 1598, when its ground lease expired, and the ➤Globe, ➤Bankside, was built from the materials.

Thersites In *Troilus and Cressida*, the most satirical and disrespectful of the Greeks assembled before Troy. His bawdiness is contrasted with Troilus's romantic nature, and he acts as a commentator, debunking the concepts of both love and of military glory. In Greek legend, he assailed the name of Agamemnon and was beaten by Odysseus (Ulysses). When he taunted Achilles, Achilles killed him.

Theseus In *A Midsummer Night's Dream*, the Duke of Athens, engaged to marry Hippolyta. He also appears in *The Two Noble Kinsmen* as husband to Hippolyta and steadfast friend to Pirithous. In Plutarch, Theseus is a lawgiver, but also celebrated for his many love affairs. After marrying Hippolyta, and fathering Hippolytus, he married Phaedra.

Thisbe In classical legend, a maiden of Babylon, loved by ►Pyramus. The two communicated secretly through a hole in the wall between their houses, their parents being opposed. Pyramus killed himself when he saw blood that he mistakenly believed to be Thisbe's. In *A Midsummer Night's Dream*, the part of "Thisby" in the interpolated play is taken by Flute.

Thomas In *Measure for Measure*, the head of an order of friars. He permits the Duke of Vienna to disguise himself as a friar of the order so that he may spy on Angelo.

Thomas, Lord Cromwell [Also, *The Life and Death of Thomas, Lord Cromwell*] An anonymous play published in 1602 as by "W. S." and included in the second issue of the third Shakespeare folio (1664), but now considered not to be Shakespeare's.

Thomas Percy, Earl of Worcester ►Worcester, Thomas Percy, Earl of.

Thump, Peter In *2 Henry VI*, an apprentice to Horner. He accuses his master of treasonable speech and in a fight with sandbags kills him. The King believes the outcome to be an indication of God's power and justice (II.iii).

Thurio In *Two Gentlemen of Verona*, a foolish rival to Valentine for Silvia. Proteus pretends to be wooing Silvia for him after Valentine has been banished, and in the final act Thurio claims Silvia, but gives her up as soon as Valentine challenges him.

Thyreus [Also, Thidias] In *Antony and Cleopatra*, a follower whom Octavius sends to Cleopatra to persuade her to desert Antony.

Timandra In *Timon of Athens*, a mistress of Alcibiades.

Time In *The Winter's Tale*, Time acts as Chorus, bridging the gap (sixteen years) between Acts III and IV.

Timon In *Timon of Athens*, the noble Athenian who is the hero of the play. Although he is at first a trusting and warm-hearted person, the ingratitude of his friends (when he loses his fortune) causes a violent reaction in him and he becomes a bitter misanthrope, only occasionally revealing glimpses of his former goodness, as in his touching words to Flavius. He dies in solitude, a bitter and cynical man. The historical Timon lived in the last part of the fifth century BC.

Timon of Athens [Full title, *The Life of Timon of Athens*]   A tragedy by Shakespeare, probably all by his hand, although some scholars have doubted this and claims for ►Middleton's collaboration have been strongly advanced. It is sometimes thought that the play is incomplete or unrevised. It was probably written between 1605 and 1608, and printed in the first folio of 1623. There is no record of performance before 1678 and this was Shadwell's adaptation (not until 1851 was there a performance of Shakespeare's play). The main source was North's translation of Plutarch's *Lives of the Noble Grecians and Romans*, from which Shakespeare used the *Life of Marcus Antonius* and the *Life of Alcibiades*. He found in the former Timon's misanthropy, the idea that he had been abandoned by his friends, the relationships with Alcibiades and Apemantus, the anecdote of the fig-tree (V.i), and the two epitaphs for the tomb. He may also have been influenced by the description of Antony's life, which mentioned his trusting nature and the sycophants who took advantage of it. *The Life of Alcibiades* supplied very much that Shakespeare did not use for his rather incomplete portrait of the soldier, but he did take the fact of Alcibiades's turning against Athens and his resolution to harm the city, and also the courtesan Timandra, although he changes the reason for Antony's leaving Athens and omits Plutarch's account of Timandra's genuine affection for Alcibiades. Another important source was Lucian of Samosata's dialogue *Timon*, which was not translated into English in Shakespeare's time, although he could have read it in Erasmus's Latin version, in Italian, or in French. From this he may have taken elements not in Plutarch, such as Timon's kindness to his friends, the hypocritical offers of money made to him only when he was not in need, and the incident of his driving away the parasites who approach him after he has dug up the unwanted gold. The character and manner of speech may have been modelled on Diogenes in John ►Lyly's play *Campaspe* (1584), in which the philosopher talks with Alexander the Great much as Apemantus does with Timon. Shakespeare probably also knew the story of Timon in William Painter's *The* ►*Palace of Pleasure* (1560), although he does not seem to have used it. An anonymous academic play called *Timon*, also based on Lucian, did exist, but it was possibly written after Shakespeare's play, and in any case Shakespeare probably never knew it.

Dramatis Personae

Timon, *a noble Athenian*
Lucius, *a flattering lord*
Lucullus, *a flattering lord*
Sempronius, *a flattering lord*
Ventidius, *a false friend of Timon*
Alcibiades, *an Athenian captain*
Apemantus, *a churlish philosopher*

Flavius, *steward to Timon*
Flaminius, *a servant to Timon*
Lucilius, *a servant to Timon*
Servilius, *a servant to Timon*
Caphis, Philotus, Titus, Lucius, *and*
   Hortensius, *servants to Timon's*
   creditors

Poet, Painter, Jeweller, and Merchant
An old Athenian
Servants to Varro and Isidore, two of
    Timon's creditors
Three Strangers
A Page

A Fool
Phrynia, *a mistress of Alcibiades*
Timandra, *a mistress of Alcibiades*
Lords, Senators, Officers, Soldiers,
    Thieves, and Attendants
Cupid and Amazons in the Masque

The Story. Timon is a wealthy and generous lord of Athens, but spends beyond his means. When he suddenly discovers that he is deeply in debt, he asks his friends, whom he has frequently entertained, for help. They, however, are only "feast-won" and refuse him. As a final gesture, Timon invites them all to a banquet at which he serves only warm water, and this he throws in their faces. Bitterly denouncing all humankind, Timon then retreats to a cave, where he lives on roots grubbed from the earth nearby. One day in his digging he discovers buried treasure, and when he learns that the great captain Alcibiades is preparing to attack Athens he shares his gold with him. Apemantus, the professional misanthrope, visits him, as well as a number of thieves, artists, and others, all anxious now to flatter him, and thus perhaps to secure some of his gold. Flavius, his faithful steward, is the only one to whom Timon speaks kindly, but he too is finally sent away and, as Alcibiades invades Athens, news comes that Timon has died alone by the sea.

Titania In A *Midsummer Night's Dream*, the Queen of the Fairies. ➤Ovid used her name (meaning "Titan's daughter") as an epithet of Diana. She quarrels with Oberon over the possession of a changeling child, and in revenge he causes her to fall in love with Bottom.

Titinius In *Julius Caesar*, a friend of Brutus and Cassius. When he joins up with Brutus's forces at Philippi, Cassius mistakenly thinks he is taken prisoner by the enemy and kills himself. Titinius stabs himself on finding Cassius's body.

Titus In *Timon of Athens*, a servant of one of Timon's creditors.

Titus Andronicus The hero of *Titus Andronicus*, a fictitious Roman general who fights against the Goths. At the beginning of the play he is a hot-tempered and tyrannical old father who kills one of his sons in a rage. He becomes the victim of Tamora, her lover Aaron, and her sons, who rape his daughter and kill two of his sons. He is driven mad and revenges himself horribly on Tamora, finally killing his daughter and then committing suicide.

Titus Andronicus [Full title, *The Tragedy of Titus Andronicus*] A tragedy, produced probably in 1592 or 1593, though it may be earlier, and published in 1594. There were two further quarto editions (1600, 1611) before the first folio of 1623. The probable source of the play is an anonymous prose tale, *The History of Titus Andronicus*, which exists only in an eighteenth-century version; this tale is closely related to a ballad, "The Lamentable and Tragical History of Titus Andronicus," printed in 1620, although it is not known for certain if the ballad was influenced by Shakespeare's play or vice versa. The prose tale describes Titus's war against the Goths and the marriage between the Goths' queen, Attava, and the Emperor of Rome. Attava has a black child by her lover, a Moor, and together they plot against Titus and his family. They have Titus's surviving sons murdered, and Attava's own sons rape and mutilate Titus's daughter, Lavinia. Titus feigns madness to secure revenge, which takes the form of cutting the throats of Attava's sons and baking them in a pie. Finally Titus kills Attava and her husband; the Moor confesses his crimes and is horribly put to death; Titus kills his daughter at her own request and then commits suicide. This tale has a few links with historical facts, but is in the main fictitious. Shakespeare's play shares the same basic features but with several changes. In particular, Shakespeare inserts the contrast between the Roman ideals of Titus and the decadence of the Emperor Saturninus, and he enlarges the Machiavellian character of the Empress's Moorish lover. The character of Titus was perhaps influenced by two portraits of the great Roman generals Scipio Africanus and Coriolanus in Plutarch's *Lives* (translated by North, 1579). Some of the names in the play also come from Plutarch. ►Seneca's tragedy, *Thyestes*, available in a translation of 1560 by Jasper Heywood, was also an important source and provided among other elements the manner of Titus's revenge on the Empress and her sons. The episode of Lavinia's rape comes from the tale of the ravished Philomela, to which Shakespeare refers, from ►Ovid, ►*Metamorphoses*, vi. The story of Philomela, her ravisher Tereus, and her sister Procne, is an important model for the structure of the play. The references to the rape of Lucrece come from Ovid's *Fasti*, which Shakespeare also used as a source for his poem, *The Rape of Lucrece*.

Dramatis Personae

Saturninus, Emperor of Rome	Aemilius, *a noble Roman*
Bassianus, *brother of the Emperor*	Alarbus, *son of Tamora*
Titus Andronicus, *Roman general*	Demetrius, *son of Tamora*
Marcus Andronicus, *tribune*	Chiron, *son of Tamora*
Lucius, *son of Titus*	Aaron, *a Moor, Tamora's lover*
Quintus, *son of Titus*	A Captain, *Tribune, Messenger, and*
Martius, *son of Titus*	Clown
Mutius, *son of Titus*	Goths and Romans
Young Lucius, *son of Lucius*	Tamora, Queen of the Goths
Publius, *son of Marcus*	Lavinia, *daughter of Titus*
Sempronius, *kinsman of Titus*	A Nurse and a black Child
Caius, *kinsman of Titus*	Senators, Tribunes, Officers, Soldiers,
Valentine, *kinsman of Titus*	and Attendants

The Story. Titus, a victorious Roman general, brings home as his captives Tamora, Queen of the Goths, and her three sons, the eldest of whom (Alarbus) is sacrificed by Titus's sons. Saturninus, the new Emperor, and Bassianus, his brother, both claim the hand of Titus's daughter, Lavinia, but Saturninus renounces Lavinia and marries Tamora, who with her lover, Aaron the Moor, is determined to be revenged on Titus for the death of her son. Her two remaining sons, Demetrius and Chiron, meet Bassianus and Lavinia in the woods. They kill Bassianus, throw his body into a pit, ravish Lavinia, and cut off her hands and tongue. Titus's sons Quintus and Martius fall into the pit and are accused of murdering Bassianus. Aaron informs Titus that they will be pardoned if Titus cuts off one of his hands and sends it as ransom. Aaron, however, returns the hand along with the heads of the two sons. Titus, driven mad, takes revenge by killing Demetrius and Chiron, and serving them baked in a pie to Tamora. He kills Lavinia, Mutius (his youngest son, who is trying to protect his sister), then Tamora, and is himself killed by Saturninus, whom Lucius, the last remaining son, then kills. Aaron, meanwhile, has been captured and is condemned by Lucius, now the new Emperor, to be set breast-deep in earth until he starves to death.

Titus Lartius In *Coriolanus*, a Roman general and supporter of Coriolanus, who opposes the Volscians.

Tom o'Bedlam Formerly, in England, a popular name for a lunatic. "Bedlam" was the colloquial name for the hospital of St Mary of Bethlehem, at London, an insane asylum that for a period was so overcrowded that many inmates, uncured but considered harmless, were dismissed and turned beggars. In *King Lear*, Edgar pretends to be one of these mendicants, calling himself "Poor Tom."

Tooley, Nicholas (d. 1623) English actor, a member of the ▶Lord Chamberlain's Men from 1594, becoming a shareholder in 1605. He is mentioned as a principal actor in the first folio (1623) of Shakespeare's plays.

Touchstone In *As You Like It*, the court fool (or professional clown) who accompanies Rosalind and Celia into the forest of Arden. His reductive view of romantic love gives a new perspective on the emotional feelings of the other characters.

Tranio In *The Taming of the Shrew*, a servant of Lucentio.

Travers In *2 Henry IV*, a retainer of Northumberland who brings the news of Hotspur's defeat.

Trebonius In *Julius Caesar*, a conspirator who (with Brutus) opposes the killing of Antony. At the time of the assassination of Caesar, he leads Antony away from the scene.

Tressel In *Richard III*, an attendant to Lady Anne.

Trinculo In *The Tempest*, a jester from Alonso's court in Naples who, with Stephano and Caliban, plans to murder Prospero.

Troilus In *Troilus and Cressida*, the youngest son of Priam and lover of Cressida. When he witnesses Cressida's unfaithfulness, he is broken-hearted and vows to kill Diomedes (who, however, escapes).

Troilus and Cressida [Full title, *The Tragedy of Troilus and Cressida*] A tragedy prob-ably written in the period 1601–02, listed in the Stationers' Register in 1603 but not published in quarto till 1609. Although the original title-page describes it as having been acted by the ►King's Men at the ►Globe, the epistle states that it had never been performed, a discrepancy still not explained. It was printed in the first folio of 1623 between the histories and the tragedies. The love-plot of *Troilus and Cressida* is based on Chaucer's narrative poem *Troilus and Criseyde*, although the characterization of the three main figures is very different, partly because of the in-fluence of Robert Henryson's sequel, *The Testament of Cresseid*, thought at that time to be by Chaucer, which Shakespeare also used. The main sequence of events in Chaucer is followed, with Shakespeare making use of such details as the scene in which Criseyde watches Troilus return from the war amid popular acclamation (Book II, ll.610–51), the emotional confusion of the lovers at their first meeting, Cressida's protestation of fidelity in IV.ii (from Book IV, ll.1534–54), and the let-ter she finally sends to Troilus after she has gone over to the Greek camp. Shake-speare's Troilus is close to Chaucer's, a young and impetuous warrior, but Pandarus is older and coarser than his medieval counterpart. The character of Cressida is strongly influenced by Henryson's poem, in which she finally becomes a leprous beggar after being mistress to a succession of Greek warriors. The war-plot of the play is influenced by other sources, John Lydgate's *The Hystorye Sege and Dystruc-cyon of Troye* (1513), Caxton's *Recuyell of the Historyes of Troye* (c. 1474), and George ►Chapman's translation of Homer, *The Seaven Bookes of the Iliades* (1598). Shake-speare's debt to Homer for *Troilus and Cressida* implies that he used more of the *Iliad* than was contained in Chapman's version, as for instance in the incidents of Achilles being moved to return to battle by the death of Patroclus and his humil-iation of the dead body of Hector. The character of the railing Thersites and the emphasis on dissension in the Greek camp also came from Homer. Lydgate and Caxton may have supplied inspiration for the encounter between Hector and Ajax in IV.v., for Andromache's dream, and for Hector's fight with the Greek in sump-tuous armour that immediately precedes his death. The idea for Ulysses's famous speech on degree (I.iii) comes from Homer, *Iliad*, Book II, but many sources have been suggested for the details of it, including Virgil, *Aeneid*, I, 430, which supplies the image of bees swarming to the hive, Thomas Elyot's *The Boke named the Gov-ernour* (1531), which also uses this image and relates it to the idea of order, the Homily on Obedience appointed to be read in churches, Hooker's *Ecclesiastical Polity* (1597), and ►Florio's translation of Montaigne's *Essais*. It is not necessary to sup-pose that Shakespeare consciously combined material from all these sources, for the ideas in Ulysses's speech were conventional ones in Shakespeare's day and the no-tion of disorder leading to the breakdown of human society, symbolized by can-nibalism, can be found also in *Coriolanus*, *King Lear*, and the Shakespearean scenes of *Sir Thomas More*. For various reasons, the play is often grouped with Shakespeare's "problem plays." It depicts a world without love, honour, or nobility of character;

the atmosphere is one of degeneracy and corruption; and it represents a deflating view of the ancient world and of epic values.

Dramatis Personae

Priam, King of Troy	Ajax, *Greek commander*
Hector, *son of Priam*	Ulysses, *Greek commander*
Troilus, *son of Priam*	Nestor, *Greek commander*
Paris, *son of Priam*	Diomedes, *Greek commander*
Deiphobus, *son of Priam*	Patroclus, *Greek commander*
Helenus, *son of Priam*	Thersites
Margarelon, *bastard son of Priam*	Alexander, *Cressida's servant*
Aeneas, *Trojan commander*	*Servants to Troilus, to Paris, to*
Antenor, *Trojan commander*	*Diomedes*
Calchas, *Trojan priest*	Helen, *wife of Menelaus*
Pandarus, *uncle of Cressida*	Andromache, *wife of Hector*
Agamemnon, *Greek general*	Cassandra, *daughter of Priam*
Menelaus, *brother of Agamemnon*	Cressida, *daughter of Calchas*
Achilles, *Greek commander*	*Trojan and Greek Soldiers*

The Story. In Troy, during the Trojan War, Troilus, the youngest son of King Priam, has fallen in love with Cressida. Pandarus, her uncle, helps them arrange meetings and otherwise encourages the romance, and they pledge eternal faithfulness. Meanwhile, Calchas, Cressida's father, who has deserted Troy for the Greeks, persuades the Greek commanders to exchange one of their prisoners for Cressida. Cressida parts reluctantly from her lover, but eventually surrenders to the amorous advances of the Greek Diomedes, and gives him the token of love that Troilus had given her at the time of their parting. Troilus, in the Greek camp under a safe conduct from Ulysses, witnesses this betrayal of their love by Cressida, and is broken-hearted. He vows to kill Diomedes, but the fight between them at the end of the play ends indecisively. The other part of the plot concerns the Greek decision to redouble their efforts to end the war, refusing to surrender Helen to the Trojans. In a council meeting, Ulysses arouses the spiritless and weary commanders and, when a challenge to personal combat comes from the Trojan warrior Hector, he suggests giving it to Ajax instead of Achilles, who is sulking in his tent. The fight between Hector and Ajax ends in a truce, and the two armies feast together. On the following day, however, the fighting continues and, when Hector kills Patroclus, Achilles is roused to avenge his friend. Coming upon Hector resting without his armour, Achilles treacherously kills him. The day ends with defeat for the Trojans.

Tubal In *The Merchant of Venice*, a Jewish friend of Shylock.

Tullus Aufidius ➤Aufidius, Tullus.

Tutin, Dorothy (1930–) British actress who has performed in Shakespearean roles for over forty years, her first being Phebe in *As You Like It* (Bristol Old Vic,

1950). She joined the ►Shakespeare Memorial Theatre Company (subsequently the ►Royal Shakespeare Company) in 1958, appearing as Juliet and Viola (1958), Cressida (1960), Desdemona (1961), and Rosalind (1967–68). More recently, she has played Queen Katherine at Chichester (1991).

Tutor to Rutland In *3 Henry VI*, the companion of Rutland. He begs Clifford not to slay his charge.

Twelfth Night [Full title, *Twelfth Night, or What You Will*] A comedy by Shakespeare, probably written in 1600 or 1601, acted in 1602, and printed in the first folio of 1623. The central situation of the play, that of a girl disguised as a page acting as emissary from the man she loves to the woman he loves, was one that Shakespeare had already used before in *The Two Gentlemen of Verona*. For *Twelfth Night*, which has been called "a masterpiece of recapitulation," he took characters and devices from several of his earlier plays including the use of identical twins mistaken for one another from *The Comedy of Errors*, the loyal friend Antonio from *The Merchant of Venice*, the comic possibilities of eavesdropping from *Much Ado About Nothing*, and the girl disguised as a boy unbeknown to the man she loves from *As You Like It*. But there are also important outside sources. There were numerous plays and prose romances available to Shakespeare that combined the device of identical twins, originally from the *Menaechmi* of Plautus, with that of the disguised girl serving her lover as a page. The plot of the Italian play, *Gl'Ingannati* (The Deceived) (1537) is very close to Shakespeare's, although its tone and mood, those of a realistic contemporary comedy, are very different; Shakespeare could have known something of it in a Latin version that was performed at Queen's College, Cambridge in 1595 under the title *Laelia*. In *Gl'Ingannati* the heroine disguises herself in order to follow a man who once loved but has now forgotten her; she is employed by him to woo the lady he loves, and this lady falls in love with her. The heroine's troubles are finally solved when her long-lost twin brother appears to woo the lady in her stead, while her old nurse meantime convinces her lover of her devotion. Other possible sources include *Gl'Inganni* (The Deceiver, 1597) by Curio Gonzaga, in which the disguised girl takes the name of Cesare, and two plays by Nicolo Secchi, *Gl' Inganni* (1562) and *L'Interesse* (1581), in the latter of which a duel is proposed in which the disguised heroine is to take part, as Viola duels with Sir Andrew. Of the available prose romances, Shakespeare may well have known versions of the story in Bandello's *Novelle* (1554) and Belleforest's *Histoires Tragiques* (1579), but the most important of these is the story of Apolonius and Silla in Barnaby ►Riche's *A Farewell to the Military Profession* (1581). In this tale Silla, the heroine, is shipwrecked, disguises herself as her brother, Silvio, and woos a wealthy widow on behalf of Apolonius, whom she loves; Silvio appears, and takes over his sister's part with the wealthy widow, getting her pregnant; the disguised Silla is accused of this deed and obliged to reveal her sex to prove her innocence. Apolonius, touched by her devotion, agrees to marry her, and Silvio marries the widow. None of these sources contained the Malvolio subplot, which is Shakespeare's invention; the character is possibly based on a real figure, Sir William Knollys, controller of the Queen's household, although Shakespeare may have found a hint for the episode of his being imprisoned in the dark and tormented by the fool from one of Riche's stories about a man who locked up his shrewish wife in a dark house to cure her temper. The subplot with Sir Toby Belch, Sir Andrew Aguecheek, and Maria is Shakespeare's invention.

Dramatis Personae

Orsino, Duke of Illyria	Feste, *a clown, Olivia's servant*
Sebastian, *brother of Viola*	A Sea Captain
Antonio, *a sea captain*	Olivia, *a rich countess*
Valentine	Viola, *in love with the Duke*
Curio	Maria, *Olivia's woman*
Sir Toby Belch, *uncle of Olivia*	Lords, Priests, Sailors, Officers,
Sir Andrew Aguecheek	Musicians, and other Attendants
Malvolio, *Olivia's servant*	

The Story. The Duke of Illyria, Orsino, is courting the wealthy countess Olivia with the aid of his page Cesario, who is really Viola disguised as a man. (Viola has been shipwrecked on the coast of Illyria and thus separated from her twin brother, Sebastian.) Olivia refuses the advances of Orsino and falls in love with Cesario (Viola), who has herself fallen in love with Orsino. In the household of Olivia, drunken Sir Toby Belch, Sir Andrew Aguecheek, the clown Feste, Fabian, and Maria plot to trick the puritanical Malvolio by leading him to believe that Olivia is in love with him. They contrive that he shall discover a letter apparently written by Olivia (but actually by Maria) that will sustain his amorous hopes, and, as the letter suggests, he appears before the astonished Olivia in yellow stockings, crossed garters, and a constant smile. Because of his strange antics he is believed mad and confined in a dark cellar, where he is tormented by Feste until Olivia orders his release. Meanwhile, Sebastian has arrived in Illyria, and Olivia, believing him to be Cesario, persuades him to marry her. After much confusion resulting from mistaking the twins, Orsino discovers his love for Viola (whom he too has hitherto thought to be a man) and decides to marry her.

Two Gentlemen of Verona, The A comedy by Shakespeare, possibly written as early as 1590–91, and first printed in the first folio of 1623. There is no record of any performance until 1672. The primary source for the story of Julia was the romance *Diana Enamorada* by Jorge de Montemayor (Valencia, 1559), which Shakespeare might perhaps have known in the original Spanish, or more likely in the French translation by Nicolas Collin (1578, 1587); an English translation by Bartholomew Young (or Yonge) was published in 1598, though it had been made sixteen years earlier. In this story Felix (the Proteus character) is sent to a foreign court so that he may not marry Felismena (Julia); Felismena follows him in male disguise and finds him wooing Celia (Silvia). She becomes his page and goes to Celia with Felix's letter, with the result that Celia falls in love with her; Shakespeare made use of this part of this story not in *Two Gentlemen of Verona* but later, with the disguised Viola and Olivia in *Twelfth Night*. Finally Celia dies when the "page" cannot return her love, and Felix goes into exile, but he is pursued, saved from death, and finally rewon by Felismena. Shakespeare changed this story in several ways. He altered the character of Felismena, who is a bold Amazonian shepherdess, for his more gentle Julia, and he added another young man, Valentine, and so provided a rival for Proteus and a happy ending for the second heroine. Some of his changes may be due to the influence of a lost play, *Felix and Felio(s?)mena*, performed in 1585, which may well have been a pastoral based on Montemayor, but he could also have found the theme of the disloyal friend in ►Lyly's *Euphues: The Anatomy of Wit* (1579). Lyly's plays supplied several ideas for *Two Gentlemen of Verona*; *Endimion* included two comic servants who foreshadow Launce and Speed, a foolish suitor, Sir Tophas, who resembles Sir Thurio, and a treatment of the conflict between love and friendship in *Euphues*. Lyly's characteristic verbal wit and logic-chopping perhaps influenced the style of *The Two Gentlemen of Verona*. The basis of Shakespeare's play is the conflict between love and friendship, a popular Renaissance theme, and Shakespeare could have found other presentations of this in Boccaccio's *La Teseide* and the *Decameron* (Day 10, Story 8), in Chaucer's *The Knight's Tale*, and in Sir Thomas Elyot's *The Book named the Governour* (1531). *The Two Gentlemen of Verona*, one of Shakespeare's earliest comedies, contains many ideas and devices that he was constantly to vary and re-use in years to come, including the disguised heroine, the movement of the main characters from court to country, the rivalry and betrayal in love, and the comic servant.

Dramatis Personae

Duke of Milan	Panthino, *Antonio's servant*
Valentine, *Gentleman of Verona*	Host, *where Julia lodges*
Proteus, *Gentleman of Verona*	Outlaws, *with Valentine*
Antonio, *father of Proteus*	Julia, *beloved of Proteus*
Thurio, *Valentine's rival*	Silvia, *beloved of Valentine*
Eglamour, *a knight*	Lucetta, *Julia's woman*
Speed, *Valentine's servant*	Servants, Musicians
Launce, *Proteus's servant*	

The Story. Valentine, one of the two Veronese gentlemen of the title, travels to the court of Milan, where he falls in love with the Duke's daughter, Silvia. His friend Proteus, the other gentleman of Verona, pledges constant faithfulness to his beloved Julia before departing for Milan, but there he, too, falls in love with Silvia. Determined to have her for himself, he betrays the confidence of his friend by informing the Duke that Valentine is about to elope with his daughter. Valentine is thereupon banished and joins a band of robbers. Proteus continues his courting of

Silvia, who rejects both him and her father's choice, the foolish Thurio. Meanwhile, Julia has arrived, disguised as a page, and offers her services to Proteus. When Silvia, in search of Valentine, flees her father's court, Proteus and his "page" follow her and rescue her from robbers. As Proteus is on the verge of raping Silvia, Valentine appears and because Proteus is so overcome with remorse, even offers to yield Silvia to Proteus. However, at this point the "page" faints, Proteus recognizes her as Julia, and realizes that she, rather than Silvia, is his true love. The Duke and Thurio arrive, but because Thurio is too cowardly to fight Valentine for Silvia, the Duke gives her to the "gentleman of Verona."

Two Noble Kinsmen, The A play now accepted as a collaboration between Shakespeare and John ►Fletcher, written between 1613 and 1614. It was not included in the first folio of 1623, which has led many scholars to regard it as not being a genuinely Shakespearean work; its first publication seems to have been in a quarto of 1634, and it was included in the second folio of ►Beaumont and Fletcher's plays (1679). It is generally accepted that Shakespeare was responsible for slightly less than half of the play, in particular the first act, most of the last, and the prose scenes in Acts II and III, while Fletcher wrote the remainder; the morris dance in III.iv. contains characters from Beaumont's *Masque of the Inner Temple* (1616). The authors' main source was Chaucer, as they acknowledge in the prologue; *The Knight's Tale* supplies the play with its main plot and characters. There are some differences, both of detail and emphasis: in *The Two Noble Kinsmen*, Theseus and Hippolyta are not yet married at the beginning of the play, though they are in Chaucer (a reminiscence perhaps of *A Midsummer Night's Dream*); the time-scheme for the events is sometimes shortened in the play, particularly in the long speeches of Emilia in I.iii and IV.ii; in Chaucer, Theseus does not decree that the loser in the combat for Emilia's love must be put to death, and partly in consequence of this the theme of loss is more insistent in the play. The addition of the subplot of the Jailer's Daughter, for which no source is known, changes the effect of the story considerably, enhancing both the theme of the unpredictable and often destructive consequences of sexual passion and also the role of women in the play.

Dramatis Personae

Theseus, Duke of Athens
Palamon, *nephew of the Theban King*
Arcite, *nephew of the Theban King*
Pirithous, *an Athenian general*
Artesius, *an Athenian captain*
Valerius, *a Theban nobleman*
Six Knights
A Herald
A Jailer
Wooer of the Jailer's Daughter

A Doctor
Brother of the Jailer
Friends of the Jailer
A Gentleman
Gerrold, *a schoolmaster*
Hippolyta, *wife of Theseus*
Emilia, *her sister*
Three Queens
The Jailer's Daughter
Servant to Emilia

*Country Wenches and Women
A Labourer, Countrymen, Messengers, a
Man Personating Hymen, Boy,*

*Executioners, Guards, Soldiers,
Attendants*

The Story. Theseus, Duke of Athens, is about to marry Hippolyta, Queen of the Amazons, when the ceremony is interrupted by the appearance of three weeping queens who beg him immediately to avenge the dishonour done to their dead husbands by the tyrant Creon of Thebes. Theseus agrees, and succeeds in overcoming Creon. The cousins, Palamon and Arcite, the "two noble kinsmen," are obliged by duty to fight on behalf of Creon, who is their uncle, although they abhor his tyranny. They are captured and imprisoned by Theseus. From their prison they catch sight of Emilia, sister to Hippolyta, and both fall in love with her. Arcite is then released by order of Theseus's friend Pirithous, but into banishment. Palamon too is released, but secretly, by the Jailer's Daughter, who has fallen in love with him. The two meet again, and prepare to fight one another for the right to woo Emilia. They are discovered by Theseus, who is at first disposed to condemn them both to death, but substitutes (at the request of Hippolyta and Emilia) another sentence: Palamon and Arcite must within a month's time each secure three knights and then engage in a tourney for the hand of Emilia. The victor will marry her, the loser will be executed. Meanwhile, the Jailer's Daughter, mad with love for Palamon, wanders in the forest and tries to drown herself. She is saved by a faithful suitor, whose love she rejects. In the tourney, Arcite is victorious, but just as Palamon is about to be executed word arrives that Arcite has been mortally injured by a fall from his horse, and as he dies he surrenders Emilia to Palamon. At the conclusion of the subplot, the Doctor persuades the Daughter's suitor to impersonate Palamon and woo her. This cures her of her madness, and she accepts him.

Tybalt   In *Romeo and Juliet*, the quarrelsome nephew of Lady Capulet, who, having discovered Romeo's presence at the Capulet ball, wishes to fight with Romeo when he later meets him in the street. Romeo refuses to fight, but Mercutio takes up the challenge, and is mortally wounded when Tybalt thrusts at him under Romeo's arm. In remorse, Romeo attacks Tybalt and kills him.

Tyrrel, Sir James   In *Richard III*, a supporter of Richard. He is ordered to kill the Princes in the Tower, but hires two murderers to do the deed for him.

U

Ulysses In *Troilus and Cressida*, one of the Greek commanders. He makes the speech on degree (I.iii) in an attempt to bring order to the Greeks. He also suggests that Achilles be made jealous of Ajax so as to get him into battle again. He goes with Troilus to see Cressida and tries to reconcile him to the situation when Troilus sees her with Diomedes.

Underwood, John (d. 1624) English actor. Originally with the ➤Children of the Revels, he joined the ➤King's Men in 1608. He is listed as a principal actor in the first folio (1623) of Shakespeare's plays.

Ur-Hamlet The name given by scholars to a lost pre-Shakespearean play about Hamlet. ("Ur" means "source"). The existence of such a play is shown by such evidence as a reference in ➤Nashe's Preface to ➤Greene's *Menaphon* (1589), a performance at ➤Newington Butts recorded in ➤Henslowe's *Diary* for June 1594, and Thomas ➤Lodge's allusion to the Ghost "which cried so miserablie... Hamlet, revenge" (*Wit's Misery*, 1596). It has often been thought that this play was by Thomas ➤Kyd, in view of Nashe's apparent allusion to this writer in his remarks and the resemblances between *Hamlet* and Kyd's own revenge play, *The Spanish Tragedy* (*c.* 1592).

Ursula In *Much Ado About Nothing*, one of Hero's gentlewomen.

Urswick, Christopher In *Richard III*, a priest who is sent with a message to Richmond (IV.v).

V

Valentine In *Titus Andronicus*, a kinsman of Titus.

Valentine In *Twelfth Night*, a gentleman attending on Orsino, Duke of Illyria.

Valentine In *The Two Gentlemen of Verona*, one of the "two gentlemen." He falls in love with Silvia when he travels to Milan, but finds himself a rival for her love with his friend Proteus, the other "gentleman."

Valeria In *Coriolanus*, a friend of Virgilia.

Valerius In *The Two Noble Kinsmen*, a Theban nobleman.

Varrius In *Antony and Cleopatra*, a friend of Pompey.

Varrius In *Measure for Measure*, a friend of the Duke. The Duke merely speaks to him, and he is not listed in the folio of 1623.

Varro In *Julius Caesar*, a servant of Brutus.

Varro In *Timon of Athens*, two servants of a usurer, who sends them to collect a debt from Timon. They are both called by the name of their master (who does not appear).

Vaughan, Sir Thomas In *Richard III*, an enemy of Richard who is executed with Rivers and Grey.

Vaux, Sir Nicholas In *Henry VIII*, a gentleman of the court who is put in charge of Buckingham when he is arrested.

Vaux, Sir William In *2 Henry VI*, a messenger who announces that Cardinal Beaufort is dying.

Venice, Duke of In *The Merchant of Venice*, the judge presiding at the trial of Antonio. He pardons Shylock on the terms suggested by Antonio.

Venice, Duke of In *Othello*, the ruler of Venice. He tries to persuade Brabantio to accept Othello as his son-in-law, and orders Othello to take charge of the expedition to Cyprus.

Ventidius In *Antony and Cleopatra*, one of Antony's generals.

Ventidius In *Timon of Athens*, a false friend of Timon.

Venus and Adonis A narrative poem by Shakespeare, printed in 1593 and dedicated to the Earl of ►Southampton, his first published work. It was immediately popular and successful, and during Shakespeare's lifetime the most often cited and quoted of all his works. It is in six-line stanzas, rhyming *ababcc*, the same form as that used by Thomas ►Lodge in *Scylla's Metamorphosis* (1598), the poem which initiated the vogue for this genre, the Ovidian brief epic, which became very fashionable in the 1590s. Such poems were based on a mythological love story, narrated in an elaborately rhetorical style, pervaded by an erotic atmosphere, and written to show the inhabitants of the classical world in a detached and often comical manner. Shakespeare's source is ►Ovid's ►*Metamorphoses*, mainly Book x, 519–59. He tells the story of Venus's unrequited love for the youth Adonis. The goddess overpowers her lover physically, and begs him at some length to return her passion, urging the naturalness of procreation in similar terms to those used in Shakespeare's Sonnets, 1–17. She points to the behaviour of his horse, which has escaped into the woods in pursuit of a mare, as a model for him to follow. He rejects her love, and instead prepares to go hunting, undeterred by her warnings of the dangers of the boar. He is gored to death. A flower springs up from his shed blood, which Venus picks before returning to her home on the island of Paphos.

Verges In *Much Ado About Nothing*, a "headborough" (a minor constable), assistant to Dogberry.

Vernon In *1 Henry VI*, an adherent of the Duke of York. He quarrels with Basset, a supporter of the Lancastrian faction, and both ask for single combat but are refused.

Vincentio In *The Taming of the Shrew*, an old gentleman of Pisa, Lucentio's father.

Vincentio, Duke of Vienna In *Measure for Measure*, the reigning Duke. Leaving Angelo to rule Vienna as his deputy, he disguises himself as a friar and becomes aware of the results of Angelo's hypocritically stringent administration. In particular, he helps Isabella out of her dilemma, and in the end proposes marriage to her.

Viola In *Twelfth Night*, a principal female character, twin sister of Sebastian. She assumes a page's disguise and the name of Cesario when she arrives in Illyria. She woos Olivia on Orsino's behalf, disguised as his page, but finds herself falling in love with him. Eventually he recognizes the quality of her devotion and marries her.

Violenta In *All's Well That Ends Well*, a Florentine woman, friend of the Widow.

Virgilia In *Coriolanus*, the wife of Coriolanus. She, with her son and Volumnia, persuade Coriolanus to spare Rome.

Voltemand In *Hamlet*, a courtier sent by Claudius on an embassy to Norway, together with Cornelius.

Volumnia   In *Coriolanus*, the mother of Coriolanus. She is a powerful woman who exerts great influence over her son. Her arguments constitute the key factor in persuading Coriolanus to give up his plan to attack Rome, and as a result she wins a "happy victory to Rome" (V.iii), but loses her son, who is killed by his Volscian allies under Aufidius (V.vi).

Volumnius   In *Julius Caesar*, a boyhood friend who refuses to hold the sword for Brutus's suicide.

Wall   In *A Midsummer Night's Dream*, the wall that separates Pyramus and Thisby (Thisbe) in the interpolated play. It is represented (with spoken lines) by Snout, the tinker.

Wanamaker, Sam   (1919–93) American theatre director and actor on stage and film. He was artistic director of the New Shakespeare Theatre, Liverpool (1957–59) and in 1959 played Iago at the ►Shakespeare Memorial Theatre, Stratford-upon-Avon. In 1970 he became executive director of the Globe Playhouse Trust, the aim of which was to establish a replica of Shakespeare's Globe on the original site. He died before the ►International Shakespeare Globe Centre opened in 1996.

Warner, Deborah   (1959–   ) British theatre director who became known for her productions with Kick Theatre, especially *King Lear* (1986) and *Coriolanus* (1987); she has also worked with the ►Royal Shakespeare Company, directing *Titus Andronicus* and *King John*. Other productions include *King Lear* (1990) and *Richard II* (1995) at the Royal National Theatre, and *Coriolanus* at the Salzburg Festival (1993).

Wart, Thomas   In *2 Henry IV*, a recruit in Falstaff's army.

Warwick, Earl of   In *2 Henry IV, Henry V*, and *1 Henry VI*, the historical Richard de Beauchamp. In *2 Henry IV*, he is a counsellor to the King and reassures him about the rebellion and the behaviour of the Prince. In *Henry V*, he is a leader of the English forces in France. In *1 Henry VI*, he plucks a white rose, indicating that he favours Richard Plantagenet.

Warwick, Earl of   In *2* and *3 Henry VI*, the historical Richard Neville, called "the Kingmaker," a member of the Yorkist faction. In *2 Henry VI*, he is convinced that Gloucester was murdered, accuses Suffolk, and later fights on the winning side at the first battle of St Albans. In *3 Henry VI*, he at first supports Edward but, when he learns that Edward has married Lady Grey instead of Lady Bona, he joins the Lancastrians, captures Edward, and returns Henry VI to the throne. He is killed at Barnet.

Warwick, Edward, Earl of   In *Richard III*, a young son of the Duke of Clarence, eventually imprisoned by Richard.

Welles, Orson   (1915–85) American actor and director of films and plays. His first Shakespearean role was Mercutio (1934), while others he played in the USA in-

clude Hamlet (1934), Brutus (1938), Falstaff (1939), and King Lear (1956), in a production which he also directed. His first stage appearance in London was as Othello in a production he himself directed in 1951. He directed several film versions
of Shakespeare, including *Macbeth* (1949), *Othello* (1951), and *Chimes at Midnight*
(stage play 1960, film 1966), a version of *1* and *2 Henry IV*, in which he played
Falstaff.

Westminster, Abbot of   In *Richard II*, a supporter of the divine right of kingship, and conspirator with Aumerle against Bolingbroke.

Westmoreland, (1st) Earl of   In *1* and *2 Henry IV* and *Henry V*, the historical
Ralph Neville (1365–1425), 1st Earl of Westmoreland, a loyal adherent of the King.
He is a leader of the royal forces, in *Henry IV* against the rebels and in *Henry V*
against the French.

Westmoreland, Earl of   In *3 Henry VI*, the historical Ralph Neville (*c.* 1404–84),
a member of the Lancastrian faction.

W. H., Mr   ➤Herbert, William; ➤Sonnets.

Whitefriars   A district in east central London, in the City of London between
the present-day Fleet Street and the river. It is named from the convent of an order
of Carmelites, established in Fleet Street in 1241. A private playhouse was opened
in the Whitefriars precinct in 1608. It was in Shakespeare's time a notorious locality.

Whitmore, Walter   A character in *2 Henry VI* who, in revenge for losing an eye
in a sea battle, beheads his prisoner, Suffolk (IV.i).

Widow   In *All's Well That Ends Well*, a Florentine woman with whom Helena
lodges, the mother of Diana.

Widow   In *The Taming of the Shrew*, the woman who marries Hortensio.

Wilkins, George   (*fl.* 1603–08) English dramatist and prose writer, an obscure figure whose works include the domestic tragedy *The Miseries of Enforced Marriage*
(1606), the pamphlet *Three Miseries of Barbary* (*c.* 1606), and the prose romance *The
Painful Adventures of Pericles, Prince of Tyre* (1608). The relationship of this last to
Shakespeare's *Pericles* is still in dispute, but he is sometimes thought to have collaborated with Shakespeare on the play. He had earlier collaborated with John Day
and Thomas Rowley on *The Travels of Three English Brothers* (1607).

William   In *As You Like It*, a country bumpkin in love with Audrey.

Williams, Michael   In *Henry V*, a soldier who encounters King Henry disguised as an English gentleman before the battle of Agincourt. He challenges the
King upon the latter's defending his faithfulness to his troops. Fluellen comes to
blows with him.

Willobie his Avisa   ➤*Avisa*.

Willoughby, Lord In *Richard II*, a deserter of the King and later a member of Bolingbroke's party.

Winchester, Bishop of In *1 Henry VI*, the historical Henry Beaufort, a son of John of Gaunt and great-uncle of Henry VI. He quarrels with Gloucester, the Protector, who accuses him of having Henry V murdered. He crowns Henry VI in Paris and later appears as a Cardinal (V.i). In *2 Henry VI*, he joins York, Suffolk, and others in accusing Gloucester of misdeeds and having him imprisoned. Gloucester is murdered, apparently on his orders, and he repents for this on his deathbed (III.iii).

The Winter's Tale A play by Shakespeare, produced *c.* 1611 and printed in the first folio of 1623. The main source was Robert ►Greene's romance *Pandosto* (1588), from which Shakespeare borrowed more words and phrases than from any other romance he used. He altered the story in several ways. He changed the names so as to make them more Greek, even giving a Greek name to his invented comic character, Autolycus. He omitted Greene's account of the growth of friendship between the Queen (Hermione) and Egistus (Polixenes) that partly motivates the jealousy of Pandosto (Leontes), thus emphasizing Hermione's total innocence and Leontes's delusion. He had Leontes's baby daughter, Perdita, left in a remote spot by an invented character, Antigonus (who is then eaten by a bear), rather than having the baby placed in a boat and cast off to sea as in Greene. He altered the ending of the story by having Hermione reappear, posing as her own statue, after sixteen years' absence; in Greene, the Queen died, and the story ended with Pandosto's sudden suicide after a reconciliation with his daughter. This change makes *The Winter's Tale* more like Shakespeare's other late plays, and emphasizes ideas that seem to have interested him at that stage of his writing. Shakespeare added four characters, Antigonus, Paulina, Autolycus, and the Clown; Antigonus and Paulina have important functions in the plot, but Autolycus, whose origins may be found in the Elizabethan cony-catching pamphlets of writers like Greene and ►Dekker, is needed mainly to evoke the atmosphere of the Bohemian countryside. The clown, son to the old shepherd who saves the baby Perdita, forms with his father a significant part of the pattern of contrasting relationships between older and younger generations, as in Leontes and Mamillius, Polixenes and Florizel. Shakespeare also changed the nature of the relationship between the two young lovers; in Greene, Dorastus (Florizel) regards his instinctive feeling for the shepherdess Fawnia (Perdita) as unworthy, since he is a prince and she of lowly rank, and Fawnia is attracted by the prospect of becoming a queen when she marries Dorastus. Shakespeare's lovers are less class-conscious. A minor source for the play is Francis Sabie's blank verse poem based on *Pandosto*, *The Fisherman's Tale* (1595). The play was revised in the Restoration, and ►Garrick produced it as *Florizel and Perdita*.

Dramatis Personae

Leontes, King of Sicilia
Mamillius, Prince of Sicilia

Camillo, *a lord of Sicilia*
Antigonus, *a lord of Sicilia*

Cleomenes, *a lord of Sicilia*

Dion, *a lord of Sicilia*

Polixenes, King of Bohemia

Florizel, Prince of Bohemia

Archidamus, *a lord of Bohemia*

An old Shepherd, reputed father of
Perdita

Clown, his son

Autolycus, *a rogue*

A Mariner

A Jailer

Hermione, *Queen to Leontes*

Perdita, *daughter to Leontes and*
Hermione

Paulina, *wife to Antigonus*

Emilia, *a lady to Hermione*

Mopsa, *a shepherdess*

Dorcas, *a shepherdess*

Lord, Ladies, and Gentlemen, Officers,
and Servants, Shepherds and
Shepherdesses, Guards

Time, as Chorus

The Story. Leontes, King of Sicilia, unjustifiably accuses his wife, Hermione, of having a love affair with his friend, Polixenes, King of Bohemia, who is visiting the court at Sicilia. Leontes tries unsuccessfully to have Polixenes poisoned, but he flees to safety; Hermione is imprisoned, and shortly thereafter gives birth to a daughter. At the trial of Hermione, the King refuses to believe the Delphic oracle, which has stated that Hermione is innocent. The king orders the baby, which he believes to be the child of Polixenes, to be abandoned; word comes of the death of the King's son, Mamillius, and Leontes then acknowledges the truth of the oracle, but apparently too late, for Paulina announces the death of Hermione. The baby, Perdita, left on the Bohemian "coast" by Antigonus, at Leontes's command, is discovered by an old shepherd, who raises her to womanhood. Sixteen years later, Florizel, the son of Polixenes, meets her and falls in love with her but, because of the opposition of his father to the marriage, flees with her to Sicilia. There the identity of Perdita is discovered, to the joy of Leontes (who has now repented of his distrust of his wife), and Polixenes, who has followed his son, is reconciled to his old friend. Leontes, however, grieves for his wife (whom he thinks dead), but Paulina offers to show him a lifelike statue of her, which turns out to be the actual Hermione. Leontes is reunited with his wife and daughter, and succession to the thrones of Sicilia and Bohemia is assured through the union of Perdita and Florizel.

Witches [Also, Weird Sisters] In *Macbeth*, three supernatural women. They appear in the first scene, setting the atmosphere of the play. They hail Macbeth as Thane of Glamis, Thane of Cawdor, and "King hereafter" (I.iii). When Macbeth learns immediately afterwards that he is indeed to become Thane of Cawdor, their words seem prophetic and act as an incentive to the murder of Duncan. Their prophecies upon the second occasion of his consulting them are ambiguous and suggest a security that is not real. The characters may be derived from the Scandinavian Norns, or Goddesses of Fate, probably by way of the Anglo-Saxon Wyrdes, though their presentation owes more to Elizabethan witchcraft pamphlets.

Wolfit, Sir Donald (1902–68) British actor-manager with an extensive career in playing and directing Shakespeare for more than thirty years. He made his debut as Biondello in *The Taming of the Shrew* (1920). In 1933 he played Hamlet in a production of the first quarto text, and in 1936 Hamlet in the received version at the ►Shakespeare Memorial Theatre, Stratford-upon-Avon. Having established his own Shakespeare Company in 1937, he toured as Hamlet, Macbeth, Shylock, and Malvolio. Other roles included Falstaff, Richard III, Iago, and especially King Lear. After 1953 he played Shakespeare on stage only in recital tours, which he continued to put on until a few years before his death.

Wolsey, Thomas, Cardinal   One of the major characters in *Henry VIII*.

Woodvile   In *1 Henry VI*, a Lieutenant of the Tower (of London).

Worcester, Thomas Percy, Earl of   In *1 Henry IV*, the younger brother of Northumberland. Suspicious of the King, he fails to tell Hotspur of the King's offer to pardon the rebels.

Wriothesley, Henry   ►Southampton, (3rd) Earl of.

Y

Yorick In *Hamlet*, the King's jester whose skull is found by the Gravediggers and is addressed elegiacally by Hamlet (V.i).

York, Archbishop of ►Rotherham, Thomas; ►Scroop, Richard.

York, Duchess of In *Richard II*, the wife of York and mother of Aumerle. She begs Henry to pardon her son's treason.

York, Duchess of In *Richard III*, the mother of Edward IV and Clarence, whose deaths she laments with Margaret and Queen Elizabeth. She joins the chorus of women cursing Richard.

York, (1st) Duke of In *Richard II*, Edmund of Langley, the historical Edmund de Langley. At first a supporter of Richard, he is left as Lord Protector during Richard's absence in Ireland. As soon as Bolingbroke demonstrates his power, however, he adheres to him, and later he reveals the part of his son Aumerle in the plot against Bolingbroke.

York, (2nd) Duke of In *Henry V*, a cousin to the King. He is killed at Agincourt. In *Richard II*, he is the Duke of Aumerle, son of the Duke of York.

York, (3rd) Duke of In *1 Henry VI*, the historical Richard Plantagenet, head of the house of York. He picks a white rose in the Temple Garden, indicating his opposition to the house of Lancaster. As regent in France, he fails to aid Talbot and condemns Joan of Arc to death. In *2 Henry VI*, he claims his right to the throne and, with the support of Warwick and Salisbury, wins the battle at St Albans and there kills Clifford. In *3 Henry VI*, he makes peace, being promised the succession to the throne at the King's death. Gloucester urges him to break his oath, and he is captured and killed by the Lancastrians at Wakefield.

York, Richard, (5th) Duke of In *Richard III*, a young boy, son of Edward IV, who is murdered in the Tower by Richard.

Yorkshire Tragedy, A A play produced and printed in 1608, based on a contemporary murder. It was formerly attributed to Shakespeare, as his name appeared in full on the title page, and it was included in the second issue of the third Shakespeare folio (1664), but is not now considered his. Some editors ascribe it to ►Middleton.

Z

Zadek, Peter (1926–   ) German theatre director, head of the Bochum Theatre (1972–75) and Deutches Schauspielhaus, Hamburg (1985–89). He is internationally known for his radical and experimental productions, which include *Othello* (1976), *Hamlet* (1977), *The Merchant of Venice* (Vienna, 1988), *Measure for Measure* (1990), and *Antony and Cleopatra* (Vienna, 1994).

Zeffirelli, Franco (1923–   ) Italian theatre and film director, whose productions of Shakespeare include *Romeo and Juliet* (Old Vic, 1960), *Much Ado About Nothing* (Old Vic, 1965), and *Othello* (Stratford-upon-Avon, 1961). He has made film versions of three Shakespeare plays with English-speaking casts: *The Taming of the Shrew* (1966) with Richard Burton and Elizabeth Taylor, *Romeo and Juliet* (1968), and *Hamlet* (1990).